THE OLYMPIC SPIRIT

100 YEARS OF THE GAMES

100
Atlanta 1996
TM, © 1992 ACOG

The Olympic Spirit was made possible through the generous support of the following Olympic Sponsors.

Thanks to their commitment, the memories of millions will live on.

   Southern Living®

The OLYMPIC SPIRIT

100 YEARS OF THE GAMES

BY SUSAN WELS

CollinsPublishersSanFrancisco
A Division of HarperCollins*Publishers*

The Olympic Spirit is published through *Southern Living* magazine, an Official Worldwide Sponsor of the 1996 Atlanta Centennial Olympic Games. *The Olympic Spirit* is published with the permission of the Atlanta Committee for the Olympic Games and bears its official marks.

The Olympic Spirit was conceived and produced by Tehabi Books, Del Mar, California.
Nancy Cash–*Managing Editor;* Andy Lewis–*Project Art Director;* Sam Lewis–*Art Director;*
Tom Lewis–*Editorial and Design Director;* Sharon Lewis–*Controller;* Chris Capen–*Project Director and President.*
Additional support for *The Olympic Spirit* was also provided by Debbie Fife–*Editor;* Kathi George–*Copy Proofer.*

For more information on the Olympic Museum, Lausanne, Switzerland please contact the Museum directly at 4121.621.66.10. For more information on *The Olympic Spirit,* including corporate customized copies, please contact Chris Capen, Project Director, Tehabi Books, 13070 Via Grimaldi, Del Mar, California 92014 USA. Telephone: (619) 481-7600.

Tehabi Books, in association with The Basic Foundation, a not-for-profit organization whose primary mission is reforestation, will facilitate the planting of two trees for every one tree used in the manufacture of this book.

Library of Congress Cataloging-in-Publication Data
Wels, Susan.
The Olympic spirit : 100 years of the games / by Susan Wels.
      p. cm.
   Includes index.
   ISBN 0-00-638279-7 (Softcover - U.S. Edition)
   ISBN 0-00-649054-9 (Softcover - Int'l Edition)
   ISBN 0-8487-1504-7 (Hardcover Edition)
   1. Olympics—History—Pictorial works. I. Title.
GV721.5.W36 1995
796.48'022'2—dc20
                     95-17442
                     CIP

10 9 8 7 6 5 4 3 2 1

This edition is printed on acid-free paper that meets the American National Standards Institute Z39.48 Standard.

Photography provided by: Olympic Museum, Lausanne, Switzerland.
                              Duomo Photography Inc., New York, New York.
                              Allsport Photography Inc., Los Angeles, California.

Color separations and film provided by Digital Pre-Press International through PrintNet.

Printed in Hong Kong through Mandarin Offset.

Photos: Cover photo design by Tehabi Books, © Duomo, David Madison, Al Tielemans;
Page 2 and opposite page: Archives, Olympic Museum Lausanne.

CONTENTS

CELEBRATING THE CENTENNIAL

As the world celebrates the one-hundredth anniversary of the modern Olympic Movement with the 1996 Centennial Olympic Games in Atlanta, it is profoundly clear that the true spirit of the Olympics—the union of sport, art, and culture—has flourished beyond the greatest dreams of their founder, Baron Pierre de Coubertin.

THE FOUNDING VISION

When Coubertin established the International Olympic Committee (IOC) in 1894 in Paris, his goal was to encourage a better understanding among nations through the linking of sport, education, art, and culture. The modern Olympic movement evolved from the ideals celebrated by the ancient Greeks, who devoted themselves to the harmonious pursuit of physical, moral, cultural, and artistic excellence and regarded the Olympic Games as the greatest expression of those values.

In 1896, the first of the modern Olympic Games were held in Athens, Greece. Since then, as Coubertin had hoped, the long tradition of the modern Games has offered an opportunity for the world's youth to gather in the spirit of friendship and learn the importance of values that transcend differences in nationality, geography, and culture.

Now, as the world gathers in Atlanta, the Centennial Games will again honor the great Olympic tradition established by Coubertin. I join you in looking forward to this exciting celebration.

Juan Antonio Samaranch
President of the International Olympic Committee

JUAN ANTONIO SAMARANCH

Perpetuating the vision of Olympic founder Pierre de Coubertin (above), Juan Antonio Samaranch (below) has guided the IOC since his election to the presidency in 1980. Opposite: Seoul, 1988. Following spread: Barcelona, 1992.

OLYMPIC DREAMS

Streams of color streak the sky. Doves scatter over a field surging with athletes, Herculean heroes, and rippling flags. And in the black Catalan night, thousands watch a white-clad archer draw his bow; a fiery arrow flashes through the dark and fills the vast Olympic cauldron with a burst of flame. With blazing symbol and ceremony, the 1992 Summer Olympics

THE PASSION TO COMPETE

opened in Barcelona, Spain. Now the torch passes to the city of Atlanta for the 1996 Centennial Olympic Games.

With their sweeping pageantry, the Olympics have remained, for the past one hundred years, one of the few rituals that regularly bring the people of the world together. During the Games, nations gather, not for combat or debate, but to celebrate the hope of peace and the shared love of competition. In the Olympics, as in any ritual, there has sometimes been friction between ideals and reality. But often enough we witness the ideal, and it never fails to astonish and move us.

The world holds its collective breath as athletes hurtle down the track, plunge perilously down mountain slopes, and flout gravity on the balance beam, the springboard, and the ice. Billions are riveted by these glimpses of pure, realized potential. In a world of virtual reality, the Olympics are one arena in which real human heroes reach levels of physical performance that the rest of us can only dream of. It's a dream that pulls us back, again and again, no matter how strident the politics of the moment or how vast the challenge of gathering together the world's family, once again, for this ultimate spectacle of sport.

LET THE GAMES BEGIN

The massive spectacles of the Olympic Opening Ceremonies rivet audiences around the world with their powerful displays of sport, art, and culture.
Opposite: Calgary, 1988.
Following spread: Los Angeles, 1984.

A century after the birth of the modern Games, the power of the Olympics is still rooted in ideals of heroism, sacrifice, and the human struggle for perfection—just as it was for the ancient Greeks, who invented the Olympic idea almost 2,800 years ago. For us, as for the Greeks, these emotional currents are stirred by the intoxicating Olympic blend of physical contests, pageantry, and art. Olympic imagery is as powerful as any secular devotion could inspire: the lighted torch, a flickering link between the modern Games and the ruins of Olympia in Greece; the cluster of five Olympic rings, a symbol taken from the ancient shrine of Apollo at Delphi; the flags and banners; and the massive, moving spectacles of the Opening and Closing Ceremonies.

But it's always the athletes—the hundreds who medal and the thousands more who don't—who make the Olympic dream personal and real. Their moments on the Olympic stage are dramatically unscripted. For those who win, it's a fragile, fleeting instant at the top. Even for an athlete like Austria's Franz Klammer, a skier who won almost every World Cup downhill race in 1975, the Olympics are the peak. "Now I've got everything," he said after winning the downhill gold in 1976. "I don't need anything else."

"There's no other feeling like winning the Olympic Games," reflected Darrell Pace, a gold-medaling archer in 1976 and 1984. "You stand on the podium and know that you are the best in the world, but you also know that you may never be there again."

For many, the journey to the Games comes at a high personal cost. "People forget how many times you lost on your way there…[and] how much training takes out of you. It's lonely in that pool," remembered swimmer Cathy Ferguson, who won twin golds in 1964. Time and youth pass quickly, too, for athletes who may wind up empty-handed at the end of their Olympic quest. Ye Qiaobo, a Chinese speed skater, wept with grief when she took the silver medal, not the gold, at the 1992 Winter Games in Albertville. "I spend so many times for skating, and I gave up so many hobbies for this," she sobbed. And now, she despaired, "I am old."

But still, the Olympic dream drives them to compete, despite the stakes and sacrifices. "These are the Olympics. You die for them," declared discus thrower Al Oerter, who competed for his third Olympic gold while suffering from agonizing injuries.

Like the athletes, the rest of us are drawn in, time and time again, by the mesmerizing spectacle and celebration of the Games—by the glory, the magic, and the hope.

BARON PIERRE DE COUBERTIN

The man who almost single-handedly willed the modern Olympics into being at the end of the last century was a canny, idealistic French aristocrat, Baron Pierre de Coubertin. Born in Paris in 1863, Coubertin was inspired by the archaeological excavations of ancient Greece and concerned about the lack of physical training among French youth. He pressed for the revival of the ancient Olympic Games and won support for launching a modern Olympic festival. In 1896, the first of the reborn Olympic Games was held in Athens. Coubertin continued to guide the Games as president of the International Olympic Committee until 1925. Opposite: Montreal, 1976. Following spread: Moscow, 1980.

Photo: Opposite and following spread © Duomo.

OLYMPIC TORCHES

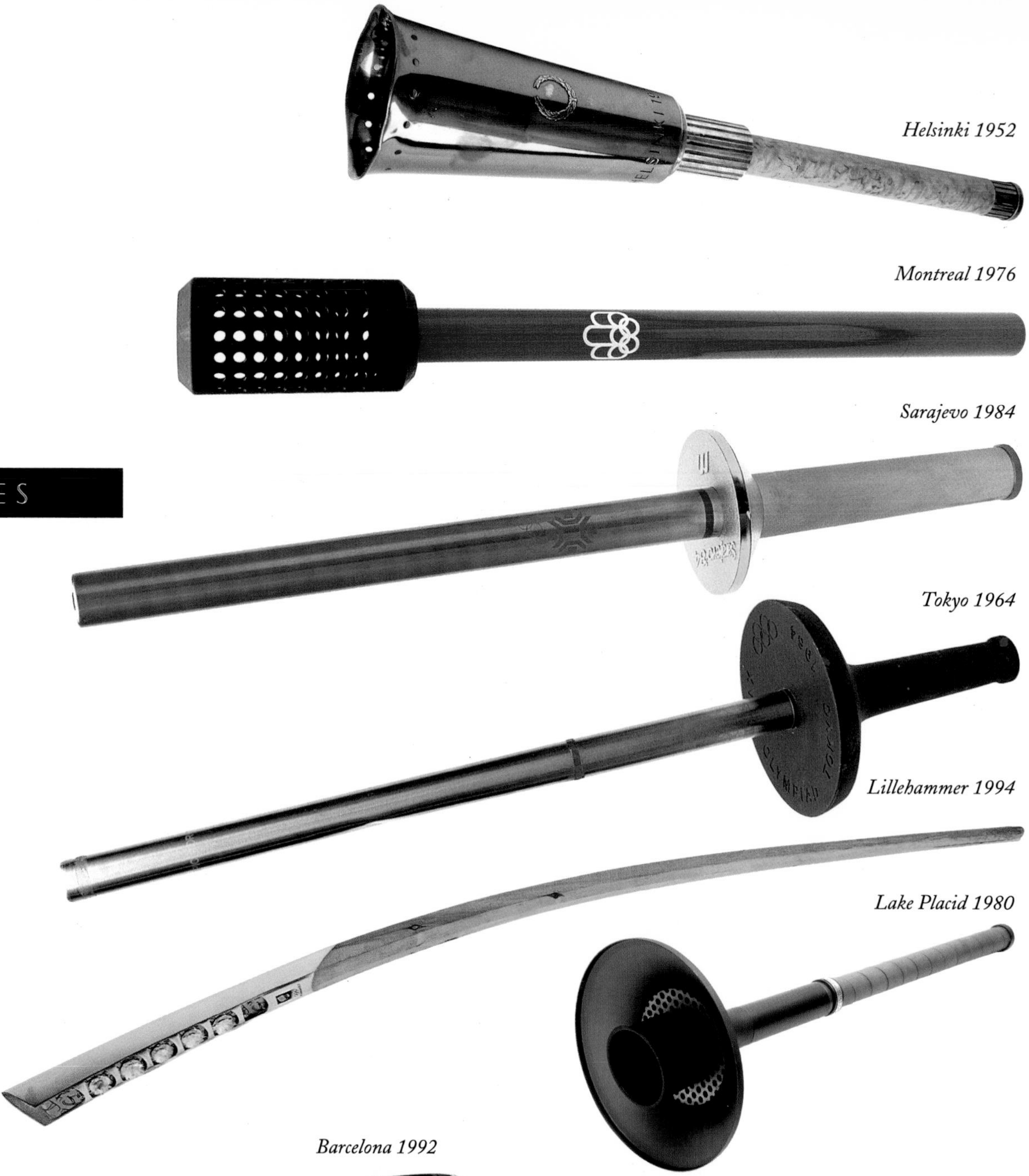

Helsinki 1952

Montreal 1976

Sarajevo 1984

Tokyo 1964

Lillehammer 1994

Lake Placid 1980

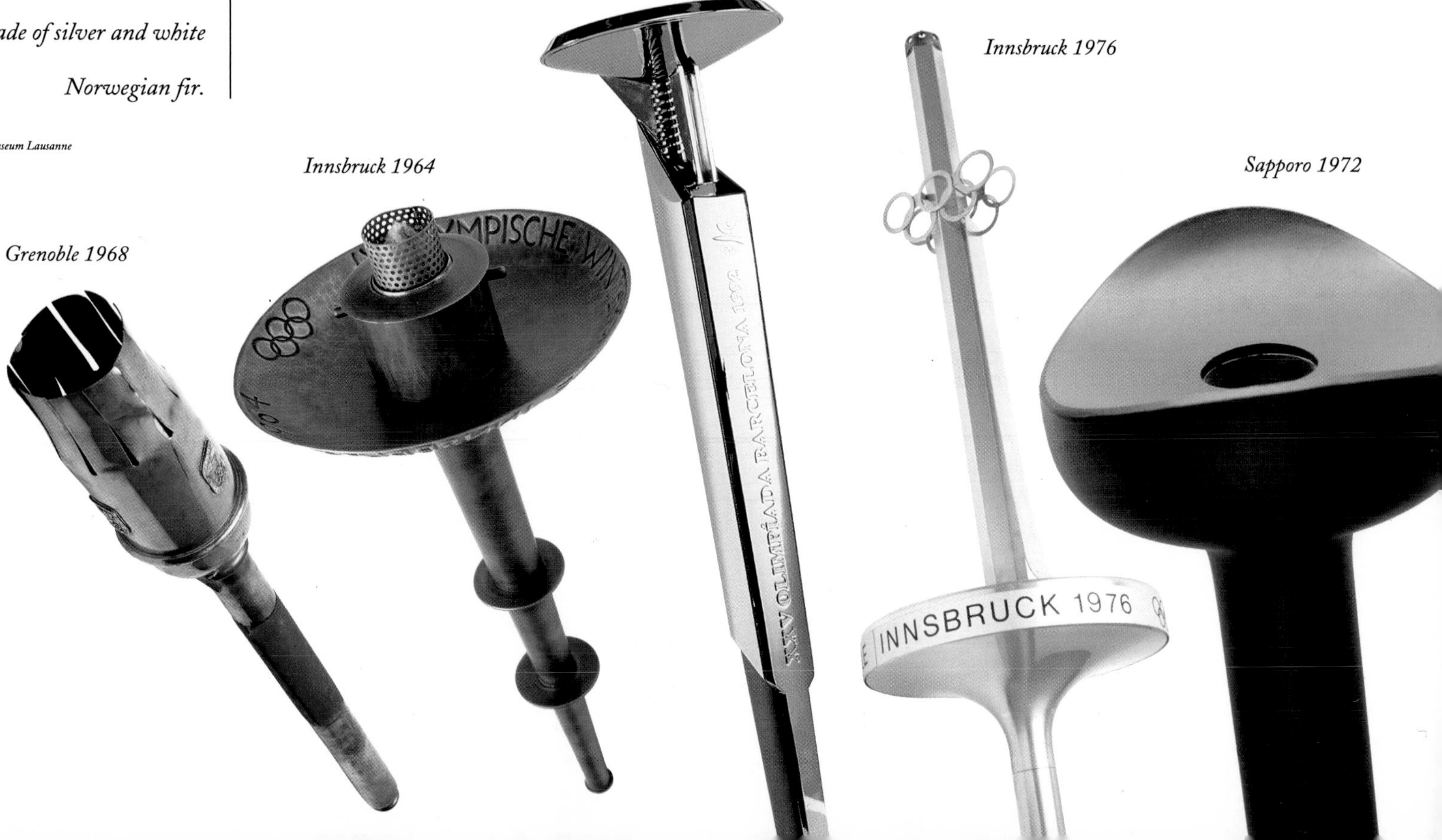

Barcelona 1992

Innsbruck 1976

Innsbruck 1964

Sapporo 1972

Grenoble 1968

When the Olympic torch relay was introduced in 1936, 3,000 runners carried torches from Olympia in Greece to the host city of Berlin. Produced by the firm of Friedrich Krupp, the stainless steel torch holders were more than two feet long and weighed 1 1/2 pounds, with specially designed wicks of incendiary magnesium. Since 1936, Olympic torches have been created for every host city, incorporating a range of technologies and cultural and design influences. For the Lillehammer Games in 1994, runners carried a curved, four-foot-long torch on a 5,000-mile relay around Norway. The Olympic flame was kept burning by six wicks in a 10-pound holder made of silver and white Norwegian fir.

Photos: Archives, Olympic Museum Lausanne

Los Angeles 1984

Munich 1972

Calgary 1980

Rome 1960

Mexico 1968

Berlin 1936

Melbourne 1956

London 1948

Cortina d'Ampezzo 1956

Squaw Valley 1960

Albertville 1992

Seoul 1988

Oslo 1952

THE LEGACY OF OLYMPIA

In the ancient Greek world, there were few qualities more prized than *arete*, the perfection of physical performance, and *kalòk'agathía*, the combination of beauty and goodness. For more than a thousand years, there was no higher expression of those virtues than victory in the sacred Games at Olympia—an athletic and religious spectacle that was

THE ANCIENT GAMES

venerated from Athens and the Aegean Islands to the Hellenic outposts of the Near East and Asia Minor.

From their historical beginnings in 776 B.C. until they were banned in A.D. 394, the ancient Games at Olympia were held every four years without interruption, despite grave threats of invasion and nearly constant warfare among the city-states of Greece. In 480 B.C., the seventy-fifth Olympic Games went on as scheduled, even while a small heroic force of Spartans struggled, unsuccessfully, to repel invading Persians at the Battle of Thermopylae. When the Persian general Mardonius wondered where the rest of the Greek forces were, he was informed that they were "celebrating the Olympic Games and watching gymnastics and horse contests." Ironically, it was in part the superb physical conditioning of the Greeks, achieved through exercise and competition, that enabled them ultimately to drive out the Persians at Plataea, near Thebes, in 479 B.C.

The Games held such a pivotal position in Hellenic life that the Greeks used the Olympic contests and the Olympiad—the four-year period between Games—as a method of dating historical events. To win a contest in the Games made the champion a hero for life, immortalized

THE PENTATHLON

In the ancient Greek Olympics, the five events of the pentathlon included running, wrestling, discus, javelin throwing, and long jump—an event in which the athletes carried semicircular jumping weights, as illustrated on this eighth-century B.C. amphora (opposite).

Photos: Above © Hermitage Museum, Saint Petersburg; Below © George Ortiz Collection, Patrick Goetelen, Geneva; Opposite © Rijks Museum van Oudheden, P.T. Bomhof.

in poetry and sculpture and entitled to free food and lodging. Even to attend the Games was considered a high honor, despite the long journey and frequently uncomfortable living conditions at Olympia. The Games attracted citizens from Greek towns and city-states, and later from colonies in Sicily, the south of Italy, Asia Minor, Spain, and Africa. The most famous artists, poets, writers, and sophists gathered at the Games, including the sculptor Phidias, whose works included

THE GREEK IDEAL

Physical beauty, paired with a well-developed mind, was the epitome of masculine virtue in classical Greece. "From the love of the beautiful," Plato counseled in the Republic, *"comes every good thing in heaven and earth."*
To cultivate the Hellenic ideal of kalòk'agathía—*the combination of beauty and goodness—Greek boys from the age of seven studied literature, music, and art and increased their grace and strength through athletic exercises. Older teenage boys, the* epheboi, *spent time in the* palaestra *and* gymnasium—*public athletic complexes established throughout Greece. There, strict instructors, called* paidotribai, *drilled them in running, wrestling, discus and javelin throwing, boxing, jumping, and ball sports, to the accompaniment of music.*
The Greek preoccupation with physical training had its roots in the constant warfare between small city-states. Each state needed a supremely fit and battle-ready corps of warriors, kept in peak condition during peacetime through rigorous athletics.

Photos: Above, Archives, Olympic Museum Lausanne, Donatsch; Right © George Ortiz Collection, Patrick Goetelen, Geneva.

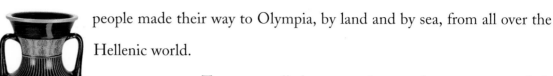

the colossal statues of Zeus at Olympia and Athena at the Parthenon in Athens, the poet Pindar, and the historian Herodotus. Every four years, as many as 40,000 people made their way to Olympia, by land and by sea, from all over the Hellenic world.

To protect all the competitors and spectators on their journeys to and from the Games, a sacred truce, the *ekecheiria*, was declared by heralds throughout Greece before every Olympic festival. The truce was strictly enforced by Olympic officials, who levied fines on anyone who broke the peace. In 420 B.C., according to Thucydides, Spartans were barred from the Games after they launched an attack during the *ekecheiria* and balked at paying the penalty demanded by officials.

Olympia itself, a fertile valley in the remote northwest corner of the Peloponnesus, was acknowledged by all Greeks to be a neutral precinct, where free citizens from every city-state could compete peacefully. No town or village had ever been established at Olympia; its groves and fields had, as early as the tenth century B.C., been set apart as the most sacred center for the worship of Zeus, the supreme god in the Greek pantheon.

Apart from Olympia's religious importance, the sanctuary had plenty of natural advantages. Unlike much of the rough and rocky landscape of Greece, Olympia was a lush, green valley watered by two rivers, the Alpheus and the Kladeus. Spreading out from the banks of the rivers was a broad plain, flanked by evergreen hills and shaded by groves of plane trees, pines, oaks, and wild olives.

According to legend, wild olive trees were once so plentiful at Olympia that Herakles made beds of their foliage to sleep on. It was a wreath woven from the branches of one of these trees, called the Crown Olive, that was the prize bestowed on every Olympic victor—the most coveted honor in all of Greece. At Thermopylae, Herodotus writes, one of the Persian leaders was amazed that Greek athletes would compete so passionately for a prize that was apparently so worthless. "What sort of men," he asked Mardonius, "have you led us to fight against, who contend not for money but purely for the sake of excelling?"

That conclusion was somewhat inaccurate, since Olympic victors actually received substantial material rewards from their city-states—including, in some cases, lifetime pensions and lavish payments for appearances. At Olympia, however, the garland of wild olive was the only reward for victory—and it was victory alone that counted. There was no prize for second or third place, and athletes prayed for "the wreath or death." Epictetus, a Greek philosopher writing in the first and second centuries A.D., described the ultimate humiliation of failure at Olympia: "In the Olympic games it is not possible for you merely to be beaten and then leave; but…you…disgrace yourself in the sight of the whole civilized world…."

For the athletes, the journey to Olympia began in the wrestling schools (*palaestrae*) and *gymnasia* found in nearly every city in Greece. In these public complexes, equipped with exercise rooms, baths, and outdoor training grounds, young men were drilled in athletics to prepare and harden them for armed combat. Those athletes who had the potential to be champions put themselves under the strict supervision of their trainers (*paidotribai*), who prescribed a demanding regimen: "You have to submit to discipline, follow a strict diet, give up sweet cakes, train under compulsion, at a fixed hour, in heat or cold; you must not drink cold water, nor wine just whenever you feel like it; you must have turned yourself over to your trainer precisely as you would to a physician."

THE OLYMPIC FLAME

Torch races—short-distance local relays of purely religious significance—were occasionally included in Greek athletic festivals, but they were never part of the Olympic program. Nevertheless, since 1936, the modern Olympic flame relay has symbolically linked the modern Games with their ancient past. At Olympia in Greece, classically robed women (following spread) ignite the flame with a parabolic mirror that focuses the rays of the sun. The flame is then traditionally passed hand to hand by torch-bearing runners until it reaches the site of the Olympic Games.

Photos: Above, Archives, Olympic Museum Lausanne, Stram; Below © Hermitage Museum, Saint Petersburg; Following page © Duomo, William R. Sallaz.

THE CROWN GAMES

The glory of the Greek gods Zeus, Poseidon, and Apollo was celebrated at the four Crown Games, the most important of all the Greek athletic festivals. Together, these Panhellenic Games, which attracted athletes from all over the Greek world, were called the periodos, *or circuit. The Olympic festival and the Nemean Games held at Nemea honored Zeus. The Isthmian Games at Corinth were held at a sanctuary of Poseidon, and the Pythian Games at Delphi were consecrated to the god Apollo. Each of these festivals featured running events, as well as the pentathlon, wrestling, boxing, the fierce pankration, and equestrian contests. Only the lesser Crown Games—the Pythian, Isthmian, and Nemean—included musical competitions in singing and the playing of the lyre and the flute.*

The prize at each of the Panhellenic Games was a simple crown of leaves: a wreath of laurel at the Pythian festival, a garland of pine branches at the Isthmian, a crown of wild celery at the Nemean, and a wreath of wild olive at Olympia. An athlete who won a crown at each of the four Games was immortalized as a hero and honored with the title periodonikos, *the "winner of the circuit."*

Photos: Above and right, Archives, Olympic Museum Lausanne, Strahm.

ANCIENT GREECE

There were ample opportunities for athletes to compete in local contests and athletic festivals. In 500 B.C. there were some fifty regularly scheduled games, and the number climbed to more than three hundred in the first century A.D. By far the most important of these contests was the *periodos,* the circuit of Crown Games: the Pythian, Isthmian, Nemean, and Olympian festivals. The greatest of all these events, which drew the very best competitors in Greece, were the Games at Olympia, dedicated to Zeus.

Six months before every Olympic festival, official heralds (*spondophoroi*) would travel throughout Greece to announce the exact dates for the coming Games—which always coincided with the second or third full moon after the summer solstice—and to declare the sacred truce to protect all travelers. The arrival of the *spondophoroi*  marked the beginning of intensive athletic training and competition in every town and city. Local judges selected the athletes who would compete at Olympia—all, by requirement, free-born citizens of pure Greek lineage who had committed no crimes of violence. About two months before the Games, these hometown champions—accompanied by a colorful procession of leading politicians, artists, merchants, and intellectuals—set off, with great pomp and circumstance, for Olympia and the city of Elis, the district that retained official control over the Games.

Situated some thirty-five miles north of Olympia, Elis was an independent, agrarian backwater. Its government oversaw the codifying of Olympic rules and appointed the Hellenodikai—judges who were the arbiters and umpires of the Olympic Games. To the Eleans' credit, they managed the Games, for the most part, strictly and fairly, even during the corrupt years of the Roman Empire; they made "painstaking and orderly arrangements; they seemed to feel themselves to be on their trial quite as much as the athletic competitors, and to be determined to make no mistakes...."

According to Olympic rules, athletes had to train in Elis, under the eyes and flashing whips of the Hellenodikai, for a period of thirty days before the Games. The judges checked athletes' qualifications, permitted them to compete or disqualified them from the Games, fined or whipped competitors for misbehavior, made sure they slept on skins on the hard ground, and enforced an austere diet of dried figs, nuts, barley bread, porridge, and fresh cheese. On the training grounds of Elis, lined with tall plane trees, the Hellenodikai also set up trial matches and paired wrestling and boxing contestants by age and ability, since there were no weight classes at Olympia.

Three days before the Games, those competitors who had successfully made it through the rigorous month of training set out by foot on a two-day procession to Olympia. By the time the athletes, judges, trainers, and other officials arrived at the sacred valley, the grounds were already teeming with spectators who had traveled to the Games from every corner of Hellas. There were few facilities to house and feed the crowds, who paid no admission for the Games and for the most part camped in tents or slept out under the stars.

The shouting, jostling crush was compounded by legions of food and drink vendors, peddlers, singers, dancers, touts, conjurers, and fortune-tellers who worked the crowd. The high-spirited scene was probably similar to the noisy chaos that one spectator observed at the Isthmian Games: "You could see and hear the accursed sophists shouting and abusing one another, and their so-called pupils fighting one another, many authors giving readings of their works which no one listens to, many poets reciting their poems..., many conjurers performing their tricks and many fortune-tellers interpreting omens, thousands of lawyers arguing cases and a host of cheap jacks selling everything under the sun."

THE FIRST FOOT RACE

The first official Olympic Games, held in 776 B.C., reportedly consisted of a single foot race. The competition, a 192-meter dash, was won by Koroibus, a cook from nearby Elis. Thirteen Olympiads later, in 724 B.C., a second foot race was added, the 400-meter diaulos—a sprint down the length of the track, around a turning post, and back. It was not until 708 B.C. that a nonrunning competition—wrestling—was officially included. By the late seventh century B.C., the Games at Olympia had evolved to include the classical roster of events, including foot races, discus and javelin throws, long jump, wrestling, boxing, chariot races, bareback horse races, and the pankration—a fierce, no-holds-barred combination of boxing and wrestling that mimicked man to man combat on the field of battle.

Photos: Above © George Ortiz Collection, Patrick Goetelen, Geneva; Below © Hermitage Museum, Saint Petersburg.

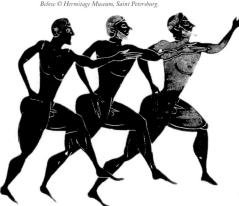

The heat, the crowds, the dust, and the flies could be so aggravating that, according to one story, a disobedient slave was threatened by his master with a visit to Olympia as punishment. According to Epictetus, "some unpleasant and hard things happen in life. And do they not happen at Olympia? Do you not swelter? Are you not cramped and crowded? Do you not bathe with discomfort? Are you not drenched whenever it rains? Do you not have your fill of tumult and shouting and other annoyances? But I fancy that you hear and endure all this by balancing it off against the memorable character of the spectacle."

The spectacle, however, was an exclusively male affair: no women were permitted, with the exception of the priestess of Demeter; and, according to the laws of Elis, any female who attempted to violate this taboo would be hurled to her certain death from a high, rocky cliff called the Tympaion. Fortunately, no female interlopers were ever caught—except for Kallipateira, who disguised herself as a male trainer to watch her son, Peisirodos, compete. When Peisirodos won his event, she jumped over a fence, uncovering her fraud in her excitement. Because Kallipateira's father, brothers, and son were all Olympic champions, her life was spared. But Olympic law was thereafter changed to require that all trainers, like athletes at the Games, had to enter the arena without clothing.

THE DISCUS

The metal discuses used at Olympia weighed up to 14 1/2 pounds. Competitors hurled them with a throwing technique similar to that used by athletes today.

Photos: Above and right, Archives, Olympic Museum Lausanne.

On opening day, the excitement at Olympia began with the arrival of the athletes, preceded by trumpeters and heralds, purple-robed Hellenodikai, priests, and delegations of officials. After making sacrifices, the procession wound its way to the council hall (*bouleterion*) with its great statue of Zeus of Oaths clutching thunderbolts in his powerful hands. Here, the athletes, their fathers and brothers, and their trainers swore over a dismembered boar to abide by all the Olympic rules. The athletes vowed that they had been in full training for ten months, and the judges pledged that they would rigidly uphold the rules and punish all offenders.

Athletes who dishonored the Games by bribery or committing other crimes were banished from Olympia or compelled to pay fines. The money collected from them paid for dozens of statues of Zeus inscribed with cautionary words such as "You win with the speed of your feet and the strength in your body, and not with money."

After the first day of oaths and celebrations, the athletic competitions commenced. In the early fifth century, when the Games assumed their classical, five-day schedule, the very first event was the two-wheeled chariot race, held in the rectangular, open-air hippodrome. This immensely popular contest was one of very few in which competitors were clothed—and in which a woman could win the crown of olive, since victory went to the wealthy owner of the winning chariot and horses, and not to the anonymous driver.

During this heart-stopping event, as many as forty chariots, each driven by a team of four horses, hurtled back and forth down a 400-meter track as they attempted to complete twelve double laps, totaling nearly nine miles. Inevitably, chariots crashed and horses panicked in the dust and commotion as they careened wildly around the single turning post at each end of the narrow, undivided race course. In one race, celebrated by Pindar, only a single charioteer out of forty competitors made it to the finish line.

THE PAIDOTRIBAI

In the gymnasia—*sports complexes which were central to the cultural life of every Greek city—athletes were rigorously drilled by whip-wielding trainers called* paidotribai.

Photo: Archives, Olympic Museum Lausanne.

After the chariot races, equestrian events continued with Olympic horse racing. Riders galloped, without saddles or stirrups, up and down the race course of the hippodrome, on turf that had been torn up by the teams of hard-charging chariots. As in the previous event, the crown of olive was awarded to the owner of the winning steed rather than to the jockey. On one occasion, the wreath was given to the owner of a mare named Breeze, who made it first to the finish line without the rider who had fallen off at the starting gate.

The second day's competitions ended with the pentathlon events—long jump, javelin and discus throwing, running, and wrestling—most of which were held in the Olympic stadium. The victor was the athlete who finished first in three of the five competitions. For the long jump, competitors carried semicircular weights, called *halteres,* which they swung forward on takeoff and backward upon landing. Made of stone or metal, the four- to nine-pound weights were used to extend the length of the jump and help the athlete land steadily on his feet. In the javelin contest, athletes hurled a blunt-tipped wooden spear, competing for the greatest distance. To help guide the javelin, competitors wrapped the shaft tightly with a leather thong, leaving a loop at one end through which they slipped one or two fingers. After a running start, the athlete hurled the javelin, which spun as the leather strap unwound. Five throws were permitted, and only the best performance counted. Similarly, pentathletes were scored on the best of five throws of the discus. Made of metal, the discuses at Olympia varied in size and heft, weighing up to 14 1/2-pounds, and were thrown using a technique similar to that employed today.

The pentathlon foot race was a 200-meter sprint down the length of the stadium, on a course of sand laid over a surface of clay. At the start of the race, the barefoot runners pushed off with their back feet from marble starting slabs, called *balbides,* which are still visible at Olympia. Finally, at the end of the second day, spectators crowded to watch the wrestling, the last event of the pentathlon. Matches were fought standing up, and victory went to the athlete who forced his opponent to the ground three times.

The morning of the third day was devoted entirely to religious processions and spectacles—culminating in the blood-soaked slaughter of a hundred oxen before the towering altar of Zeus, an enormous mound of ash rising

THE STRIGIL

To protect their skin, athletes rubbed their bodies with olive oil and covered themselves with dust. After training or competition, and before bathing, they scraped the oil and dirt from their bodies with a curved implement called a strigil.

Photos: Below © Hermitage Museum, Saint Petersburg; Bottom, Archives, Olympic Museum Lausanne.

HORSE RACING

Equestrian contests provided some of the most exciting moments of the ancient Olympic Games. During the horse racing event, riders galloped bareback up and down the 400-meter race track in the hippodrome. In the two-wheeled chariot race, one of the most dramatic competitions, dozens of four-horse teams charged twelve times up and down the undivided track, careening around a single turning post at each end of the course.

Photos: Right © George Ortiz Collection, Patrick Goetelen, Geneva; Below, Archives, Olympic Museum Lausanne.

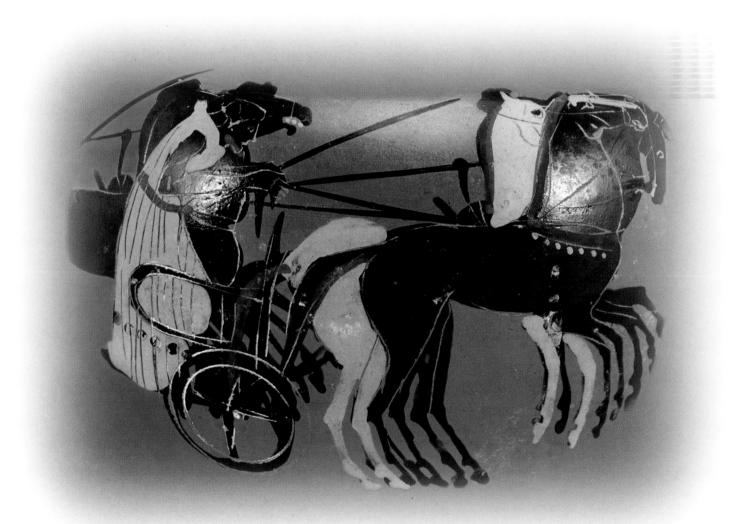

twenty-two feet high. The thighs of the slaughtered creatures were burned on a fire of white poplar at the top of the ash mound; the remains were reserved for feasting at the conclusion of the Games. Competition then resumed in the afternoon, when youths aged twelve through seventeen matched their speed and strength in sprints, wrestling, and boxing events.

The fourth day at Olympia was the very last day of competition. In the stadium, four to eight runners at a time competed in foot races—the 200-meter *stade* sprint, the 400-meter *diaulos* race, and the 4,800-meter *dolichos* long-distance event. An athlete who won all three races earned the title *Triastes*, a rare honor conferred four times on one champion, Leonidas of Rhodes.

The day ended with the hugely popular body-contact sports: wrestling, boxing, and the ferocious *pankration*. There were no weight classes or time limits for any of these brutal sports. Wrestlers, their thickly muscled bodies rubbed with oil and sand to toughen and protect their skin, gripped each other on a platform in the center of the stadium and struggled to force each other to the ground. Milo of Kroton, a champion with legendary strength who won the wrestling at Olympia six times, reportedly trained for this grueling event by ingesting a daily diet of twenty pounds each of bread and wheat and eighteen pints of wine.

Even more popular with the spectators was boxing, the bloodiest of all the Olympic combat sports. Boxers wrapped their fists tightly with narrow strips of leather and pummeled each other brutally until one was knocked unconscious or gave up by raising his right hand. Over time, leather thongs were replaced by fist coverings weighted or spiked with metal, and boxers were often beaten beyond recognition. One man named Olympikos, wrote Lucillius in the first century A.D., "used to have nose, chin, forehead, ears, and eyelids. But then he enrolled in the guild of boxing...."

The most demanding and highly regarded body-contact sport was the *pankration*, a combination of wrestling and boxing in which nearly every imaginable move was permitted, from kicking and trampling to punching and strangling. Only biting and eye gouging were forbidden. One pankratist, nicknamed "Mr. Fingertips," would bend his opponent's fingertips back and not let go until the victim gave up in agony. Another pankratist, overcome during a match by pain from a broken toe, tapped his opponent's shoulder in surrender—only to discover that he had already strangled his adversary to death. The judges awarded the wreath of olive to the corpse.

The final, somewhat comic, event of the Olympic Games was the race in armor—a 400-meter foot race in which contestants ran up and down the length of the stadium clad only in helmets, shields, and leg armor. The festival concluded on the evening of the fifth day with the reading of the list of winners and the crowning of the champions with the garlands of wild olive.

Olympic victory was considered so glorious that in A.D. 67—more than two hundred years after Greece had become a Roman province—the Emperor Nero made special arrangements to compete in the Olympic Games, proclaiming himself winner in six events. Under the emperor's absurd orders, the festival included musical and poetic competitions—unheard of at Olympia—and a ten-horse chariot race in which Nero had himself declared the victor even after he had ridiculously fallen out of his chariot. These Games were later expunged from the Olympic record.

By A.D. 324, however, when Christianity became the state religion of the Roman Empire, the influence and integrity of the Olympic Games had seriously degenerated. Professional athletes performed at Olympia, and the Games, which had become rife with bribery, resembled more of a circus rather than a sacred festival. In A.D. 394, the Games were banned as a pagan rite by Emperor Theodosius I. The temples and altars were tumbled and the statues melted down. The next year, the Goths, led by Alaric, swept through Olympia, and its ruin was completed by devastating earthquakes in A.D. 522 and 551. Eventually, nearly all traces of the sanctuary were erased by the river Kladeus, which changed its course and buried Olympia under twenty feet of earth and rubble. It was more than fourteen hundred years before the German archaeologist Ernst Curtius began to clear away the debris and bring the lost ruins and spirit of Olympia to light.

THE HALTERES

Long jumpers at Olympia used stone or metal weights, called halteres, *to extend their leaps. Jumpers swung the four- to nine-pound weights forward to shoulder height on takeoff and backwards, to the knees, on landing.*

Photos: Below © George Ortiz Collection, Yoram Lehmann, Jerusalem; Opposite, Archives, Olympic Museum Lausanne.

THE GAMES OF SUMMER

After racing for hours over twenty-five miles of rugged ravines and twisting mountain paths, Spiridon Loues pounded exhaustedly into the white marble Panathenean Stadium in Athens. Alone, with the closest runner a full seven minutes behind him, he was suddenly swept up by the thunderous cheers of 140,000 spectators who packed

FROM ATHENS TO ATLANTA

the stadium to the rims, swarmed over the surrounding hills, and showered the field around him with hats and flowers.

On that April day a century ago, Loues—a twenty-five-year-old Greek shepherd—carried some of Olympia's ancient magic into the modern world. He was the first Olympic champion from Greece in nearly fifteen centuries—the winner of the first marathon in the very first of the modern Olympic Games, held in Athens in 1896. He had raced along the route taken in 490 B.C., according to legend, by the Olympian Pheidippides, who died after running from Marathon to Athens with news of Greek victory in battle. But Loues, flanked in his exultant last lap by two princes of Greece, claimed a victory rich in history for himself and for his country, the birthplace of the ancient Games.

Loues wasn't the first winner of those first modern Olympics. That place in history belongs to American James Connolly—an undergraduate who had dropped out of Harvard to compete, paid his own travel expenses to the Games, and captured the first Olympic title in the triple jump. But when Loues won the marathon for Greece on the fifth day and was crowned with a wreath of wild olive leaves from Olympia, it was a moment that profoundly fused past and present, 1,500 years of history,

1992 BARCELONA

CARL LEWIS, USA

At the Los Angeles Summer Games in 1984, American track phenomenon Carl Lewis became the first Olympic athlete to duplicate Jesse Owens's golds in four events. Lewis earned two more golds in 1988 and two again in 1992.

Photos: Above © Duomo, Steven E. Sutton; Below, Archives, Olympic Museum Lausanne; Opposite © Duomo, David Madison.

with the sweaty, cheering, raucous reality of modern life. The Olympics were reborn—and from that day on they belonged not just to the Greek world but to the whole world.

To be sure, the Athens Games were in many ways a rough revival of the Olympic spirit. Most of the world knew or cared little about these Games. Although 311 athletes from thirteen nations competed in nine sports, three-quarters of the competitors were Greek. America's patched-together team was made up largely of college students who had mistakenly arrived just a day before the Games began—forgetting that there was a twelve-day difference between the Greek and American calendars. Great Britain's squad included two employees from its embassy in Athens, as well as a tourist named John Boland, who signed up for the tennis tournaments and won.

Germany's athletes were strong contenders in gymnastics and clinched the wrestling title, while France's Paul Masson pedaled to victory in three cycling events. America's squad of athletic club recruits managed to thoroughly dominate the track and field events. In one distressing upset for the Greeks, Robert Garrett, a shot-putter from Princeton, outhurled a popular Greek champion in the discus throw, even though Garrett had never seen a discus before setting foot in Greece. U.S. swimmer Gardner Williams, however, didn't have quite as much success adapting to Greek sport. Olympic swimming races were held in the choppy Bay of Zea, where the waters had cooled to an icy 55 degrees Fahrenheit. Used to the warmer temperatures of indoor pools, Williams plunged in, announced he was "freezing," and quit the competition.

Overall, the first Olympic Games were a roaring success, and Greece lobbied hard to remain the exclusive host of all subsequent Games. But Baron Pierre de Coubertin opposed the idea and succeeded in moving the second Olympiad to Paris in 1900. The Paris plans, however, were a disaster from the beginning. That year, the French capital was also hosting the enormous Universal Exposition. The Olympic Games were tacked onto the event as an afterthought and were for the most part ill-organized,

---

1896 ATHENS

SPIRIDON LOUES, GRE

In the first of the modern Olympic Games, Spiridon Loues, a twenty-five-year-old Greek shepherd from the village of Amaroussion, won the 25-mile marathon race with a seven-minute lead. He was joined in his victory lap around the stadium by the royal princes of Greece and was offered rewards of free food, lodging, shaves, and hats.

Photos: Left and above, Archives, Olympic Museum Lausanne.

1896 ATHENS

PANAGIOTIS PARASKEVOPOLOUS, GRE

The discus event in Athens was a major upset for the Greeks, whose champion, Panagiotis Paraskevopolous, was beaten by American Robert Garrett—a Princeton student who had never seen a discus before he arrived in Athens for the Games.

Photo: Archives, Olympic Museum Lausanne.

unpromoted, and ignored. The word "Olympics" never even
appeared in the official program, which billed the competition
as an "International Championship." Fewer than a thousand spectators attended, and some competitors had no idea that they were
participating in the Olympic Games. The athletic spectacle
itself had all the glamour of a brewery picnic. Events
were held over five months and were staged in vari-
ous parts of the city, many of them much more
suitable for Sunday strolls than for track and field
events. Jumpers had to dig their own landing
pits with the spikes of their shoes, and hammer and discus throwers ended up hurling
shots into the trees.

Despite the innumerable problems, teams from twenty-two countries
entered the Paris Games, with France
sponsoring the largest contingent.

Thirteen new sports were added, including golf,
rowing, and water polo, and women were allowed to compete in
Olympic events for the first time, though solely in lawn tennis and
golf. Champions included U.S. standing-jump champion Ray Ewry—
the "Rubber Man"—who collected three gold medals in Paris and went
on to win another seven in 1904, 1906, and 1908. Ewry's gold-medal har-
vest in Paris was topped by U.S. track star Alvin Kraenzlein, who introduced the technique of hurdling with one leg extended and swept four
individual golds in track and field events.

Although the Paris Olympics were an admitted flop, the
next Olympiad did nothing to improve the fortunes or the image of
the Games. The 1904 Olympics were originally destined for Chicago,
but President Theodore Roosevelt urged that they be held in St. Louis,

1904 ST. LOUIS

ETIENNE DESMARTEAU, CAN

*Etienne Desmarteau, a
Montreal policeman, was fired
for leaving work to compete in
the Olympics. He was welcomed
back on the job, however, after
he beat a New York City
policeman to win the gold in
the 56-pound weight throw.*

Photo: Archives, Olympic Museum
Lausanne / NOC / CAN.

Missouri, in conjunction with the Louisiana Purchase Exhibition. Once again, the thunder of the Games was stolen by massive civic entertainment. The event was billed as "a fair where there are also sports." And this time, because the Olympics were located so far from Europe, only twelve nations took part. Even Coubertin declined to make the trip. The carnival-like atmosphere sank to grotesque lows during a two-day Olympic "Anthropological Days" demonstration, in which African

Pygmies, Patagonians, and Philippine Igorots and Moros were recruited from sideshows at the World's Fair to compete in mud fights, pole climbing, and other "native games."

Official Olympic sports had their troubles, too. At least partly because of their overwhelming numbers, American athletes grabbed 238 out of 284 Olympic medals. And a wretchedly organized marathon tested athletes' endurance beyond ordinary limits. The race was staged in scorching heat, and runners had to gasp and dodge their way through the constant, dust-kicking traffic of bicycles, horses, and automobiles that clung to them along the route. One competitor, a Zulu tribesman named Lentauw, was forced to take a sudden detour when two large dogs chased him through a cornfield. The race was ultimately won by a Boston brass worker named Thomas Hicks, who swallowed small doses of strychnine along the way to numb the pain of running and had to be revived by four doctors after crossing the finish line.

To recover from the dismal experiences of Paris and St. Louis, Coubertin sanctioned the first— and only—interim Olympic Games, held in Athens in April 1906. Greeks enthusiastically welcomed the Games back, even during an unofficial Olympic year, and managed the event with energetic efficiency. Spectators packed the Panathenean Stadium, and twenty countries competed, including the first official American Olympic team. Although the

1904 ST. LOUIS

WOMEN'S BOXING

Boxing debuted at the 1904 Olympic Games, and women's boxing was a demonstration sport.

Photo: Archives, Olympic Museum
Lausanne / AIO Athens.

1904 ST. LOUIS

THE "NATIVE GAMES"

In a demeaning sideshow event called "Anthropological Days," Pygmies, Patagonians, Kaffirs, and other "savages" were called on by Olympic organizers in St. Louis to participate in "native" contests such as archery, pole climbing, and mud fights.

Photos: Above and left, Archives, Olympic Museum Lausanne;
Below, Archives, Olympic Museum Lausanne / AIO Athens.

1904 ST. LOUIS

RALPH ROSE, USA

A 6-foot, 6-inch Californian, Ralph Rose won the shot put and took silver in the discus in 1904. He went on to win two more shot put golds in 1908 and 1912.

Photo: Archives, Olympic Museum Lausanne.

1904 ST. LOUIS

RAY EWRY, USA

Ray Ewry spent his childhood partly paralyzed by polio and confined to a wheelchair. Determined to overcome his handicap, he exercised to strengthen his legs and amazingly won ten gold medals in Olympic jumping events from 1900 through 1908, including three-gold sweeps in both 1900 and 1904.

Photo: Archives, Olympic Museum Lausanne.

1908 LONDON

3,000-METER STEEPLECHASE

Runners splashed through a water jump in the chilly 1908 Olympic Games in London (opposite). The steeplechase event, which included seven water jumps and twenty-eight solid hurdles, was won by Arthur Russell of Great Britain.

Photo: Archives, Olympic Museum Lausanne.

results of these interim Games are not counted in the Olympic record, they succeeded in reviving the flagging Olympic spirit and reassured organizers that the modern Games did, in fact, have a future.

Buoyed by success in Athens, the regular Olympic schedule picked up again in London in July 1908, after Rome declined to host the Games for financial reasons. Many modern Olympic traditions originated in this fourth Olympiad. For the first time, only nations, not individuals, were permitted to enter, and athletes representing twenty-three countries paraded behind their flags during the opening ceremonies. Beginning with the London Games, medals were awarded for third-place finishers, and women's participation was expanded to archery and gymnastics demonstrations.

Throughout the Games, however, the weather was miserably wet and cold, and there were fractious disputes among teams, including accusations of bad sportsmanship and chauvinism—particularly since all the judges were British. British spectators, by the same token, were aghast at the enthusiastic rooting of Americans, who cheered victory by tooting kazoos and singing "There'll be a Hot Time in the Old Town Tonight." In a legendary marathon incident that nearly strained international relations between America and Britain, the first runner to stagger into Shepherd's Bush Stadium, Dorando Pietri—a candymaker from Capri—collapsed on the track and was dragged over the finish line by overexcited English officials. After screams of unfair officiating, America's Johnny Hayes—the first to cross the tape under his own leg power—was finally awarded the gold medal. In another strange footnote to the marathon, Princess Mary requested that the race begin beneath the royal nursery windows at Windsor—a move that permanently lengthened the official international marathon distance from about twenty-five miles to twenty-six miles, 385 yards.

1912 STOCKHOLM

PATRICK MCDONALD, USA

At 6-feet, 4-inches and 350 pounds, Pat McDonald made his presence felt at the 1912 Olympic Games, where he beat out Ralph Rose for a shot put gold. McDonald made his living as a New York City policeman, directing traffic in Times Square.

Photo: Archives, Olympic Museum Lausanne.

Throughout the events, Great Britain captured the greatest number of medals, although the United States again dominated track and field. In the 110-meter hurdles, American Forrest Smithson shattered the world's record while, according to some accounts, clutching a Bible in his hand to protest the scheduling of the race on Sunday, and U.S. swimmer Charles Daniels earned his fourth individual Olympic gold in the 100-meter freestyle, adding to the three he had previously collected in 1904 and 1906.

After the poisonous squabbling and alleged jingoism of the London Games, many skeptics concluded that the Olympics did more to cause international strife than to encourage world peace. But the well-organized 1912 Olympics in Stockholm restored some of the luster to the Games. At Coubertin's urging, the number of sports was trimmed back from twenty-one to fourteen. Public address systems and electric timing systems were introduced, and there was high-profile press coverage of the athletic spectacle. Women competed in swimming, and the 100-meter freestyle was snared by Australia's Fanny Durack, who hauled through the water wearing a bulky woolen bathing suit. Boxing, however, was stricken from the program for the first and only time in Olympic history, since the sport was banned in Sweden.

The most impressive marathons took place not on the road but in the wrestling arena. The final bout of the light-heavy-weight event went on for a grueling nine hours, and Finnish and Russian middleweights grappled for nearly twelve hours under a brutal sun. In men's swimming events, America's Duke Kahanamoku—who introduced the flutter kick and Hawaiian crawl in international competition—sprinted to a gold medal in the 100-meter freestyle race. George Patton, future World War II general—then a lieutenant at West Point—ranked fifth in a new event, the modern pentathlon. And there were astonishing per-formances in track and field. Hannes Kolehmainen, a vegetarian bricklayer, became the first of the famous "Flying Finns" when he flashed to gold medals in three cross-country races.

1912 STOCKHOLM

KENNETH MCARTHUR, SAF

Victorious Kenneth McArthur, a thirty-year-old South African policeman, was carried off the field by his proud countrymen after winning the marathon, held in brutally hot weather. Francisco Lazaro, a Portuguese runner, collapsed during the race and died in the hospital the next day.

Photos: Below and right Archives, Olympic Museum Lausanne.

1912 STOCKHOLM

JIM THORPE, USA

One of the greatest Olympians of all time was the astonishing Jim Thorpe. Part Irish, part French, and part Native American, Thorpe easily swept gold medals in the grueling pentathlon and decathlon events. Sweden's King Gustav V declared him "the greatest athlete in the world." Six months later, however, a newspaper reported that Thorpe had accepted $25 a week for playing minor-league baseball, and he was stripped of all his Olympic medals. His record was not reinstated until 1982, nearly thirty years after his death.

Photo: Archives, Olympic Museum Lausanne.

1924 PARIS

ERIC LIDDELL, GBR

Celebrated in the movie Chariots of Fire, Eric Liddell was a Scottish divinity student who flashed past his rivals to take gold in the 400 meters. "I do not like to be beaten," he was often heard to say.

Photo: Archives, Olympic Museum Lausanne.

1912 STOCKHOLM

JOHAN "HANNES" KOLEHMAINEN, FIN

When "Hannes the Mighty" Kolehmainen raced to victory in Stockholm in the 5,000-, 8,000-, and 10,000-meter races, Finland pulled ahead of the pack as a world power in distance running. Kolehmainen went on to triumph in the marathon in the 1920 games.

Photo: Archives, Olympic Museum Lausanne.

But dwarfing all other competitors was U.S. collegiate track and football star Jim Thorpe. Part Sac and Fox Indian, Thorpe—whose tribal name was Wa-Tho-Huck or Bright Path—had never thrown a javelin until two months before the Games. But he easily mastered both the decathlon and pentathlon in an unmatched display of all-around athletic prowess. Sweden's King Gustav V declared the Oklahoman "the greatest athlete in the world." Six months later, however, a Boston newspaper reported that Thorpe had been paid $25 a week for playing minor-league baseball in Rocky Mount, North Carolina, and Thorpe was heartbreakingly stripped of all his medals. It wasn't until 1982—nearly thirty years after his death—that Thorpe's record was officially reinstated by the International Olympic Committe (IOC).

The cataclysmic upheaval of World War I postponed the next Olympic Games until 1920, when they were held in the war-ravaged city of Antwerp, Belgium. Despite persistent rain, the economic toll of war, and the exclusion of Germany, Austria, Hungary, Bulgaria, and Turkey, the Antwerp Games managed to revive the Olympics after a savage eight-year interruption. This time America's domination of track and field was challenged by the fleet-footed Finns. But French military veteran Joseph Guillemot—who had been badly gassed in combat during World War I—edged past Paavo Nurmi, Finland's "mechanical Frankenstein," in the 5,000-meter run. Another war veteran, Great Britain's Albert Hill, scored golds in the 800- and 1,500-meter races, while the silver in the 1,500 was clinched by teammate Philip Baker, who went on to receive the Nobel Peace Prize in 1959. In the pool, Duke Kahanamoku splashed to a second freestyle gold, and Ethelda Bleibtry, who had suffered from childhood polio, swam to two individual gold medals in world-record times.

Paris was given a second chance to host the Olympics in 1924. Eager to repair their city's Olympic image, the French hosts took pains to prepare carefully for the event. Again, Germany was encouraged to stay home, but athletes from forty-four other nations converged on the French capital, and more than 600,000 spectators jammed the Games. The hometown team took honors in cycling and fencing, and Great Britain's Eric Liddell and Harold Abrahams—later mythologized in the movie *Chariots of Fire*—paced to golds in the 400- and 100-meter races. In his second Olympic appearance, the "Flying Finn," Paavo Nurmi—who had drilled

1924 PARIS

JOHNNY WEISSMULLER, USA

Born in Romania, Johnny Weissmuller was four when his family emigrated to the U.S. At age twenty, he swam off with three gold medals in the 1924 Olympics and took two more Olympic pool titles in 1928. Weissmuller's greatest fame came after 1932, when he starred in Tarzan the Ape Man, *the first of his eighteen Tarzan movie roles.*

Photo: Archives, Olympic Museum Lausanne.

himself by outracing the mail train at home in Turku, Finland—stunned spectators by taking five gold medals in track and field events, even though he had injured his legs during training. In brutally hot weather, Nurmi trotted coolly over stony, thistle-choked paths to the finish in the 10,000-meter cross-country, while twenty-four of his thirty-eight rivals collapsed in exhaustion along the route. U.S. sharpshooter Carl Osburn raised his Olympic medal total to eleven, including five golds. A member of the winning U.S. rowing team was a 6-foot, 4-inch Ivy League sculler named Benjamin Spock, and Tarzan-to-be Johnny Weissmuller, winner of sixty-seven world records, streaked to three golds in freestyle swimming.

Germany finally rejoined the Olympic Games in Amsterdam in 1928, where, for the first time, the Olympic flame burned throughout the competitions. Nurmi and Weissmuller each added another gold to their collections, but the Games were generally disappointing for the U.S., whose historic preeminence in track and field continued to decline. India, on the other hand, began its brilliant domination of field hockey, which lasted until 1960. And Uruguay scored its second gold in soccer, an immensely popular event mobbed by more than 200,000 fans. It was a landmark Olympics for women, too, who for the first time were allowed to compete in gymnastics and five track and field events. In swimming, Germany's Hilde Schrader breaststroked so quickly past her rivals on her way to gold and a new world record that she ripped the straps of her bathing suit in the process. "I would have gone even faster," she confided, "if I had not been so embarrassed."

1928 AMSTERDAM

PERCY WILLIAMS, CAN

A former waiter from Vancouver, Percy Williams, 20, took home golds for Canada in both the 100- and 200-meter sprints. "That boy doesn't run— he flies," declared U.S. competitor Charley Paddock.

Photo: Archives, Olympic Museum Lausanne.

1928 AMSTERDAM

PAAVO NURMI, FIN

"Flying Finn" Paavo Nurmi captured the 10,000-meter gold in 1928 by six-tenths of a second—bringing his Olympic gold medal total to nine. The nearly invincible Nurmi had raced off with three golds in the 1920 Games and scored five more in 1924 in Paris.

Photo: Archives, Olympic Museum Lausanne.

JUAN CARLOS ZABALA, ARG

Twenty-year-old Juan Carlos Zabala of Argentina collapsed after crossing the finish line first in the 1932 Olympic marathon. He had a 19-second lead over his nearest competitor, Sam Ferris of Great Britain.

Photo: Archives, Olympic Museum Lausanne /
International News Photos.

JAPANESE SWIM TEAM

Seizing the spotlight in Los Angeles was an astonishingly young team of Japanese swimmers, who captured four pool titles. The 100-meter freestyle winner, Yasuji Miyazaki, was just seventeen years old. Teammate Masaji Kiyokawa, who nailed the 100-meter backstroke, was sixteen, and Kusuo Kitamura, the 1,500-meter freestyle champ, was only fourteen years of age.

Photo: Archives, Olympic Museum Lausanne.

Just three years after the New York stock market crash, in the midst of global economic depression, Los Angeles successfully secured the 1932 Olympic Games. The city had overcome the less-than-happy legacy of the previous American Olympics in St. Louis by promising bountiful financial and organizational resources. Because of the expense of traveling to Los Angeles from Europe, however, only thirty-seven nations participated, compared to forty-six in Amsterdam. But crowds were enormous, the weather was warm, and local authorities even winked at Prohibition laws by allowing French athletes to bring in their own wine.

The hands-down queen of the Los Angeles Olympic Games was Mildred "Babe" Didrikson, who personally embodied the Olympic motto "Faster, Higher, Stronger" by sweeping gold medals in both hurdles and the javelin and scoring silver in the high jump. Under special Olympic rules for women, these were the only three events she was permitted to enter, even though she had qualified for five. Didrickson—who apparently earned her nickname because she could slug a baseball like Babe Ruth—later launched a phenomenally successful career as a professional golfer, winning the world championship four times under her married name, Babe Zaharias. Another superwoman, Ohio resident Stella Walsh, competed for her native country of Poland and ran off with the gold in the 100-meter race. Walsh stunned the public again, forty-eight years later, when an autopsy revealed that she was, in actuality, a man.

The International Amateur Athletic Foundation barred Finland's phenomenal Nurmi from the Los Angeles Games, accusing him of professionalism. But there was no lack of excitement when Swedish strongmen muscled six gold medals in wrestling, and Japanese swimmers made a splash by sweeping up four individual golds. Italy brought home two gold medals in cycling—including one claimed by Attilio Pavesi, who kept himself fueled on the individual road race, according to one report, by wearing a bib packed with spaghetti, sweet rolls, bananas, and cheese sandwiches.

Standing firm against a firestorm of controversy and the threat by many countries to boycott the event, the IOC insisted on holding the 1936 Games in Berlin

1932 LOS ANGELES

LOS ANGELES COLISEUM

In the middle of the Great Depression, the Los Angeles Olympics opened glamorously under sunny July skies in the specially refurbished Coliseum. Four thousand doves were released, and nearly 100,000 people attended the majestic opening ceremonies. "It was like a fantasyland," remembered Evelyne Hall, a hurdler from Chicago. "Nobody thought about their problems."

Photo: Archives, Olympic Museum Lausanne.

1932 LOS ANGELES

BABE DIDRIKSON, USA

Mildred "Babe" Didrikson took gold medals in the hurdles and the javelin and a silver in the high jump—the only three events she was permitted to enter under special rules for women. Asked by a reporter if there was anything she didn't play, Didrikson responded dryly, "Yeah. Dolls."

Photo: Archives, Olympic Museum Lausanne.

under the ominous aegis of Hitler's Nazi Party. For the Nazi organizers, these Games became a virtual festival of propaganda—spectacular in presentation and chilling in their political overtones. The *Hindenburg* airship hovered over the massive new stadium, which had seating for 110,000 people, as athletes marched to music composed by Richard Strauss and the throng sang "Deutschland über alles." Reichsführer Adolf Hitler, dressed in a brown uniform, conspicuously attended nearly every event, and anti-Semitic signs that had been displayed around the city were temporarily removed during the Games—convincing credulous Olympic officials that their decision to trust Nazi goodwill had been correct. Taking a thoroughly rose-colored view of the monumental political event, Avery Brundage, then president of the American Olympic Committee, proclaimed, "No nation since ancient Greece has captured the true Olympic spirit as has Germany."

It was the athletes, through the sheer power of their physical performance, who subverted the Nazis' desire to present the Games as a symbol of Aryan supremacy. The ten African American stars of the U.S. track and field team—considered subhuman by Nazi organizers—outscored all their competitors. And more than any other athlete, Jesse Owens, the black American track phenomenon, dominated the Berlin Olympics. Owens, the grandson of slaves, seized four gold medals and set records in the 200-meter dash, broad jump, and 400-meter relay. In another blow to Nazi racial theories, Germany's only Jewish competitor, fencer Helène Mayer—who had been promised complete "Aryan" status if she returned from the U.S. to compete for Germany—was beaten to the gold by another Jewish swordswoman, Hungary's Ilona Elek.

Following behind the once-again dominant Americans in track and field were the Finns, who swept the 5,000 and 10,000 meters and the steeplechase. New Zealand's Jack Lovelock set a new world record in the 1,500-meter run, while

---

1936 BERLIN

JESSE OWENS, USA

The son of an Alabama cotton picker, Jesse Owens, 22, infuriated the Nazi organizers of the 1936 Berlin Games with his superb track and field performance. Flying in the face of Nazi claims that blacks were inferior to Aryan supermen, Owens outshone every other athlete at the Games, winning four gold medals in ten days in the 100 meters, 200 meters, broad jump, and 400-meter relay.

Photos: Archives, Olympic Museum Lausanne.

1936 BERLIN

THE BERLIN OLYMPICS

In the first torch ceremony of the Olympic Games, a runner triumphantly carried the Olympic flame into the center of Berlin to light the brazier in the Reichssportfeld during the 1936 Opening Ceremonies. The lavish spectacle, attended by Hitler, Göring, and Goebbels, featured music by Richard Strauss, the release of 20,000 doves, and the hovering presence of the airship Hindenburg, which suspended the Olympic flag over the massive stadium.

Photo: Archives, Olympic Museum Lausanne.

1948 LONDON

FANNY BLANKERS-KOEN, HOL

*Holland's "Magnificent Mama"
Fanny Blankers-Koen flashed
through track and field events in
London's postwar "austerity
Olympics." Blankers-Koen, thirty
years old and the mother of two,
bolted to four gold medals in the
100 meters, the 80-meter
hurdles, the 200 meters, and the
400-meter relay.*

Photo: Archives, Olympic Museum Lausanne / O.P.A.

France's Robert Charpentier dominated cycling, winning three gold medals. The Dutch eclipsed other competitors in women's swimming events, but the springboard diving gold was won by a thirteen-year-old child wonder, America's Marjorie Gestring.

World War II obliterated any chance of holding Olympic Games as originally planned in Tokyo in 1940 or London in 1944. In 1948, however, despite endless rain, food rationing, housing shortages, and the damage wreaked by Hitler's bombs, London managed to stage a postwar "austerity Olympics." For the first time, athletes from communist countries were included in the list of fifty-nine participating nations.

The wonder woman at the London Games was Holland's "Magnificent Mama," Francina "Fanny" Blankers-Koen. The thirty-year-old mother of two dashed to four golds on the soggy track in the 100- and 200-meter races, the 80-meter hurdles, and the 400-meter team relay. Seventeen-year-old American decathlete Bob Mathias, a future congressman, became the youngest male athlete to win an individual gold medal—despite the fact that he had never even attempted two of his events, the javelin and pole vault, until four months before the Games.

Finland, a country with a tradition of legendary athletes, hosted its first Olympic Games in 1952 in its capital, Helsinki. Allied fighter bombers were pounding communist forces in Korea in a hot war, and Cold War politics added treacherous new rivalries to the Games. After an absence of forty years, Russian athletes under the flag of the Soviet Union took part for the first time, but they and other Eastern Bloc competitors kept to themselves in a separate Olympic village, surrounded by barbed wire and draped with mammoth images of Stalin. Adding to nationalist tensions, Taiwan boycotted the Games because mainland Chinese athletes were competing.

For athletes and spectators, however, the Games had rich moments. In his second Olympics, the teeth-gnashing, arm-waving Czech Army captain Emil Zatopek—nicknamed "the Beast of Prague"—zoomed past rivals to win three golds in the 5,000 and 10,000 meters and the marathon. "He runs," an observer said, "like a man who has just been stabbed in the heart." Zatopek, who spoke five languages, was known for

1948 LONDON

BOB MATHIAS, USA

*Only seventeen years old, Bob
Mathias clinched the 1948
Olympic decathlon—despite
the fact that, until a few
months before the Games, he
had never thrown a javelin,
pole vaulted, or run a 1,500-
meter race, and he had hardly
ever broad jumped or raced
400 meters. He took the
Olympic decathlon title
again in 1952.*

Photo: Archives, Olympic Museum
Lausanne / Olympia-Kuva.

1952 HELSINKI

EMIL ZATOPEK, CZE

Emil Zatopek (below), "the Beast of Prague," left rivals in the dust, streaking to gold medals in the 5,000 meters, the 10,000 meters, and the marathon. Zatopek, a captain in the Czech Army, was known for his grimacing, grunting racing style. "He runs," an observer said, "like a man who has just been stabbed in the heart."

Photo: Archives, Olympic Museum Lausanne.

A. FERREIRA DA SILVA, BRA

In Helsinki, Adhemar Ferreira da Silva (opposite)—a Brazilian world-record-holding leaper who spoke seven languages fluently—scored a gold medal and new world record in the triple jump. In six jumps during the event, da Silva smashed his own world record four times. He repeated his win in 1956.

Photo: Archives, Olympic Museum Lausanne / Olympia-Kuva.

running ten to twenty-five miles a day, frequently in bulky army boots. Minutes after he won the 5,000, his wife, Dana, scored the gold in the javelin. Another unforgettable family moment occurred when, overcome by emotion, the father of a French freestyle winner leaped into the pool completely clothed, still wearing his beret.

Australia's Marjorie Jackson bolted to world records in the 100 and 200 meters, and Bob Mathias owned the decathlon for a second consecutive time. In the shooting events, Hungary's resourceful Károly Takács bagged his second gold in the rapid-fire pistol. The formerly right-handed marksman had lost his pistol hand in 1938 in a grenade accident; he scored his two Olympic golds after teaching himself to fire with his left.

In 1956, when the Games were held in Melbourne, Australia, more than a shift in seasons threw Olympic plans off-kilter. The wet-weather Games were held in November and December to coincide with summer in the Southern Hemisphere, and because of Australia's strict animal quarantine laws, the equestrian events had to be held in Stockholm. More calamitous, however, were the escalating military conflicts around the world. Brutal shooting wars, including the Suez crisis and the Soviet invasion of Hungary, eroded most semblance of international goodwill and led to a bitter Olympic boycott by Spain, Switzerland, the Netherlands, Egypt, Iraq, and Lebanon. And this time the communist Chinese refused to compete when nationalist China was invited.

HAMIT KAPLAN, TUR

Super heavyweight Hamit Kaplan of Anatolia muscled a gold medal in freestyle wrestling at the Melbourne Games, breaking Russia's winning streak. Kaplan went on to take a silver in 1960 and a bronze in 1964.

Photo: Archives, Olympic Museum Lausanne.

Political snarling spilled over into a vicious water polo semifinal between the Soviet Union and Hungary, which turned into a bloody "boxing match under water." For at least one couple, however, love conquered Cold War jitters. Soon after the Games, American Harold Connolly, Melbourne's gold-medalist in the hammer throw, wed the Czech Olympic women's discus champion, Olga Fikotova, with Emil Zatopek standing by as best man.

Australia's powerful swimmers stormed the pool in Melbourne, racking up eight golds. On the track, sprinters Betty Cuthbert from Australia and Bobby Joe Morrow from the U.S. each picked up three gold medals, and Ukrainian Vladimir

ABEBE BIKILA, ETH

A member of Emperor Haile Selassie's Palace Guard, Abebe Bikila of Ethiopia first raced barefoot for twenty-six miles, 385 yards to victory in the Olympic marathon in Rome. He repeated his performance—with shoes on—in Tokyo in 1964 (below).

Photo: Archives, Olympic Museum Lausanne.

WILMA RUDOLPH, USA

The nineteen-year-old sprinter Wilma Rudolph overcame enormous odds just to reach the 1960 Olympic Games in Rome. Due to polio and other crippling diseases, Rudolph could not walk without a leg brace until she was eleven. Despite these overwhelming challenges, Rudolph effortlessly captured gold medals in three events in Rome, including the prestigious 100-meter dash.

Photo: Archives, Olympic Museum Lausanne.

RAFER JOHNSON, USA

In the decathlon in the 1960 Games, Rafer Johnson waged a titanic battle in the ten events against his rival and former UCLA teammate, Yang Chuan-Kwang, who was competing for Taiwan. Johnson took home the gold and the title as the best overall athlete in the world.

Photo: Archives, Olympic Museum Lausanne.

Kuts flashed to the USSR's first two titles in men's track and field events. America's legendary discus star Al Oerter threw for his first of four consecutive wins, Soviet gymnast Larisa Latynina snatched four titles, and USSR wrestlers took five Greco-Roman golds.

After the political powder keg of Melbourne, the Olympics moved relatively peacefully to Rome in 1960. Television cameras beamed the competitions around the world, and Olympic performances peaked. Like the racers of ancient Greece, Ethiopia's Abebe Bikila sprinted barefoot down the Appian Way to the finish line in the torch-lit moonlight marathon, capturing the gold in record time. Bikila, one of Emperor Haile Selassie's palace guards, was unwilted by the twenty-six-mile slog: "I could have gone around the course again without any difficulty," he declared.

In their second Olympic appearance, Soviet athletes came on strong. Boris Shakhlin took four golds in the gymnastic events, and the Soviet women's massive sweep of track and field golds, led by sisters Tamara and Irina Press, was only stopped by American racing legend Wilma Rudolph. One of twenty-two children in her family, the amazing Rudolph—known as "Skeeter" to her friends—had suffered from a crippling string of childhood ailments, including malnutrition, polio, double pneumonia, and scarlet fever, and wore a leg brace from the age of six. But Rudolph kicked off her orthopedic shoes at age eleven, and after training and competing relentlessly in high school and college, she exploded on the track at Rome, claiming triple golds in the 100- and 200-meter sprints and the 400-meter relay. But the athlete who attracted the most attention at the Games was a charismatic eighteen-year-old boxer named Cassius Marcellus Clay, who later changed his name to Muhammad Ali. After the light heavyweight slugged his way to the championship title, he wore his beloved Olympic medal so much that the gold finish started wearing off.

In an exhausting battle of near-equals, America's Rafer Johnson edged to decathlon gold over his UCLA teammate, Yang Chuan-Kwang, who was competing for Taiwan. And in one of the first signs of emerging Olympic dope scandals, Danish cyclist Knut Jensen died of a drug overdose after a grueling 100-kilometer road race.

In 1964, the Olympic Games traveled to Tokyo, the first Asian city to host the Games. Largely recovered from the devastation of World War II, the city managed the event with skill and precision despite continuing

1960 ROME

CASSIUS CLAY, USA

At age eighteen, boxer Cassius Marcellus Clay—who later changed his name to Muhammad Ali—charmed his fellow athletes in Rome and pummeled Poland's Zbigniew Pietrzykowski to claim the light heavyweight Olympic gold. Clay wore his prized gold medal so frequently that the gold finish started wearing off.

Photos: Above, Archives, Olympic Museum Lausanne; Below © Allsport / Archives, Olympic Museum Lausanne.

political storms. South Africa was excluded from the Games because of its apartheid policies, Indonesia was barred for having hosted the unsanctioned Games of the New Emergent Forces in 1962, and North Korea withdrew its team in protest. But, once again, the heroics of the athletes claimed center stage. U.S. boxer Joe Frazier battled his German opponent Hans Huber with a broken right hand to take heavyweight gold. Abebe Bikila, this time wearing shoes, swept his second marathon title—only forty days after he'd had an appendectomy. Australia's swimming sensation Dawn Fraser seized her third consecutive gold in the 100-meter freestyle, despite neck injuries she had suffered in a serious car crash. And incredibly, Al Oerter, in terrible pain from torn cartilage in his ribs, a slipped cervical disk, and internal hemorrhaging, braced himself with bandages to hurl the discus for a third gold medal.

Controversy clung to the Mexico City Games in 1968, the first Olympics to be staged in Latin America. Many athletes worried about the high altitude of the city—7,573 feet above sea level—and in fact there were cases of severe exhaustion among Olympians who had trained for endurance events near sea level. Others fretted about drug tests that were administered for the first time. Despite the balloons and cheerful mariachi bands celebrating Mexico's "Peace Olympics," serious political problems again shadowed the Games. The Soviets had invaded Czechoslovakia two months earlier. Ten days before the Games, massive student riots at the University of Mexico had been brutally suppressed by government troops, resulting in hundreds of deaths and injuries. And two American track medalists—Tommie Smith and John Carlos—were suspended after stepping shoeless onto the medal stand, as a symbol of black poverty in the U.S., and raising black-gloved fists in a black power salute when the American anthem was played.

But for many, the most astounding moments of the Games took place in competition. American long jumper Bob Beamon left spectators speechless when he flew an incredible 29 feet, 2 1/2 inches—outdistancing the world record by nearly two feet and setting a new record that remained unbroken for twenty-three years. Beamon's gold-winning teammate Dick Fosbury also took track and field performance to new levels with his groundbreaking running high-jump technique, the

1968 MEXICO CITY

BOB BEAMON, USA

In the high-altitude Mexico City Games, Bob Beamon, a twenty-two-year-old long jumper from New York City, soared nearly two feet past the world record. His leap of 29-feet, 2 1/2-inches set a staggering new record that remained unbroken for twenty-three years.

Photos: Above © Allsport; Right, Archives, Olympic Museum Lausanne.

1972 MUNICH

OLGA KORBUT, SOV

Tiny, 85-pound Olga Korbut finished seventh in Munich in the women's all-around gymnastics competition. But she stole spectators' hearts, won golds in the floor exercises and the balance beam—on which she introduced the back flip—and set a new, diminutive size standard in women's gymnastics.

Photo: Archives, Olympic Museum Lausanne.

1972 MUNICH

VASSILY ALEXEYEV, SOV

Super-strongman Vassily Alexeyev—a 337-pound mining engineer who was seen breakfasting on a steak and twenty-six fried eggs—snatched Olympic gold with feats that included heaving a 562-pound barbell. Alexeyev, who set eighty world records from 1970 to 1977, repeated his Olympic win in 1976.

Photo: Archives, Olympic Museum Lausanne.

backward "Fosbury Flop." Meanwhile, U.S. boxer George Foreman took the super heavyweight championship, Czech gymnast Vera Cáslavská swept four golds, and discus star Al Oerter slipped and tore a thigh muscle on the rain-soaked field, and then hurled his way to a fourth consecutive Olympic title. In his first Olympic appearance, eighteen-year-old Mark Spitz won two relay golds. And Kenya's Kipchoge Keino, a Nandi tribesman who raced in Mexico City with a raging gall bladder infection, blasted across the tape in the 1,500-meter race—after first jogging a mile to the stadium to escape a traffic jam.

Political turmoil took a hideous turn four years later, when a terrorist massacre bloodily eclipsed the 1972 Olympic Games in Munich. On September 5, with a worldwide audience of a billion people focused on the Games, eight Palestinian guerrillas from the Black September group invaded the quarters of the Israeli team in the Olympic village, murdering two Israelis immediately and taking nine others hostage. The terrorists made their way to the airport, where all the Israeli captives and three of the terrorists were killed during a failed rescue attempt; the other Palestinians were captured.

1972 MUNICH

MARK SPITZ, USA

Mark Spitz splashed to Olympic history and worldwide celebrity in 1972, when he captured an incredible seven gold medals— the most that had ever been won by any athlete in a single Olympics. Spitz's phenomenal performance in Munich brought his gold medal collection to nine, including the two golds he won in the Mexico City Games.

To many, it seemed impossible that the Olympics could go on, that the gaze of the world could turn from the bloody murder of the athletes to the entertaining spectacle of sport. But the Games did go on, with the consent of the Israelis, the very next day, after a morning memorial service attended by 80,000 people in Munich's main stadium. *New York Times* sportswriter Red Smith reflected the anguished sentiments of many when he commented that Olympic organizers had "ruled that a little blood must not be allowed to interrupt play."

The Munich Games were forever scarred in the world's memory, however, despite the determination of the West Germans to stage a cheerful, relaxed gala and the superb performances of Olympic athletes. In the first week of the Games, Mark Spitz set seven world records and swept seven Olympic golds—the most ever won by an individual in a single Games. Fifteen-year-old Shane Gould grabbed three glittering swimming golds for Australia. And Soviet sprite Olga Korbut—4-feet, 11-inches and 85 pounds—stole the gymnastics show, scoring gold in two events and shifting the sport's spotlight from balletic women to daring, agile waifs. Aleksandr Medved, the 231-pound Minsk muscleman, held his own

NADIA COMANECI, ROM

With peerless grace and courage, Romanian gymnast Nadia Comaneci, 14, captivated spectators and judges in the Montreal Olympics—scoring an unheard-of seven perfect 10s, three golds, a silver, and a bronze.

"SUGAR" RAY LEONARD, USA

Named after the celebrated
singer Ray Charles, Maryland-
born "Sugar" Ray Leonard rose
to stardom himself after he
outpunched Cuba's Andrés
Aldama for the light
welterweight gold in Montreal.

Photo: © Duomo.

against 412-pound opponent, America's Chris Taylor, to take his third consecutive freestyle wrestling gold. Kip Keino added a gold in the 3,000-meter steeplechase. And the Soviet basketball team elbowed aside the Americans to win the Olympic title 51–50, ending America's thirty-six-year winning streak.

Four years later, with the help of $100 million worth of security forces, the physical safety of the athletes was ensured at the 1976 Olympic Games in Montreal. These were, however, the most expensive Olympics ever held, and among the most contentious. The Taiwanese boycotted because Canada would not recognize their country as the Republic of China. And immediately before the Games, twenty nations, mainly from Africa, withdrew from competition, refusing to share the Olympic stage with New Zealand because its rugby team had toured South Africa.

But once again, athletic performances were brilliant. Although Czech cyclists suffered a setback when their wheels and spare tires were mistakenly collected as garbage and crushed in a compactor, team champion Anton Tkac went on to pedal to the gold in the 100-meter sprint. The West Germans—who had filled their tires with helium—flew past rivals to capture the 4000-meter team pursuit title. American boxers—including "Sugar" Ray Leonard and the Spinks brothers, Michael and Leon—outpounded the competition. Bruce Jenner blasted through ten events to claim the decathlon title, Edwin Moses surged to the gold in the 400-meter hurdles, and Cuba's "El Caballo," Alberto Juantorena, swept the 400- and 800-meter dashes. The U.S. took back the basketball title, while East Germany's Kornelia Ender and America's John Naber each lapped up four swimming golds.

COE, WELLS, AND OVETT, GBR

Great Britain stormed to
triple golds in track and field
at the 1980 Games. Allan
Wells, a Scottish marine
engineer, was the first runner
from Great Britain to win the
100 meters since Harold
Abrahams dashed to the title
in 1924. And arch racing
rivals Steven Ovett and
Sebastian Coe each took home
a gold—Ovett in the 800
meters and Coe in the 1,500
meters. Coe repeated his
1,500-meter win in 1984.

Photo: © Duomo.

With fearless, flawless grace, fourteen-year-old Romanian gymnast Nadia Comaneci performed the never-before-imagined, winning seven scores of perfect 10s and three Olympic golds. In another astonishing display, Japanese gymnast Shun Fujimoto heroically ignored his fractured right leg, encased in a hip-to-ankle cast, and helped his team score a gold in the combined exercises after flying off the rings in a triple somersault and landing, bravely, in excruciating pain. The Soviet Union's Nikolai Andrianov gathered up the most medals of the Games, including four gymnastics golds.

1980 MOSCOW

ALEKSANDR DITIATIN. SOV

When he captured three golds, four silvers, and a bronze in 1980, Soviet gymnast Aleksandr Ditiatin made history for the home team, winning the most medals of any athlete in a single Olympics.

Photo: ©Allsport, Tony Duffy.

Since its reentry into competition in 1952, the USSR had emerged as an immense Olympic power, and it planned to celebrate its place in Olympic history by hosting spectacular Games in Moscow in 1980. Although eighty-one countries participated in what turned out to be an orderly, high-security event, the United States and dozens of other non-communist nations—including Japan and the Federal Republic of Germany—shunned the Games to protest the USSR's invasion of Afghanistan in December 1979. With about half the expected athletes competing, the Moscow Games turned into a virtual tug-of-war between the Eastern Bloc powerhouses—the USSR and East Germany—which together took 50 percent of all the medals.

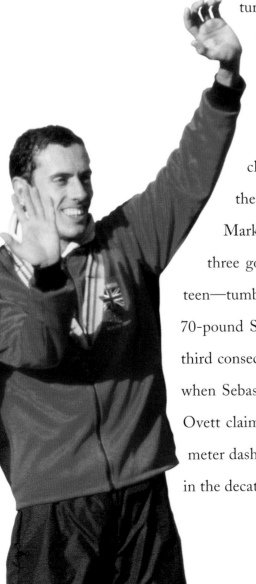

East German swimmers—led by freestyler Barbara Krause, a state police official—churned through the pool to claim twenty-six medals, and the USSR's Aleksandr Ditiatin—the only male Olympic gymnast to score a perfect 10—surpassed Mark Spitz's bounty by collecting eight gymnastics medals, including three golds. Nadia Comaneci, however—no longer an urchin at eighteen—tumbled off the parallel bars and her gymnastics throne, surpassed by 70-pound Soviet star Yelena Davydova. Cuba's Teofilo Stevenson took his third consecutive boxing title. And Great Britain raised its Olympic profile when Sebastian Coe stormed first to the finish in the 1,500 meters, Steve Ovett claimed gold in the 800-meter race, Allan Wells won the first 100-meter dash for Great Britain since 1924, and Daley Thompson scored gold in the decathlon.

At the next Olympiad, the Soviets, along with sixteen of their allied nations, turned the tables on the U.S. by boycotting the 1984 Games in Los Angeles. Libya also dropped out of competition after two Libyan journalists were barred from entering the United States. But athletes from 140 other nations competed in a pageant marked by high Hollywood production values, copious commercial sponsorship, and a touch of scandal when eleven Olympic athletes flunked their drug tests.

The first gold medal of the Games went to communist China's pistol champion—a fertilizer salesman and slingshot whiz named Xu Haifeng. America's Joan Benoit paced easily to a win in the first Olympic women's marathon. And there was melodrama in the women's 3,000-meter race, when U.S. favorite Mary Decker and Great Britain's barefoot front-runner Zola Budd collided painfully on the track, allowing Romania's Maricica Puica to breeze by them to the gold. Italy's crack cycling team sped past rivals on aerodynamic, spokeless disk wheels to win the road race in record time, even after stopping to change a wheel. U.S. track phenomenon Carl Lewis matched Jesse Owens's four-gold sweep and screeched to the finish line in the 100 meters a full eight feet ahead of his nearest rival. U.S. hurdler Edwin Moses nailed his second Olympic gold, and Portugal's Carlos Lopes left marathon rivals in the dust, easily clinching the gold medal despite the fact that he had been struck by a car while training only fifteen days before.

Gymnast Mary Lou Retton, under 4-feet, 9-inches tall, turned in a towering performance. Retton captured the coveted all-around gymnastics crown, squeaking by Romania's balletic Ecaterina Szabo, who had taken three gold medals. Peerless diver Greg Louganis soared past his competitors for gold in both the platform and springboard competitions. American cyclists, who had come home empty-handed from the Games since 1912, zoomed to four golds. U.S. biking champs included Connie Carpenter-Phinney, winner of the first Olympic women's road race, who had competed as a speed skater in Sapporo. And super heavyweight Jeff Blatnick struggled back from cancer surgery to win the first U.S. gold in Greco-Roman wrestling.

1984 LOS ANGELES

LI NING, CHN

Powerful Li Ning, 21, led China's high-flying gymnastics team in 1984. Li, who as a child practiced handsprings all the way to school, struck gold in the pommel horse, rings, and floor exercise events. "I didn't come all this way," Li said, "to fail."

Photo: © Duomo, Steven E. Sutton.

1984 LOS ANGELES

MARY DECKER AND ZOLA BUDD

Just after Great Britain's favorite, Zola Budd, passed America's Mary Decker in the 3,000 meters in Los Angeles, the two accidentally collided, sending Decker sprawling across the track with a pulled hip muscle and dashed Olympic hopes. Although Budd stayed on her bare feet, she was beaten to the finish line by Romania's Maricica Puica.

Photo: © Duomo, David Madison.

Following spread: 1984 Olympics, Los Angeles Coliseum.

Photo: © Duomo, Steven E. Sutton.

1984 LOS ANGELES

DALEY THOMPSON. USA

In Los Angeles, Great Britain's Francis "Daley" Thompson clung onto the Olympic decathlon title he had first captured in 1980. It was the third Olympics for the half-Scottish, half-Nigerian super-athlete, who outscored German rival Jürgen Hingsen for the gold.

Photo: © Allsport, Steve Powell.

1984 LOS ANGELES

JOAN BENOIT. USA

Waving her white painter's cap, America's Joan Benoit paced easily to victory in the marathon with a 400-meter edge over her closest competitor, Norway's Grete Waitz. Benoit had pulled well ahead of her rivals after only fourteen minutes, and the Maine native never let up, keeping her commanding lead for the next two hours and ten minutes.

Photo: © Duomo, David Madison.

1984 LOS ANGELES

EDWIN MOSES, USA

Super-hurdler Edwin Moses had scored gold in the 1976 Olympics, and by the time the 1984 Games rolled around he had won an astonishing 102 consecutive races. He added to his streak in Los Angeles, capturing his second gold in the 400-meter hurdles. Moses, who had studied physics on an academic scholarship at Morehouse College, started hurdling as a hobby and honed an unstoppable, thirteen-step pace between hurdles. His streak finally came to an end in 1987, after 107 wins.

Photo: © Duomo, Steven E. Sutton.

1984 LOS ANGELES

GABRIELE ANDERSEN-SCHEISS. SWI

In a harrowing moment of the 1984 Olympic marathon, Switzerland's Gaby Andersen-Scheiss, who worked as a ski instructor in Idaho, stumbled into the stadium, overcome by heat prostration. Nevertheless, she refused medical attention and staggered to the finish line in thirty-seventh place. Within two hours, she had fully recovered from her ordeal.

Photo: © Duomo, David Madison.

Following spread: Australian cycling team, 1984.

Photo: © Duomo.

1988 SEOUL

JACKIE JOYNER KERSEE, USA

Regarded as the world's greatest female athlete, Jackie Joyner Kersee dominated the heptathlon and long jump competitions in Seoul, striking gold in both events. She powered to gold in the heptathlon again in Barcelona in 1992.

Photo: © Duomo, Steven E. Sutton.

The 1988 Games moved to the bustling megalopolis of Seoul, South Korea. These magnificently organized Games were the first in twelve years in which both Americans and Soviets competed, but North Korea—joined by a number of hard-line allies including Cuba, Albania, and Ethiopia—turned its back on the Games, claiming that it had the right to host half of the events. And Olympic competitions were marred by ugly boxing disputes and continuing drug controversies. In one ringside disaster, a New Zealand referee, Keith Walker, was physically attacked by South Korean boxing officials and security guards who were incensed over what they believed to be biased judging. And Canada's Olympic hopes soared, and then crashed, with the fortunes of sprinter Ben Johnson. In the 100 meters, the Jamaican-born runner flashed past his racing rival, Carl Lewis, to take the gold. But three days later, Johnson was forced to forfeit his medal after testing positive for steroids. Four other medalists—two Bulgarian weightlifters, a Hungarian lifter, and a British judo expert—were also caught in the drug-testing web.

Churning up the track in Seoul was Florence Griffith Joyner, as famous for her running as for the racing outfits she designed herself. "Flo-Jo"—bank teller, beautician, and wife of 1984 Olympic triple-jump cham-pion Al Joyner—galloped across the finish line to three gold medals, while her fleet-footed sister-in-law, Jackie Joyner Kersee, triumphed in the heptathlon and long jump. Family feats were shared by Soviet husband and wife Viktor and Olga Bryzgin, who each breezed to a gold medal on the track.

Once again, Soviet hoopsters spiked the U.S. and Yugoslavia to take the title, but U.S. women scored their own basketball gold. In the water, East German pool shark Kristin Otto stroked to six gold medals. America's "big fish," 6-foot, 7-inch Matt Biondi, reeled in five, ranking him second only to Mark Spitz.

MATT BIONDI, USA

The "big fish" at the Seoul Games was American swimmer Matt Biondi. His haul included five golds, ranking him second only to Mark Spitz, who swam away with seven gold medals in 1972. At the Barcelona Games in 1992, Biondi added a sixth gold in the 400-meter freestyle relay.

Photo: © Duomo.

1992 BARCELONA

THE DREAM TEAM, USA

In Barcelona, for the first time, Olympic basketball was open to professional players—and the U.S. assembled the most magnificent team ever, with a roster of hoop idols including "Magic" Johnson (below), Michael Jordan (right), Larry Bird, Patrick Ewing, and Charles Barkley. Not surprisingly, the "Dream Team" outscored all rivals and claimed Olympic gold.

Photo: Below © Duomo, Mitchell Layton; Right © Duomo, Al Tielemans.

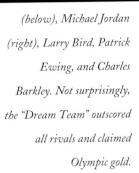

Tennis returned to the Games after a sixty-four-year absence, featuring a lineup of high-paid pros, and the new Olympic sport of table tennis was aced by the Chinese and Koreans. Greg Louganis—who only months before had been diagnosed HIV-positive—reprised his platform and springboard golds despite a fever, an injured hand, and four stitches in his head from hitting the board during a dive.

In 1992, the world's best athletes came together again, beneath blue skies and a blazing Mediterranean sun, at the Olympic Games in Barcelona, Spain. With no boycotts or Cold War skirmishes marring the event for the first time in twenty years, a record 12,000 athletes from 172 nations took part, and South Africa was welcomed back after twenty-eight years of Olympic exile. The opening ceremonies threw a spotlight on the world's newly fractured political fault lines. Twelve former Soviet republics paraded together under separate flags and the rubric Unified Team, while Latvia, Estonia, and Lithuania entered as independent nations. Yugoslavia had been torn apart, and its athletes competed as Croats or Independent Olympic Participants. The shifting kaleidoscope of nations included new Olympic members such as the Himalayan nation of Bhutan, whose archers had never before traveled on a plane or seen the sea.

Now politically independent—but athletically dominant as ever—the Unified Team swept forty-five Olympic golds. The hometown Spanish squad clinched an amazing thirteen gold medals—after capturing a total of four in the entire history of the Games. Paraskevi Patoulidou leaped to the gold in the women's 100-meter hurdles, becoming Greece's first track medalist since 1896. Hungarian swimmers triumphed, too—Tamas Darnyi stroked to double golds in the men's races, and Krisztina Egerszegi tripled in the women's. Russia's 6-foot, 6-inch Aleksandr Popov splashed past Matt Biondi to take two freestyle titles.

For U.S. diver Mark Lenzi—who took up his sport after watching Greg Louganis's 1984 Olympic performance on television—the Barcelona Games turned to gold when he inherited his idol's springboard title. Competing in a wicked wind, Carl Lewis claimed his third gold medal in the long jump—surpassing Mike Powell, who had broken Bob Beamon's super jump record in 1991. Hurdler Kevin Young achieved his dream of breaking Edwin Moses's nine-year-old world record,

1992 BARCELONA

TATIANA GUTSU, EUN

Despite a tumble from the balance beam, the Unified Team's Tatiana Gutsu, 15, substituted for injured teammate Roza Galieva in the all-around women's gymnastics competition and scored Barcelona gold.

Photo: © Allsport, Tony Duffy.

and Jackie Joyner Kersee whipped through the heptathlon—holding tight to her title as the greatest female athlete in the world.

But towering above all the other champions was smiling, 6-foot, 9-inch Earvin "Magic" Johnson—former star point guard of the Los Angeles Lakers—who led America's basketball "Dream Team" to the hoop of gold in Barcelona. For the first time, Olympic basketball competition permitted the participation of professional players. And Johnson had persuaded a host of fellow NBA superstars—including Michael Jordan, Larry Bird, Patrick Ewing, and Charles Barkley—to join him on the Olympic courts. A year before, Johnson stunned the world by announcing that he had tested positive for HIV. Now he was shooting for Olympic gold, and thousands of fans were pressing to touch him, screaming "Ma-jeek" everywhere he went in Barcelona. To no one's surprise, Johnson and the "Dream Team" crushed all comers and went home with gold around their necks. For Johnson—who was named the NBA's Most Valuable Player three times— it was, he confided, a magnificent moment. "It's sort of hard to put into words what [winning the Olympics] means....I've won every championship there is to win. You can throw them all in a hat, and it'll never compare to this."

1992 BARCELONA

PETER FARKAS, HUN

Hungary's Peter Farkas powered to gold in the Greco-Roman wrestling 181-pound class. His countryman, Tibor Komáromi, had silvered in the event in 1988.

Photo: © Allsport, G. Vandystadt.

1992 BARCELONA

FERMIN CACHO RUIZ, SPA

Spain's Fermin Cacho Ruiz sprinted to the finish in the 1,500 meters and joyfully captured the gold medal for the home team.

Photo: © Duomo, Steven E. Sutton.

Photo: © Duomo.

1988 SEOUL

GREG LOUGANIS, USA

After gashing his head on the diving board during the preliminaries in Seoul, unstoppable Greg Louganis (left) went on to win the springboard and platform titles. It was the second set of diving golds for Louganis, who had mastered the two events in Los Angeles.

Photo: © Duomo.

1992 BARCELONA

MANUEL ESTIARTE, SPA

Led by high-powered offensive player Manuel Estiarte (opposite), the highest goal scorer in the Los Angeles and Seoul Olympics— Spain's water polo team was favored to win, but was forced to settle for silver after being edged out by the Italian squad.

Photo: © Allsport, Tony Duffy.

1992 BARCELONA

SOCCER

Following spread: The Spanish home team swept past Poland in the gold-medal soccer match in Barcelona, taking Spain's first-ever Olympic title in the event.

Photo: © Allsport.

1896 - 1992

Blending Olympic symbolism with the spirit of the host cities, the posters of the Summer Olympic Games are

THE SUMMER OLYMPIC POSTERS

part of the "National Art Exhibitions" called for by the Olympic charter. One of the posters— announcing the 1912 Olympic Games in Stockholm—was considered so daring that it was not distributed in a number of countries. The poster created for the 1952 Helsinki Games features the image of the great Finnish runner Paavo Nurmi, winner of nine Olympic gold medals. The Olympic symbol of five intertwining rings, featured on all of the posters after 1928, was taken from an altar at the ancient Greek city of Delphi and symbolizes the brotherhood of nations.

Photos: Archives, Olympic Museum Lausanne.

Athens 1896

Paris 1900

Paris 1924

Amsterdam 1928

Melbourne 1956

Rome 1960

Moscow 1980

Los Angeles 1984

St. Louis 1904

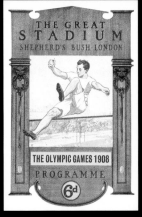

London 1908

Stockholm 1912

Antwerp 1920

Los Angeles 1932

Berlin 1936

London 1948

Helsinki 1952

Tokyo 1964

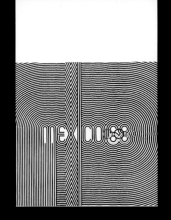

Mexico City 1968

Munich 1972

Montreal 1976

Seoul 1988

Barcelona 1992

THE GAMES OF WINTER

Mix the power and skill of Olympic sport with the slick speed of ice and snow. Add the unpredictability of weather and the vertical velocity of mountain slopes, and you have the Winter Games—the ultimate test of world-class athletes and the elements.

The Winter Olympics are younger than their sister Games of Summer. **FROM CHAMONIX TO LILLEHAMMER** There were, of course, no snowbound sports played on the sweltering fields of Olympia in Greece. Perhaps because there was neither mythology nor classical tradition to shape them, the Winter Games have typically been more informal and convivial than the warm-weather Olympiads. A smaller corps of athletes, many of whom know each other well, compete in Winter Olympic sports, and small nations like Norway are regularly big winners. But despite the cozy, winter-carnival intimacy of these Games, they are heightened by an extra element of danger. When speeds are magnified by gravity and ice, when control is routinely traded for acceleration, risk is a cold companion that haunts the most seasoned competitors.

Initially, Pierre de Coubertin, the founder of the modern Games, had no interest in adding winter competitions to the Olympic program. But the growing cadre of snow-sport enthusiasts clamored for the inclusion of cold-weather events, and in 1924 the Winter Olympic Games—initially titled "International Sports Week"—debuted in the little Alpine resort of Chamonix in France.

The opening of those first Winter Olympics, like many since, was hair-raising due to freakish swings in weather. A month before the Games, there was no snow at all in Chamonix. Then, overnight, there was

1976 INNSBRUCK

FRANZ KLAMMER, AUT

On the treacherous Patscherkofel downhill course in Innsbruck, Austria, hometown hero Franz Klammer, 22, flew to the finish line at speeds up to eighty miles per hour—edging Switzerland's Bernhard Russi for the Olympic gold by four-tenths of a second.

Photos: Above © Duomo, William R. Sallaz; Below, Archives, Olympic Museum Lausanne; Opposite © Duomo.

so much snow that it buried the skating rink, which had to be excavated by hand. A few weeks later, torrential rains transformed the ice stadium into a lake, but a freeze followed, and the Games began.

As they would in many subsequent Winter Olympics, Scandinavians dominated the sixteen competitive events. Their edge in Nordic skiing, ski jumping, and skating had been finely honed in the Nordic Games, inaugurated in 1901, and in Norway's celebrated Holmenkollen, an annual week of ski jumping and cross-country competitions. To no one's surprise, Finland's champion speed skater, Clas Thunberg, hurtled away with three gold medals, while Norway's Thorleif Haug raced to three golds in Nordic skiing. Sweden's Gillis Grafström won his second gold medal in figure skating, which had first been unseasonably featured in the 1908 and 1920 Summer Olympic Games.

Canada, the country that invented ice hockey, captured the second of many wins in its national sport, which had been introduced in the 1920 Summer Olympics in Antwerp. The lone U.S. winner was Charles Jewtraw, who streaked to the gold—the first medal of the Games—in the 500-meter skating race. And, although she was unknown at the time, the most famous competitor at Chamonix was not a medalist at all. It was an eleven-year-old Norwegian named Sonja Henie, who finished at the bottom of the list in women's figure skating.

Henie had, amazingly, clinched the skating championship of Norway just a few weeks before the Games—defeating many older, much more seasoned competitors. Although she didn't distinguish herself in her first Olympic competition, it proved to be an experience that helped prepare her for one of the most successful skating careers of all time. By 1928, when the second Winter Games opened in St. Moritz, Switzerland, Henie had drilled herself in ballet as well as skating and, at the tender age of thirteen, had already captured the world championship. Henie never practiced more than three hours a day—"I'd simply go nuts," she said. But she still managed to transfix Olympic crowds in St. Moritz

1924 CHAMONIX

CURLING

The sport of curling, which originated in Scotland more than four centuries ago, was featured at the first Winter Olympic Games in 1924. Players slide 42-pound granite stones across the ice toward fixed targets, using brooms to smooth the ice and help direct the moving stones. Curling reappeared as an Olympic demonstration sport in 1988 in Calgary, and it will be reintroduced as an official Winter Olympic event at the 1998 Games in Nagano.

Photo: © Presse Sport.

1924 CHAMONIX

BOBSLEDDING

The first official international bobsled race was held at the 1924 Winter Games. The Swiss team clinched the four-man event; two-man racing was introduced in 1932.

Photos: Left © Presse Sport; Opposite, Archives, Olympic Museum Lausanne.

1924 CHAMONIX

HERMA VON SZABO-PLANCK, AUT

At the first Winter Games, Austria's Herma von Szabo-Planck skated off with the women's figure skating title. In last place was a Norwegian girl named Sonja Henie.

Photo: Archives, Olympic Museum Lausanne.

1924 CHAMONIX

SONJA HENIE, NOR

One of the greatest figure skaters ever was Norway's ice queen, Sonja Henie. Henie was just eleven years old and already Norway's national skating champion when she entered the first Winter Olympic Games in 1924. Although she didn't do well in Chamonix, she went on to gold-medaling performances in 1928, 1932, and 1936. After she retired from competition following the 1936 Games, Henie bewitched movie audiences in a new Hollywood career.

Photo: © Presse Sport.

with her near-perfect figures and imaginative "Dying Swan" routine, which shattered tradition by incorporating the fluid movements of ballet. Henie skated off with the gold—a feat she repeated at the next two Winter Games. In 1936 she retired from competition—after amassing nearly 1,500 trophies, cups, and medals—and launched a new, smashingly successful career as a Hollywood movie star.

Things didn't go quite so smoothly for all the other athletes at St. Moritz. Weird weather again bedeviled the Games: first a warm spell and no snow, and then heavy rain, forced the cancellation of some bobsled and speed skating events. On one day, the thermometer bounced between 0 and 77 degrees Fahrenheit, confounding cross-country athletes dependent on temperature-sensitive ski waxes. And once again, Gillis Grafström won the men's figure skating gold, Canada easily dispatched its rivals in ice hockey, and the Scandinavians, particularly the Norwegians, went home clutching most of the medals. The U.S., however, began its two-decades-long domination of the bobsled run, and brothers Jennison and John Heaton from New Haven, Connecticut, hurtled head-first to gold and silver wins on a heavy sled, the skeleton toboggan, in a rare event called the Cresta Run, held only in St. Moritz.

Americans did better in the 1932 Winter Games, held for the first time on home turf at the Adirondack resort of Lake Placid, New York. Franklin Roosevelt, then New York's governor, opened the Olympics, and his wife, Eleanor, gamely rattled down the bob run. But right on cue, weather again menaced the events. Tons of snow had to be trucked down from Canada, and due to rain, several ski jumpers splashed down in an unexpected pond. Because of the distance from Europe, only seventeen nations competed, compared to twenty-five in St. Moritz. But the masses of spectators—more than 78,000—made up for the

1948 ST. MORITZ

REIDAR LIAKLEV, NOR

Norwegian racers dashed off with three out of four speed skating golds in St. Moritz. Reidar Liaklev snatched the title in the 5,000 meters. His Swedish rival Åke Seyffarth ran into trouble when he collided with an overeager photographer on the ice.

Photos: Above and below, Archives, Olympic Museum Lausanne.

1948 ST. MORITZ

BARBARA ANN SCOTT, CAN

Nineteen-year-old Barbara Ann Scott, the reigning world champion, captured the women's figure skating gold for Canada in 1948. To prove to Olympic officials that she hadn't turned professional, the Ottawa native returned a canary-yellow car that had been presented to her by hometown officials.

Photo: Archives, Olympic Museum Lausanne.

lack of international competitors. They mobbed the figure skating events, which Henie won again, and the U.S.-dominated bobsled runs. One of the winning U.S. bobbers was Eddie Eagan, a gold-medal-winning light heavyweight boxer in the 1920 Summer Games who landed another gold by switching Olympic sports and seasons. The Canadians scored another win in ice hockey, and the Scandinavians wrapped up the skiing competitions. Sparking controversy, American and Canadian speed skaters dominated their events due to the imposition of North American Rules, which called for rough-and-tumble mass starts instead of skaters racing in pairs against the clock.

1948 ST. MORITZ

DICK BUTTON, USA

With his perfectly executed double axel jump—a move he had mastered only two days before—Dick Button, eighteen, wowed judges and won the men's figure skating gold in the St. Moritz Winter Games.

Photo: Archives, Olympic Museum Lausanne.

Traditional speed skating rules, favoring the Europeans, were reinstated when the Winter Games crossed the Atlantic again in 1936. This time the host was Germany, which had fallen under Adolf Hitler's domination in 1933. The Führer himself, his mustache white with snowflakes, opened the Games attended by his propaganda minister, Joseph Goebbels, and his aviation minister, Hermann Göring. Despite the grim presence of Nazi troops and heavy rain, the events—held in the twin Bavarian villages of Garmisch and Partenkirchen—were a popular success, drawing half a million spectators and athletes from twenty-eight countries. The undisputed king of the ice was Norwegian speed skater Ivar Ballangrud, who streaked away with three gold medals. The ice queen, once again, was Sonja Henie, who ended her amateur career with a third figure skating gold—this time edging out a fifteen-year-old British skater named Cecilia Colledge.

The biggest surprise of the Games was the trouncing of Canada's champion ice hockey team by the British, whose lineup on the ice mainly consisted of British-born Canadians. Despite Hitler's racist policies, Germany's ice hockey team included star player Rudi Ball—a Jewish

1952 OSLO

HALLGEIR BRENDEN, NOR

In Oslo, the 15-kilometer Nordic skiing title was claimed by the host country's national steeplechase champion, Hallgeir Brenden—a lumberjack and farmer who repeated his gold-medaling performance in 1956.

Photo: Archives, Olympic Museum Lausanne.

TONI SAILER, AUT

*Austria's Anton "Toni"
Sailer, the Kitzbühel
cannonball, dominated the
1956 Winter Games,
capturing the downhill triple
crown with huge leads over
his competitors.*

Photo: Archives, Olympic Museum Lausanne.

1952 OSLO

STEIN ERIKSEN, NOR

*Norwegian heartthrob Stein
Eriksen zigzagged to victory in
the 1952 Olympic giant slalom.
In 1954, after winning the
world combined alpine
championship title, he launched
a career as a sought-after ski
instructor in the U.S., where he
was known for his debonair style
on and off the slopes.*

Photo: Archives, Olympic Museum Lausanne.

CAROL HEISS, USA

In her second Olympic appearance, America's Carol Heiss, 20, easily skated away with the women's figure skating title at the Squaw Valley Games. Her future brother-in-law, David Jenkins, captured the men's figure skating gold—a title previously held by his brother and Heiss's soon-to-be husband, Hayes Alan Jenkins, who gold-medaled in 1956.

Photos: Below and right, Archives, Olympic Museum Lausanne.

athlete who, after fleeing to France to escape Nazi anti-Semitism, was recruited to play for the Fatherland. Scandinavians again clinched the Nordic skiing competitions, and Norwegian ski jumper Birger Ruud, who had won in 1932, scored his second gold in the event. Later, during World War II, Ruud and his two brothers were imprisoned in a concentration camp for refusing to assist the Nazis.

With the world gripped by war and its terrible aftermath for much of the next decade, the Winter Games did not resume until 1948, when they returned to the neutral Swiss mountain resort of St. Moritz. Notably absent from the Games were teams from defeated Germany and Japan, but athletes from twenty-eight other nations competed—including, for the first time, teams from Denmark, Chile, Iceland, Lebanon, and Korea. The war might have been over, but there was plenty of squabbling around the snow-packed Alpine town. American bobsledders claimed that their equipment had been sabotaged, and a hockey game between Sweden and Canada ended in a raging fist-fight. Major disputes broke out when the U.S. entered two rival ice hockey teams—one by the Amateur Hockey Association and another by the American Olympic Committee.

On more amicable notes, Alpine (downhill) skiing events, which had first been introduced in 1936, drew nearly twice as many competing teams as the Nordic (cross-country) skiing races. France's Henri Oreiller hurtled to two golds in the downhill events, and America's pigtailed Gretchen Fraser snatched a surprise gold in the women's slalom. U.S. figure skater Dick Button, an eighteen-year-old Harvard freshman, made his Olympic debut at St. Moritz, where his athletic style and powerful double axel jump—a move he'd mastered only two days before—landed him the gold. And Canada's favorite, Barbara Ann Scott, captured the women's figure skating gold after agreeing to return a canary-yellow car—a gift from the City of Ottawa—to put to rest accusations of professionalism.

Germany and Japan were invited back to the Winter Games in 1952, hosted by Oslo. Good weather and good spirits prevailed, and the Games were an indisputable victory party for the Norwegians. Their teams swept up seven golds, including three won by speed skating truck driver Hjalmar Anderson. Next best, surprisingly, was the U.S., whose four-gold record was led by nineteen-year-old downhiller Andrea Mead Lawrence. The young Vermonter beat out Europe's fastest skiers for gold medals in both the slalom and giant slalom, and Dick

Button nailed his second gold in figure skating with a jaw-dropping triple-loop jump. The Germans set a record of sorts, too. Giving new meaning to the term "heavy sledding," their bobsled team thundered to two gold medals—partly because their two-man crew weighed in at more than five hundred and twenty pounds, and their hefty four-man team tipped the scales at well over one thousand pounds. After the Games, Olympic officials announced new weight limits of two hundred and twenty pounds per man. "It's diet or quit," lamented one of the record-busting bobbers.

In 1956, for the first time, there was a massive global audience for the Winter Games, as television beamed images of Olympic skiers and skaters around the world. Although the balmy-weather Games were held in the slush-filled Italian ski resort of Cortina d' Ampezzo, they were owned, hands down, by skier Toni Sailer—Austria's Kitzbühel cannonball. The twenty-year-old plumber and future movie star *wedeled* to victory in all three Alpine events, outracing the other skiers by huge margins. The Soviets had a lot to celebrate, too. At Cortina, their very first Winter Olympics, they claimed sixteen medals—the most of any country—and took golds in

ice hockey and speed skating. The pairs skating event, however, was most notable for its surly spectators. Unhappy with the judging, the crowd took to hurling oranges at the officials, forcing crews to clear smashed fruit from the rink three times before skating could resume. American wins were limited to the figure skating singles golds, won by Hayes Jenkins and Tenley Albright. Although stoic Albright had fallen less than two weeks before the Games, slashing her right ankle to the bone with her skate blade, her father, a Boston surgeon, had flown to Cortina to stitch her up so she wouldn't miss the competition. Albright became a surgeon herself after ending her skating career.

The decision by the International Olympic Committee to hold the 1960 Winter Games at Squaw Valley, California, ignited a storm of controversy. The remote site, forty miles from Reno in the Sierra Nevada Mountains, had absolutely no facilities—everything, from skating rinks to ski runs, lifts, and lodging, had to be built from scratch. The organizers also decided to strike bobsled races from the Games, on the grounds that the small number

1968 GRENOBLE

JEAN-CLAUDE KILLY, FRA

France's skiing superstar Jean-Claude Killy repeated Toni Sailer's remarkable triple-gold sweep in 1968. With his glamorous style, breakneck speed, and technical virtuosity, Killy dominated the 1968 Grenoble Games.

Photos: Left and below, Archives, Olympic Museum Lausanne.

of teams competing didn't justify the steep cost of constructing a bob run. But despite disputes, heavy snow, and the heating up of the Cold War, the Games proceeded smoothly in an informal and remarkably congenial setting. Walt Disney staged opening ceremonies filled with school bands and balloons and presided over by Vice President Richard Nixon. And, a year before the Berlin Wall went up, the East and West German athletes competed as one team, using Beethoven's Ninth Symphony in their victory ceremonies, rather than their respective national anthems.

Soviet schoolteacher Lydia Skoblikova clinched two of the women's speed skating races—the first ever held in the Olympics. Scandinavians dominated Nordic skiing, Canadian downhiller Anne Heggtveit nailed the slalom, and Americans—this time, David Jenkins and Carol Heiss—again took the figure skating honors. By far the biggest surprise of the Games was America's shocking capture of the Olympic hockey title. Riding an amazing lucky streak, the underdog U.S. "Team of Destiny"—a patchwork crew that included a fireman, two carpenters, a couple of insurance agents, and an ad salesman—came out of nowhere to sweep past traditional hockey powers, including Czechoslovakia, Canada, and the Soviets, to score the winning gold.

Luck, however, at first seemed to turn against the next Winter Olympic Games, held in Innsbruck, Austria, in 1964. Two athletes, an Australian skier and a Polish-born British luger, were killed in training accidents. And a mere week before the opening ceremonies, the slopes were still agonizingly bare of snow. Fortunately, 3,000 Austrian troops accomplished what the weather wouldn't, hauling 40,000 cubic meters of snow to Olympic ski runs and carting 20,000 bricks of ice from Alpine peaks to line the luge and bobsled runs.

The events themselves were a triumph, once again, for Soviet athletes. Lydia Skoblikova bettered her 1960 wins, picking off all four speed skating golds, and teammate Claudia Boyarskikh took three golds in Nordic skiing. The Soviets also reclaimed the ice hockey championship, and the passionate pairs skaters, Ludmilla Belousova and Oleg Protopopov—known for their legendary "death spiral"—captured their first figure skating gold. The unofficial hero of the Games, however, was Italy's world champion bobsledder, Eugenio Monti. When the British bob team sheared a bolt on their sled, Monti—who had just come down the run—pulled a bolt out of his own so that his competitors could race. The British shot down the chute to win the gold.

1968 GRENOBLE

NANCY GREENE, CAN

In her third Olympics, Canada's Nancy Greene charged down the slopes to score gold in the women's giant slalom. Greene, from Rossland, British Columbia, won Canada's first women's alpine gold since Anne Heggtveit raced to victory in the slalom in the 1960 Winter Games.

Photos: Below and right, Archives, Olympic Museum Lausanne.

1972 SAPPORO

YUKIO KASAYA, JPN

In Sapporo, ski jumper Yukio Kasaya, a local champion from the island of Hokkaido, won the second Winter Games medal ever for Japan when he soared to the gold in the normal hill competition. Teammates Akitsugu Konno and Seiji Aochi made it a clean sweep for Japan when they captured the silver and bronze in the event.

Photo: Archives, Olympic Museum Lausanne.

1972 SAPPORO

ERHARD KELLER, GER

After racing to the speed skating gold in the 500 meters at Grenoble in 1968, West Germany's Erhard Keller held onto his Olympic title in 1972. In the 500, Keller outpaced the Netherlands's Ard Schenk who won every other men's speed skating event at the Sapporo Games.

Photo: Archives, Olympic Museum Lausanne.

1976 INNSBRUCK

KARL SCHNABL, AUT

Following spread: Austria claimed its first gold medal in ski jumping when Karl Schnabl took first place on Innsbruck's 90-meter hill. Fellow Austrian Ernst Vettori duplicated Schnabl's feat in Albertville in 1992.

Photo: © Duomo.

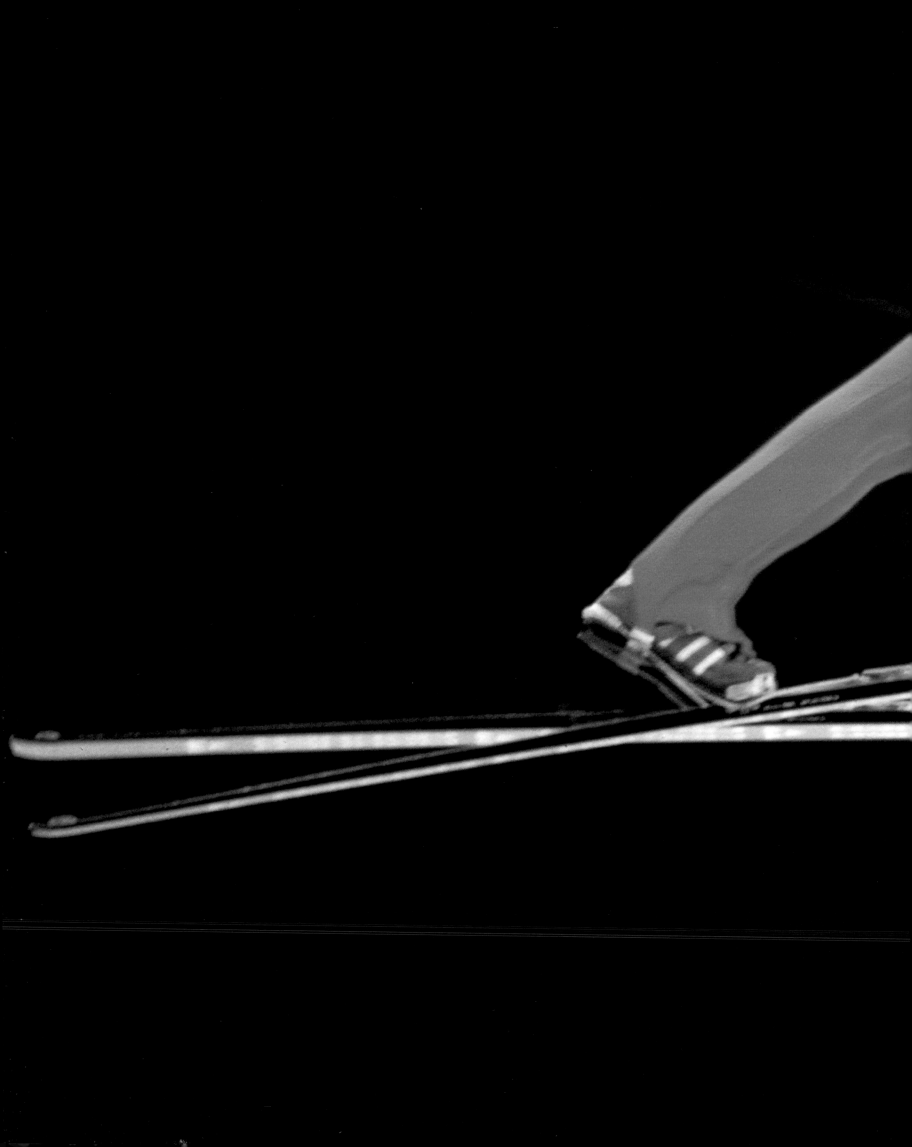

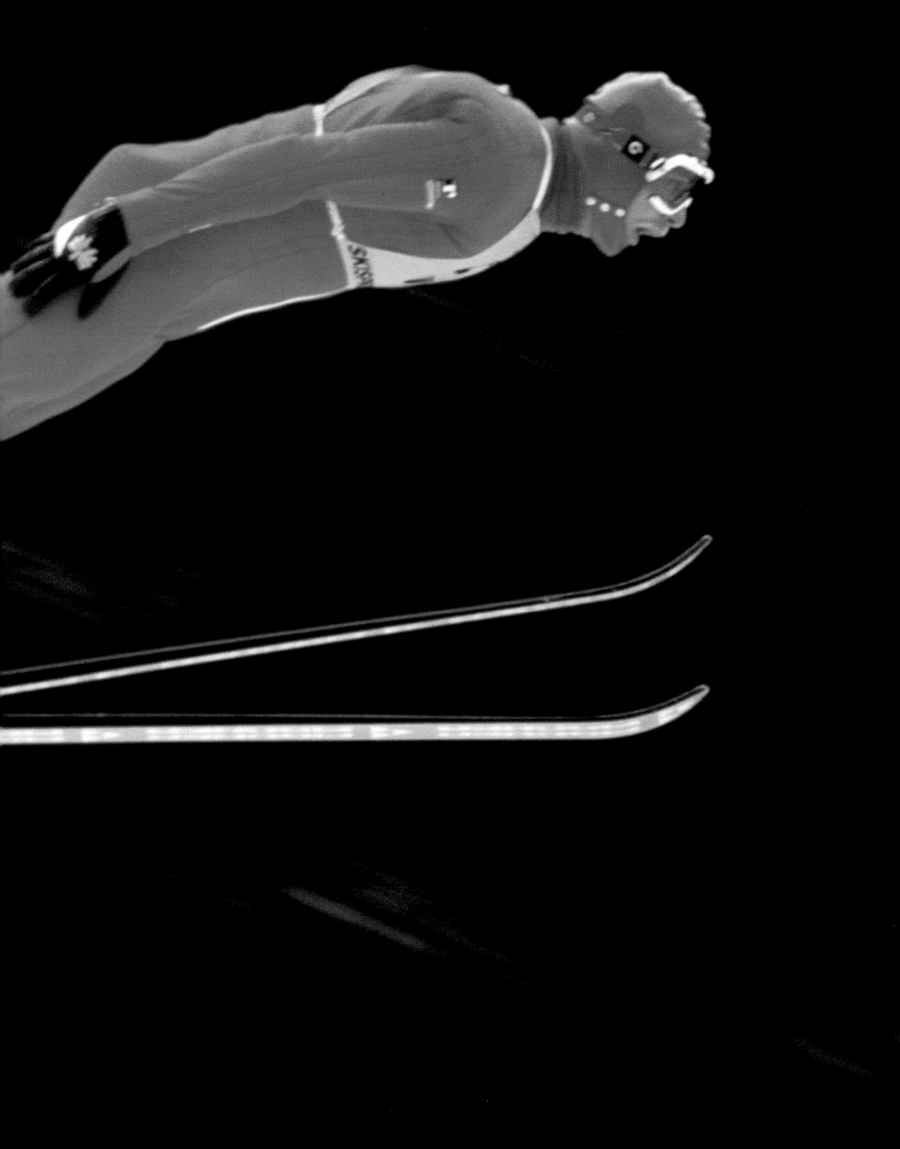

Monti finally got his own gold medals at the Grenoble Winter Games in 1968. But virtually all the athletes competing in the French Alps were overshadowed by "Le Superman," French ski god Jean-Claude Killy. Combining precision and explosive speed, Killy zipped off with all three gold medals in the Alpine—matching Toni Sailer's 1956 feat—despite record-setting winds, thick fog, and a haze of controversy surrounding the giant slalom race. The arguments arose after Austria's Karl Schranz had cut short his second run, having missed two gates. Officials allowed him to ski the course again after he claimed that he had been distracted by a shadowy figure, possibly a course policeman, who had mysteriously crossed the track. Schranz's time for the last run would have earned him the gold, but the French protested. After deliberating for hours, the Olympic jury determined that Schranz had missed a gate before the distraction occurred. They awarded the gold medal to Killy, giving him the third jewel in his triple crown.

There were other controversies, too, at the Grenoble Games. Female athletes were required to undergo gender tests for the first time. The East German women were disqualified from the luge event for heating the runners of their sled, prompting their officials to complain of a "capitalist revanchist plot." And the International Olympic Committee clashed with top downhill skiers, insisting that they remove their brand-name-adorned equipment before posing for news and television cameras. But the quarrels didn't tarnish the bright spots of the Games. Canada's Nancy Greene zigzagged through the gates to claim the giant slalom gold, and for the first time a non-Scandinavian, Italy's Franco Nones, captured an individual Nordic skiing title. Figure skater Peggy Fleming, battling the flu and wearing a costume stitched together by her mother, won America's only gold medal. And British speed skater David Bodington earned top points in sportsmanship when he voluntarily dived onto the ice and out of competition to avoid injuring a rival who'd fallen in his lane.

1976 INNSBRUCK

DOROTHY HAMILL, USA

With her fluid skating style and signature wedge haircut, America's Dorothy Hamill glided to the women's figure skating gold in 1976.

Photos: Below and right, Archives, Olympic Museum Lausanne.

1980 LAKE PLACID

ICE HOCKEY

In a stunning upset for the Soviet Union, which had dominated Olympic ice hockey since 1956, an upstart U.S. team scored Olympic gold—jubilantly duplicating America's unexpected "miracle on ice" win over the Soviet champions in 1960.

Photo: © Duomo, Paul J. Sutton.

Unfortunately, however, the fog of controversy that had shrouded Grenoble continued to hover over the 1972 Winter Olympics at Sapporo, the first ever held in Asia. The IOC threw Karl Schranz, Austria's ski hero, out of the Games, choosing to make an example of him for appearing in commercial advertising. Furious, the Austrian team pulled out altogether, then reentered at Schranz's urging. The Canadians joined the near-frenzied debate over amateurism, boycotting the ice hockey competition to protest state sponsorship of Eastern European teams.

But the Games, held in the pristine shadow of Mount Eniwa, ended happily for the Japanese, whose home team amazingly swept three medals in ski-jumping events. The men's speed skating races were wrapped up by the flying Dutchman, Ard Schenk, who glided off with three gold medals, and the women's races were dominated by two Americans from Northbrook, Illinois, Anne Henning and Dianne Holum. Another U.S. competitor, Barbara Cochran, edged her rivals by a sheer two-hundredths of a second to take gold in the slalom.

Denver, Colorado, was tapped to host the 1976 Winter Olympics, but voters got cold feet and vetoed financing for the event. So the Games went to Innsbruck for a second time. Local ski hero Franz Klammer schussed off with the gold medal for Austria in the downhill, and West Germany's Rosi Mittermaier starred in the women's slalom and downhill. The Soviets dominated speed and pairs skating, ice dancing made its Olympic debut, and America's Dorothy Hamill—as famous for her signature haircut as for her seamless style on ice—won the figure skating gold.

Four years later, in 1980, the Winter Games returned to Lake Placid, New York, but there was little that was placid about these Games. Billed as "An Olympics in Perspective," they were the first Winter Games attended by a team from the People's Republic of China.

1980 LAKE PLACID

ERIC HEIDEN, USA

Super-speed skater Eric Heiden from West Allis, Wisconsin, swept gold medals in all five men's events at Lake Placid, dominating both the short sprints and the long-distance endurance races.

Photo: © Duomo, Steven E. Sutton.

1984 SARAJEVO

KATARINA WITT, GDR

East Germany's brilliant Katarina Witt dramatically captured gold in women's figure skating in 1984 (opposite) and decisively repeated her triumph in 1988 (below)—becoming the first since Sonja Henie to take the Olympic title in two consecutive Winter Games.

Photos: Below and right © Duomo, Paul J. Sutton.

1984 SARAJEVO

TORVILL & DEAN, GBR

The British ice-dancing duo of Jayne Torvill and Christopher Dean captivated spectators in Sarajevo, winning twelve perfect scores and dancing off with the gold medal to the music of Ravel's Bolero.

Transportation was frozen by a bus system strike that left irate Olympic spectators stranded in frigid

cold and prompted the governor of New York to declare a limited state of emergency. Bad luck also

hit U.S. pairs skaters Randy Gardner and Tai Babilonia, who were forced to leave the ice after

Gardner, suffering from a groin injury, fell four times in warm-ups. But

nothing—not even the major concussion he'd suffered five months

earlier—could stop Sweden's Arctic skiing phenomenon, Ingemar

Stenmark, who rocketed to golds in both the slalom and giant slalom on mountain

courses packed with man-made snow. And nobody has ever matched the spectacular

winning streak of U.S. speed skater Eric Heiden, who shut out competitors by sweeping

five individual gold medals, the most of any Winter Olympian in a single year. In a stu-

pefying climax to the Games, an inexperienced U.S. hockey team somehow managed a

repeat performance of the American team's stunning 1960 "miracle on ice," boosting

the country's bruised national pride and breaking the Soviets' sixteen-year-long streak

of wins.

Surrounded by the pine-forested Dinaric Mountains, Sarajevo, Yugoslavia,

was chosen to host the Winter Games in 1984.

Until then, the city had been most famous as

the place where the Archduke Ferdinand of Austria

had been assassinated, igniting World War I. The beginning of

the Winter Games, unfortunately, was not a great deal more auspi-

cious. Flags flew at half-mast to mark the death of Soviet premier Yuri

Andropov, and Sarajevo was at first buried by snow, then blinded by fog, and

blasted by 120-mile-per-hour gusts

that shredded the Alpine schedule. But when the

cold white curtain parted, the focus turned to spectacular performances. West

Germany careened to a win in the two-man luge event, propelled by 244-pound slider Hans

Stangassinger. Bill Johnson captured America's first downhill gold, while teammate Phil Mahre won

the slalom, trailed by his silver-medaling twin brother, Steve.

But the biggest stars at Sarajevo were on skates. East German women swept the speed

skating events, and Canada's Gaetan Boucher took two golds in the men's races. Most of the media

---

1988 CALGARY

MICHAEL EDWARDS, GBR

The most dazzling Olympic ski-jumping performance in Calgary belonged to Finland's Matti "Nuke-'em" Nykänen, who scored triple golds in the event. But folk-hero status was awarded to Great Britain's sole entrant, Michael "Eddie the Eagle" Edwards. The twenty-four-year-old plasterer from Cheltenham, England, had started jumping only two years earlier and collected the lowest scores of any Olympic ski jumper, alarming spectators along the course with his frighteningly shaky landings.

Photos: Left, Archives, Olympic Museum Lausanne;
Below © Duomo.

Photo: © Duomo, Steven E. Sutton.

1988 CALGARY

PIRMIN ZURBRIGGEN, SWI

Swiss skier Pirmin Zurbriggen was favored to take gold in all five Olympic Alpine events in Calgary, but he went home to the Valais Alps with only one gold medal in the downhill, having narrowly edged teammate Peter Müller.

1988 CALGARY

BONNIE BLAIR, USA

America's enduring Bonnie "the Blur" Blair—a speed skating powerhouse from Champagne, Illinois—flashed to her first 500-meter gold medal in Calgary, then went on to collect four more Olympic gold medals in the 500- and 1,000-meter races in the Albertville and Lillehammer Games.

Photo: © Duomo, David Madison.

1988 CALGARY

ALBERTO TOMBA, ITA

Alberto Tomba, Italy's skiing superstar, thrilled fans by streaking to double golds in both the slalom and giant slalom in Calgary. "La Bomba" returned to the Games for a second giant slalom win in Albertville in 1992.

Photo: © Duomo, William R. Sallaz.

Following spread: U.S. luger Erica Terwilliger competing in Albertville in 1992.

Photo: © Duomo, Paul J. Sutton.

attention focused on the brilliant, dramatic Katarina Witt, East Germany's figure skating prima donna, and the astonishing performance of Great Britain's ice-dancing royal couple, Jayne Torvill and Christopher Dean. Nottingham's "T & D" miraculously skated off with twelve perfect scores, while America's Scott Hamilton squeaked by Canada's Brian Orser for the men's figure skating title.

On his home turf at the windy Calgary Winter Games in 1988, Orser had a second chance to duel for the figure skating gold—this time against his good friend America's Brian Boitano in a matchup that was billed as the "Battle of the Brians." Though Boitano edged Orser for the title, Canada got in its licks when Elizabeth Manley beat out America's Debi Thomas for the women's silver. Skating seductively to Bizet's *Carmen*, Katarina Witt dazzled spectators for her second gold in the event, ranking her as the first woman since Henie to take the figure skating title in two consecutive Games.

On the slick downhill slopes, blasted by howling chinook gales, Italian heartthrob Alberto Tomba raced to victory in the slalom and giant slalom, while France's Franck Piccard took the gold in the new super giant slalom—scoring the first downhill victory for France since Killy's golds in 1968. Despite the wicked winds, Finland's irascible ski jumper Matti "Nuke-'em" Nykänen soared to two gold-medal distances and a third team jumping gold. Jamaica's first-ever bobsled team—including a reggae singer and a helicopter pilot—rumbled down the chute, and America's Bonnie "the Blur" Blair outpaced her rivals to the gold in women's speed skating. But favored U.S. skater Dan Jansen tragically slipped and fell in the 500-meter race just hours after learning that his twenty-seven-year-old sister, Jane, had lost her life to leukemia. Four days later, while competing in the 1,000-meter speed skating event, Jansen, hobbled by grief, caught an edge and agonizingly crashed to the ice again.

1992 ALBERTVILLE

VEGARD ULVANG, NOR

Vegard "the Viking" Ulvang, Norway's adventurer-hero from the Arctic Circle, raced to three Nordic skiing golds in Albertville. In his spare time, Ulvang has ridden across Outer Mongolia on horseback, skied across Greenland, and climbed the highest mountain peaks in North America, South America, and Africa.

Photos: © Duomo, Paul J. Sutton.

1992 ALBERTVILLE

JAMAICAN BOBSLED TEAM

Driven to compete, the Jamaican bobsled team made its second Olympic appearance at the Winter Games in Albertville. The team, which attracted worldwide attention in Calgary in 1988, originally gained its bobbing skills by practicing on pushcarts in the snowless Blue Mountains of Jamaica. At the 1994 Lillehammer Games, the Jamaican four-man team finished in fourteenth place, beating the U.S.

Photos: Above, Archives, Olympic Museum Lausanne; Opposite © Duomo, David Madison.

KRISTI YAMAGUCHI, USA

Kristi Yamaguchi, 20, gracefully twirled and jumped to America's first gold in women's figure skating since Dorothy Hamill won the Olympic title in 1976. Born with clubfeet—an impairment that was corrected— Yamaguchi grew up in Fremont, California, playing with a Dorothy Hamill doll.

Photo: © Duomo, David Madison.

BIATHLON

The demanding biathlon event, which combines Nordic skiing and riflery, was introduced as a Winter Olympic sport in 1960. Biathletes must demonstrate enormous physical control by skiing vigorously, then shooting at targets fifty meters away. Moldova's Gherhi Vasilii competed in the 1994 Olympic men's biathlon, which was dominated by the Russians.

Photo: © Duomo, David Madison.

Blair and Jansen had a second shot at gold medals four years later at the 1992 Winter Olympics in Albertville, France. Again, Blair flashed past her competitors, this time snaring two golds. And again, Jansen crumbled. This time it was sheer lack of speed that tripped him up—he finished fourth in the 500-meter and twenty-sixth in the 1,000-meter race. But despite the speed skating reprise, winds of change whipped through other Olympic event sites, scattered across 620 square miles of sun-glazed Alpine peaks. Athletes from the now-bloodied country that was Yugoslavia took part

under the emblems of Yugoslavia, Croatia, and Slovenia. Most Olympians from the former Soviet republics competed as the Unified Team—without an anthem or a superpower budget but with enough talent to muscle golds in ice hockey, men's figure skating, pairs skating, ice dancing, and five Nordic events, including the first-ever women's ski-and-shoot biathlon.

The bone-quaking sport of freestyle mogul skiing debuted as an Olympic medal event, won by America's Donna Weinbrecht and France's Edgar Grospiron. In the ice rink, America's Kristi Yamaguchi—who had grown up playing with a Dorothy Hamill doll—calmly outperformed four top-ranked rivals to win the first U.S. women's figure skating gold since 1976. And up on the sun-splashed Savoie slopes, it was total Tomba-mania as frenzied Italians roared for their Alpine idol, "La Bomba." Not one to disappoint, Alberto Tomba zipped through the gates to a gold in the giant slalom—and a record as the first Olympic downhiller to take two consecutive golds in the same event. His teammate, Deborah Compagnoni, sped off with another gold for Italy in the super giant slalom.

Two years later in Lillehammer, Norway—the first Games on a new Olympic schedule that alternates summer and winter events every two years—Compagnoni did it again, this time in the giant slalom. America's Diann Roffe-Steinrotter swooped down Kvitfjell Mountain for a gold in the Super G, and the downhill belonged to her ballistic teammate Tommy Moe. There was no question, though, that the Games themselves belonged to the Norwegians, who swept twenty-six medals—including ten

1994 LILLEHAMMER

CATHY TURNER, USA

At Lillehammer, Cathy Turner—a part-time singer and songwriter—clinched her second gold medal in 500-meter short-track speed skating. The collision-prone, pack-skating event debuted at the 1992 Winter Games in Albertville, where Turner took the title.

Photos: Left, Archives, Olympic Museum Lausanne; Below © Duomo, William R. Sallaz.

Following spread: Tommy Moe speeds to gold in Lillehammer in 1994.

Photo: © Duomo, Al Tielemans.

golds, the most of any nation. While the off-rink melodrama of U.S. figure skaters Tonya Harding and Nancy Kerrigan enthralled much of the media, Oksana Baiul, a Ukrainian teenager, shimmered on the ice and upstaged her competitors for the gold—even while skating with three stitches in her leg and a bruised spine from a tumble she had taken in practice.

Under the vast arched timbers of the Vikingskipet skating hall, Norway's speed skating sensation, Johann Olav Koss, scored triple golds in the 1,500-, 5,000-, and 10,000-meter races. America's Bonnie Blair retired—declining to compete in the 1998 Games in Nagano, Japan—after bolting to her fifth Olympic gold in the 1,000-meter sprint. And in the best Cinderella story of these—or perhaps any—Olympic Games, star-crossed skater Dan Jansen, beaten in his best event, the 500-meters, finally glided to a gold medal and a new world record in the 1,000—his very last Olympic race. As the hearts of millions went out in happiness to Jansen, the lights went out inside the Viking ship, and he skated a breathtaking victory lap alone with his baby daughter, Jane, cradled in his arms. The rapture of that moment wasn't about medal counts or winning or national Olympic pride. As a Japanese coach had mused earlier, touching his hand to his chest and pondering Jansen's anguishing Olympic journey, "The gold medal is, maybe, in the heart."

1994 LILLEHAMMER

BRIAN BOITANO, USA

U.S. Olympic figure skating champion Brian Boitano—who had edged his good friend, Canadian favorite Brian Orser, for the gold medal in the 1988 Calgary Games—returned to the Olympics in 1994. This time, however, Boitano went home empty-handed after taking a spill during his triple axel combination.

Photo: © Duomo, Paul J. Sutton.

1994 LILLEHAMMER

OKSANA BAIUL, UKR

Braving painful leg injuries, Ukrainian figure skating star Oksana Baiul, 16, enchanted judges with a flawlessly expressive routine and upstaged American favorite Nancy Kerrigan for the Olympic gold.

Photo: © Duomo, Al Tielemans.

1994 LILLEHAMMER

DAN JANSEN, USA

Victory was sweet for star-crossed U.S. speed skater Dan Jansen (opposite), who finally claimed gold in Lillehammer in the 1,000 meters—his very last Olympic race—after failing to medal at the Calgary and Albertville Winter Games.

1994 LILLEHAMMER

SKI JUMPING

German and Norwegian ski jumpers glided to gold medals in 1994. The Germans, led by Jens Weissflog, dominated the team jumping and large hill competitions, while Espen Bredesen took the title in the normal hill jump, clinching Norway's first gold in ski jumping since 1964.

1994 LILLEHAMMER

JOHANN OLAV KOSS, NOR

Local hero Johann Olav Koss stormed to triple golds for Norway in three speed skating events—the 1,500-, 5,000-, and 10,000-meter races. Koss clinched his first Olympic gold at Albertville in the 1,500 meters.

Chamonix 1924

St. Moritz 1928

Since the very first Winter Olympics at Chamonix, France, in 1924, the

THE WINTER OLYMPIC POSTERS

intimate, snow-swept spirit of the Games has been conveyed in posters produced by Olympic host towns in Europe, North America, and Asia. The first Winter Games poster was created by the Paris-Lyon-Méditerranée railway, which subsidized construction of the skating rink and other facilities in Chamonix.

Photos: Archives, Olympic Museum Lausanne.

Cortina d'Ampezzo 1956

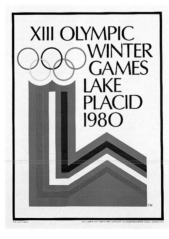

Squaw Valley 1960

Lake Placid 1980

Sarajevo 1984

Lake Placid 1932

Garmisch-Partenkirchen 1936

St. Moritz 1948

Oslo 1952

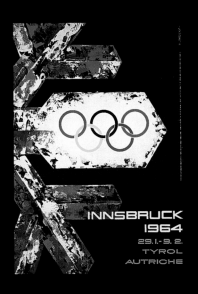

Innsbruck 1964

Grenoble 1968

Sapporo 1972

Innsbruck 1976

Calgary 1988

Albertville 1992

ARTS AND THE ATHLETES

Linked with the grueling effort and exhilaration of Olympic sport is the spellbinding beauty of performance. The sinewed bodies of the athletes, pushing with profound grace the limits of the elements and human will, have fascinated artists since ancient times. Olympic champions have inspired lasting ideals of physical beauty and, in

art and architecture, moving collective expressions of human aspiration. Today, with television broadcasts of Olympic pageantry, triumphs, and failures reaching virtually every corner of the planet, the Olympic Games are also an awesome dramatic spectacle—in effect, world theater played out before an audience of half the human race.

In ancient Greece, where the Olympic Games were born more than twenty-seven centuries ago, art and physical performance were intertwined. Both the artist and the athlete were inspired by the goal of striving, as much as humanly possible, for godlike perfection. Athletes oiled their muscles and trained rigorously to the music of flutes in wrestling, discus, running, and other disciplines. While they practiced, artists watched, carefully observing the beauty of anatomy in motion and using that knowledge to create some of the world's greatest examples of figurative sculpture.

Art in Greece was intended for public display, and Olympia, where the ancient Games were played, was crammed with sculpture immortalizing the athletes, mythological heroes, and the gods to whom the Games were consecrated. The aesthetic setting of the Games was

ANATOMY IN MOTION

In ancient Greece, the physical beauty of Olympic athletes—exemplified in recent times by the muscular grace of diver Greg Louganis (opposite), and pole vaulter Sergei Bubka (below)—inspired some of the world's greatest achievements in figurative art.

Photos: Above, Archives, Olympic Museum Lausanne; Below and right © Duomo, Steven E. Sutton.

OLYMPIC INSPIRATION

*Since the founding of the
modern Games in 1896,
painting, sculpture, and other
visual and performance arts
have been an integral part of
the Olympic experience.*

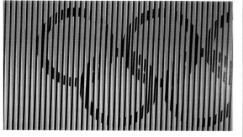

*Above: Lithograph by
Venezuelan optic artist Carlos
Cruz Díez. "Suite Olympic
Centennial," Olympic Museum,
Lausanne, Switzerland. Below:
Jesse Owens, 1942, modeled
from life by Joseph Brown.
Ohio State University,
Columbus, Ohio.*

Photos: Above and all stamps, Archives, Olympic
Museum Lausanne; Below © Joseph Brown, courtesy of
the National Sculpture Society.

enhanced by monumental architecture, particularly the towering Temple of Zeus, constructed in the mid-fifth century B.C. Behind its soaring columns and sculpted pediments loomed the colossal seated statue of the god Zeus, one of the Seven Wonders of the World. Now perished, the statue was created of wood overlain with gold and ivory by the famed sculptor Phidias, who kept his workshop at Olympia. The influence of the Olympic Games on Hellenic art was so strong that, according to one scholar, Greece's greatest aesthetic achievements would never have been possible if the Games had not existed.

When Pierre de Coubertin revived the Olympics in 1894, his goal was not simply to reestablish what he saw as the classical link between physical training, competition, and national leadership. He also sought to rekindle the Greek spiritual connection between art and sport. The universal messages of the Games, Coubertin saw, needed to be communicated through artistic symbols and ceremony, such as the dramatic flight of doves that opened the very first of the modern Games in Athens in 1896. In that spirit, other icons and rituals followed. The Olympic flag, with its design of five interlacing rings representing the five participating continents, was raised for the first time at the 1920 Olympics in Antwerp, and the Olympic oath was first movingly pronounced there by the Belgian fencer Victor Boin. The Olympic flame first blazed at the 1928 Games in Amsterdam, and in 1936, at the Berlin Olympics, it was first carried hand to hand from Olympia in Greece in a fiery relay that recalled the ceremonial torch races of ancient Hellas.

For Coubertin, however, the relationship of art and Olympic sport was more fundamental than these symbolic gestures. Reflecting this conviction, he added a clause to the Olympic charter stating that cultural events "of an equal standard" should be organized in conjunction with the Games. In 1906, he convened a conference in Paris to explore the connection of art, literature, and sport and the ways in which they might be formally combined in celebration of the revived Olympic Games. The conference recommended that, in addition to athletic contests, the Olympics should include official competitions in five aesthetic areas: architecture, sculpture, painting, music, and literature. Quadrennial prizes would be awarded for the best new works that found their inspiration in sport.

These artistic competitions were officially included in the 1912 Olympics in

Stockholm, and they were part of every Olympic program over the next three decades. After the 1948 Games in London, however, they were abandoned. The mediocre quality of many of the entries was one reason. It was also plain that the majority of spectators were interested chiefly, if not exclusively, in Olympic sports events. Although Olympiads after 1948 jettisoned the artistic competitions, they continued to celebrate the link between sport and art in exhibitions, performances, dramatic ceremonial displays, and often spectacular works of architectural design.

In Mexico City in 1968, the Games were coupled with a year-long Cultural Olympiad that drew painters, poets, sculptors, musicians, and performers from five continents and featured a

massive exposition of children's art. Spectators at the Munich Olympics in 1972 passed under a colossal sky sculpture by Otto Piene called *Olympic Rainbow*— an inflated, two-thousand-foot-long arch, made up of five colored, helium-filled tubes. And the 1992 Games in Barcelona took place surrounded by installations of more than fifty new commissioned works of urban sculpture created by artists such as Richard Serra, Ellsworth Kelly, Roy Lichtenstein, and Antoni Tàpies.

Perhaps the ultimate Olympic art celebration took place in Los Angeles in 1984. The city's 10-week Olympic Arts Festival, planned in conjunction with the twenty-third Olympiad, brought together nearly a hundred exhibits and performances from more than twenty countries. Fusing traditional and avant-garde artistic currents from Asia and the West, the Festival attracted artists ranging from the Korean National Dance Company and the Royal Opera of Covent Garden to Australia's free-form Circus Oz, the provocative Pina Bausch Wuppertaler Tanztheater from the Federal Republic of Germany, and China's traditional Central Ensemble of National Music.

Inspiring and often technically daring works of architecture have also conveyed the artistic energy of numerous Olympiads since 1948. For many cities, the prospect of hosting the Olympic Games sparked a renaissance and redesign of urban spaces, led by the construction of new stadiums, swimming pools, and other sports facilities. Beginning with the Helsinki Games in 1952, however, Olympic architecture broke out of its largely functional tradition with spirited, modern structures of unified design. Eight years later, the drama of the Olympic Games in Rome was staged in daringly engineered, domed sports palaces designed by Pier Luigi Nervi—as well as in the

DRAMA AND SPECTACLE

At the 1984 Summer Olympic Games, the Los Angeles Coliseum was packed with 93,000 spectators for the $6 million Opening Ceremonies spectacular. The extravaganza featured 10,000 performers, flags, and pageantry, including a choir of 960 voices and 84 baby grand pianos (below).
Following spread: 1984 Opening Ceremonies in Sarajevo.

Photos: Below and following spread
© Duomo, Steven E. Sutton.

OLYMPIC ARCHITECTURE

*For many host cities, the
Olympic Games have led to a
renaissance in urban
architecture and the construction
of groundbreaking new
stadiums and other sports
facilities. Below, top to bottom:
St. Jordi Hall in Barcelona,
Spain; the Vikingskipet Olympic
skating rink in Hamar,
Norway; the Gymnastics Hall
in Seoul, South Korea; and the
Gjøvik Olympic Cavern Arena,
in Lillehammer, Norway.*

Photos: Below © Duomo, Steven E. Sutton.

spectacular environs of the city's ancient architectural masterpieces.  Gymnasts performed in the elaborately arched Baths of Caracalla, while wrestlers grappled in the colossal Basilica of Maxentius, and marathoners paced to the finish line beneath the soaring span of the Arch of Constantine.

In Munich in 1972, a boldly designed, curving lattice of steel cables and acrylic glass towered over the Olympic stadiums and titanic swimming pool, which had sufficient  seating to accommodate 10,000 spectators. Munich's "Olympiaplatz," a vast sports park built for the Games, remains one of the city's most frequented recreational areas. By contrast, the 1984 Olympics in Los Angeles produced no new architectural landmarks. Existing civic and university buildings were used as settings for the Games; however, their exteriors were temporarily transformed by the illusions of bold color, three-dimensional graphics, scaffolding, tents, fabric, paper, and mylar. Like a stage set, the dazzling façade came down when the Games left town.

For Seoul, South Korea, hosting the 1988 Olympics was a catalyst for reimagining the city center and experimenting with inventive architectural design. The city's gymnastic and fencing stadiums were capped by revolutionary fabric roofs supported by radiating webs of tension cables. These groundbreaking "tensegrity" domes, based on the theoretical work of the pioneering architect and engineer R. Buckminster Fuller, were the first such structures ever built. New architectural technology and forms also created a striking setting for the 1994 Winter Olympic Games in Lillehammer, Norway. Designed to resemble the capsized hull of a Viking ship, the roof of the Olympic skating rink in Hamar, south of Lillehammer, was supported by the longest expanse of wooden beams of any structure in the world.

WORLD THEATER

*The dramatic spectacles of the
Opening Ceremonies are
watched by billions of spectators
around the world. Opposite:
The pageantry of the Opening
Ceremonies of the 1992 Summer
Olympic Games in Barcelona.*

Photo: Opposite © Duomo, David Madison.

Architectural and geological engineering records were also broken in the construction of the Gjøvik Olympic Cavern Arena, a 6,000-seat underground hockey rink hewn out of the red rock side of Hovdetoppen mountain.

Architecture and design set the stage on which the Olympic drama is played out. But the beauty of the human form and the struggle and

grace of competition form the emotional heart of the art of the Games. Modern Olympic moments frozen in figurative images, such as Joseph Brown's bronze statue of track paragon Jesse Owens pounding to the finish line, capture the drama of athletes pushing themselves beyond the limits of ordinary humans. In cinema, as well, artists have attempted to frame riveting Olympic images. The most masterly example ever produced is German filmmaker Leni Riefenstahl's documentary *Olympia* (1938). Despite her uncritical admiration for Adolf Hitler, Riefenstahl's four-hour film of the lavish, propagandist 1936 Berlin Games is a romantic, moving tribute to Olympic sport. In contrast to Riefenstahl's mythic glorification of the Games, another masterpiece—Kon Ichikawa's intimate film *Tokyo Olympiad*, produced in 1964—documents instead the lonely anxiety of the athletes as they struggle to excel.

The twin emotions of agony and rapture that drive Olympic athletes to compete also compel us to watch, transfixed, as whole lifetimes of effort climax in a single Olympic moment. It is a melodrama as cathartic as any scripted piece of theater. For a few weeks every four years, the athletes wear our nation's colors on their sleeves and carry our hopes with them into competition. Perhaps nowhere is this collective aspiration—for success and peace and the ideal of fair play—more potently expressed than in the spectacle of the Opening Ceremonies.

It is mesmerizing theater, amplified by Olympic pageants that stretch the limits of the imagination. In Moscow in 1980, 16,000 performers filled the stadium during a four-hour opening spectacle. Four years later, in Los Angeles, the Games opened with the release of millions of white and gold balloons and a cinematic evocation of American history and culture by 10,000 performers, including more than eighty pianists. In 1988, the Seoul Opening Ceremonies awed 70,000 spectators and a television audience of nearly three billion, as a cast of nearly 14,000 performed Koreran rituals and dances. Children rolled metaphorical hoops of hope, and *tae kwon do* experts split pieces of wood as a symbol of shattering barriers among the people of the world. At the

Performers dressed as trolls and elves surround a glowing image of the earth during the Opening Ceremonies of the 1994 Winter Olympic Games in Lillehammer (opposite). The avant-garde Opening Ceremonies of the 1992 Albertville Winter Games (below) featured stiltwalkers, bungee jumpers, and women bedecked in transparent plastic bubbles.

Photos: Opposite © Duomo, David Madison; Below © Duomo, Steven E. Sutton.

climax of the spectacle, a high school student, university student, and teacher were raised to the top of a 95-foot column called the World Tree to kindle the Olympic flame.

The magic was unbroken by Barcelona in 1992, where the Games opened with a $28 million allegorical confection of robots, fighter jets, sea monsters, Spanish dancers, and operatic tenors.

The opening of the Winter Games that year in Albertville, France, was equally spectacular and exuberantly avant-garde. Eight stunt planes streamed rainbows of colored smoke, and sixty-four rollerbladers—one for each participating nation—carried emblems of the Olympic teams. The athletes themselves were led into the stadium by women costumed in transparent plastic bubbles filled with simulated snowflakes. Stilt walkers, dancers, jugglers, and acrobats spilled out of three fifteen-foot-high cornucopias, bungee jumpers ricocheted off the ground, and gigantic, inflated, neon green and yellow worms wiggled in the Alpine night. Olympic fantasy opened the 1994 Lillehammer Winter Games as well. Trolls, elves, and other creatures from Norse myths teemed around a giant egg-shaped globe that rose into the sky, surrounded by a silent flock of doves.

These spectacles echo the real, electrifying moments of competition, but the most gripping beauty and drama of the Games takes place in the stadiums and pools and on the tracks and icy slopes. Artists mirror the hope and emotional spirit of these instants. To paraphrase the critic George Jean Nathan, art is a tangible dream—and Olympic art, from figurative images to fantastic pageantry, gives moving form to the dream of Olympic glory.

In the most dramatic moment of the 1992 Opening Ceremonies in Barcelona, Antonio Rebollo—a polio-stricken archer from Madrid—fired a flaming arrow through the night sky to set ablaze the Olympic cauldron.

Photo: © Duomo, David Madison.

LAUSANNE

THE OLYMPIC MUSEUM

Opened in 1993 in Lausanne, Switzerland, the Olympic Museum celebrates the tradition of the Games with extensive exhibitions of Olympic artwork, memorabilia, and historical artifacts. Designed by Pedro Ramirez Vásquez of Mexico City and Jean-Pierre Cahen of Lausanne, the new museum, located on the shore of Lake Geneva, contains five stories of collections ranging from Greek antiquities to specimens of all the Olympic torches carried since 1936. Works by artists *such as Auguste Rodin and Antoni Tàpies, along with exhibitions of Olympic stamps, coins, pins, and medals; Olympic equipment; and a vast library of books, photographs, film, and video all document the history and culture of the Olympic Games.*

Photos: Above, Archives, Olympic Museum Lausanne, Donatsch / Prahn; Far right, Archives, Olympic Museum Lausanne, Donatsch; Left and right, Archives, Olympic Museum Lausanne.

Athens 1896

Athens 1896

Paris 1900

St. Louis 1904

London 1908

London 1908

Stockholm 1912

Stockholm 1912

Stockholm 1912

Antwerp 1920

Paris 1924

Paris 1924

Amsterdam 1928

Amsterdam 1928

Los Angeles 1932

Berlin 1936

Berlin 1936

Berlin 1936

Berlin 1936

Melbourne 1956

Rome 1960

Rome 1960

Rome 1960

Tokyo 1964

Mexico City 1968

Munich 1972

Montreal 1976

Moscow 1980

Moscow 1980

Los Angeles 1984

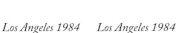
Los Angeles 1984   *Los Angeles 1984*   *Seoul 1988*   *Barcelona 1992*   *Barcelona 1992*

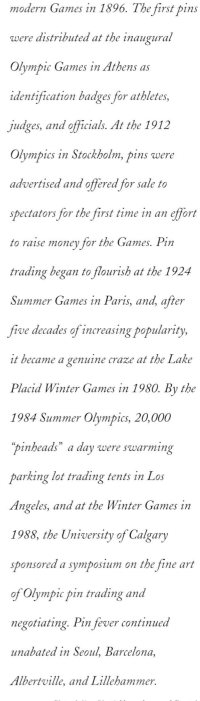

One of the most popular side events at the Olympic Games is the sport of pin trading. The history of Olympic pins goes back to the beginning of the

OLYMPIC PINS

modern Games in 1896. The first pins were distributed at the inaugural Olympic Games in Athens as identification badges for athletes, judges, and officials. At the 1912 Olympics in Stockholm, pins were advertised and offered for sale to spectators for the first time in an effort to raise money for the Games. Pin trading began to flourish at the 1924 Summer Games in Paris, and, after five decades of increasing popularity, it became a genuine craze at the Lake Placid Winter Games in 1980. By the 1984 Summer Olympics, 20,000 "pinheads" a day were swarming parking lot trading tents in Los Angeles, and at the Winter Games in 1988, the University of Calgary sponsored a symposium on the fine art of Olympic pin trading and negotiating. Pin fever continued unabated in Seoul, Barcelona, Albertville, and Lillehammer.

Photos: Archives, Olympic Museum Lausanne, J. Donatsch.

Athens 1896

Paris 1900

St. Louis 1904

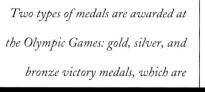

Two types of medals are awarded at the Olympic Games: gold, silver, and bronze victory medals, which are

THE COMMEMORATIVE MEDALS

presented to the winners, and Olympic commemorative medals (right), which are awarded, along with diplomas, to all competitors and Olympic and team officials participating in the Games. In addition, special medals have also been produced during certain Olympiads, such as the Olympic Medal of King Gustav V, which was distributed to members of the Swedish royal family, dignitaries, and Swedish medalists during the 1912 Olympics. A similar royal medal, bearing the likeness of Belgium's King Albert, was minted for the Antwerp Olympic Games in 1920.

Photos: Archives, Olympic Museum Lausanne.

Los Angeles 1932

Berlin 1936

London 1948

Munich 1972

Montreal 1976

Moscow 1980

THE WINTER GAMES 1924–1994

Chamonix 1924

St. Moritz 1928

Lake Placid 1932

Innsbruck 1964

Grenoble 1968

Sapporo 1972

Innsbruck 1976

London 1908

Stockholm 1912

Antwerp 1920

Paris 1924

Amsterdam 1928

Helsinki 1952

Melbourne 1956

Rome 1960

Tokyo 1964

Mexico City 1968

Los Angeles 1984

Seoul 1988

Barcelona 1992

Garmisch–Partenkirchen 1936

St. Moritz 1948

Oslo 1952

Cortina d'Ampezzo 1956

Squaw Valley 1960

Lake Placid 1980

Sarajevo 1984

Calgary 1988

Albertville 1992

Lillehammer 1994

TRAINING AND TECHNOLOGY

Luge is a sport for speed demons. Flat on their backs, free-falling down serpentine ice chutes at screamingly fast speeds up to seventy-five miles per hour, lugers abandon themselves like human bullets to the power of velocity. Sliding is all about big speed, big adrenaline rushes, and big risks. Winning an Olympic medal in luge, however, is an altogether

different matter. What separates a gold medalist from an also-ran is not a huge margin of daring and speed, but a hairsbreadth of an advantage—hundredths, sometimes thousandths, of a second. For sliders, gaining that edge can come down to a tough choice between raising their heads for an instant to see where in the world they're going, thereby risking a millisecond of air drag, and keeping their bodies as unwaveringly flat and aerodynamic as a rocket—and possibly risking a bone-jarring crash into the side of the chute.

Helping athletes achieve that sometimes decisive extra measure of performance is the mission of sports science and technology. It's a discipline that first took off in the 1950s, when Eastern European nations seized the lead in developing scientifically based methods for training their athletes. As a result of their sophisticated approaches, the USSR and the German Democratic Republic swept many of the medals at the 1976 Olympic Games in Montreal—provoking the western nations to scurry to launch sports science programs of their own. As a result, biomechanists, physiologists, engineers, computer scientists, and psychologists have been pooling their scientific expertise to give elite athletes the

THE LUGE START

The most critical moment of the luge run is the start, when athletes paddle across the ice before plunging down the chute. By shaving a tenth of a second off the start with faster, more efficient moves, sliders can cut three-tenths of a second off their finishing times.

Photos: Above © Duomo, David Madison;
Below © Duomo, Steven E. Sutton.

MEASURING PERFORMANCE

At the U.S. Olympic Training Center in Colorado Springs, sports scientists gauge athletes' physiological responses to the stress of exercise. Swimmers (opposite) are tested for the efficiency of their oxygen intake in a 50,000-gallon flume tank, in which they swim against an artificial current. Cyclists' heart rates and oxygen intake are tested on stationary equipment (below) in the sports phsyiology lab.

Photos: Opposite © Duomo, David Madison; Below © Duomo.

benefit of every advance in training, equipment, technique, and mental preparation—details that can lead to a hair-splitting advantage in Olympic competition.

For American lugers—upstarts in a sport dominated for decades by the Germans, the Austrians, and the Italians—the focus of research is the start, the most pivotal moment in the race. Before they plunge down the chute, sliders sit on their sleds and push off from stationary handles, then accelerate by paddling across the ice with metal-spiked gloves before positioning themselves flat on their backs. A mere tenth of a second saved during the luge start can shave three-tenths of a second off a competitor's finishing time.

In Lake Placid, New York, biomechanists are working to boost the efficiency of every aspect of the sliders' starting motions and techniques. High-speed video cameras record athletes' balance and timing, while strain gauges on the start handles and accelerometers attached to the sled measure horizontal and vertical forces, paddling symmetry, and velocity as sliders hurtle across the ice. Telemetry systems are being designed that will instantaneously transmit the data to a computer, so that lugers will receive immediate feedback on the speed and effectiveness of their starts. The goal of all the scientific data is to fine-tune athletes' individual training programs and techniques—helping them approach, and possibly achieve, ideal levels of performance.

In boating sports such as rowing, canoeing, and kayaking, real-time biomechanical information is already being gathered and relayed to coaches and athletes for instant analysis. With this data, athletes can work to maximize the propulsion power of their oar

Cross-country ski boot

strokes and minimize the drag created by air and water as their boats speed over 500- to 2,000-meter courses.

SKATES

Over the years, ice skates have been uniquely modified for speed, maneuverability, and precision. Speed skates, for example, have no toe pick—a design feature that is essential for athletes executing the sudden stops and jumps required in figure skating routines.

Photos: All footwear, Archives, Olympic Museum Lausanne, J. Donatsch.

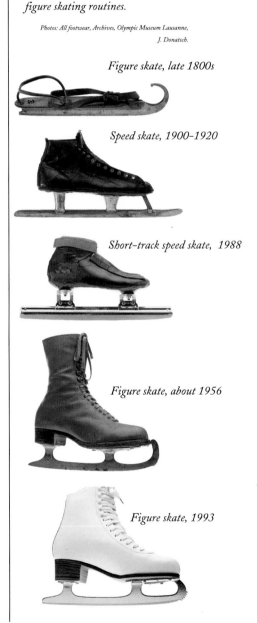

Figure skate, late 1800s

Speed skate, 1900-1920

Short-track speed skate, 1988

Figure skate, about 1956

Figure skate, 1993

3·D GRAPHICS

Biomechanists are harnessing computer technology to analyze the performance of elite athletes. The three-dimensional chart below graphs the progression of movements made by a skater while performing the difficult triple axel jump. The graphic can be rotated on the computer screen to display the maneuver from a variety of angles.

Photo: © U.S. Olympic Training Center.

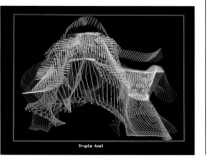

Improving on the early lead of East German scientists, who developed an effective but ungainly 100-pound assemblage of onboard scientific instruments, American engineers have outfitted a two-person rowing shell with a featherweight, pound and a half of sensitive equipment that measures the force and angle of the oars, the speed of the boat, and acceleration. Additional instruments will also gauge boat dynamics, as well as the oarsman's heart rate and body position. Data is transmitted real-time, by radio telemetry, to a computer carried on the coach's boat, so that training instructions can be refined, minute by minute, to maximize performance.

In addition to instrumentation, biomechanists rely on the visual impact of video enhanced by computer software. Sports scientists have long been using high-speed film and video to capture detailed views of athletes in action. Over the last few years, however, biomechanists have paired video cameras with computerized digital technology to create three-dimensional, stick-figure-like graphics of an athlete's every move. During the 1992 Olympics in Barcelona, for example, high-speed video cameras recorded a wide range of competitions, including pole vaulting, javelin throwing, ring gymnastics, and the men's 100-meter freestyle swimming event. The video images were then digitized and studied to understand the motions used by the best-performing athletes.

In figure skating, biomechanists have created three-dimensional graphics of every move that skaters use in the difficult, three-and-a-half revolution, triple axel jump—a maneuver mastered by Canadian champion Brian Orser and American gold medalist Brian Boitano in the 1988 Calgary Winter Games. Sports scientists are also using digitized images to give Olympic weight lifters a vivid, visual description of their positioning and the crucial symmetry of their lifting motions.

The quicker an athlete receives performance feedback, the more useful it is in training. Video digitizing, however, can be a very time-consuming process, so scientists are turning to other forms of computer-enhanced imaging to give athletes and coaches faster input. Within an hour, for example, decathletes can view a still video image of their shot-put throw, overlaid by computer-generated graphics that point out the height, angle, and velocity of their release. In ice dancing, a sport with an important aesthetic component, partners can study similar images, produced minutes after they leave the ice, that visually quantify key elements of their performance, such as their alignment and angle of lean.

Boxing shoe

DIGITIZED IMAGES

Using high-speed video cameras and computerized digital technology, biomechanists are able to create stick-figure-like images of every motion used by top-performing athletes in the long jump, figure skating triple axel, pole vault, javelin throw, and a wide range of other elite competitions. Athletes and their coaches study the images to learn the most effective motions and positioning.

Photos: *Above left © Duomo, Steven E. Sutton;*
Above right © Paul J. Sutton;
Below © U.S. Olympic Training Center.

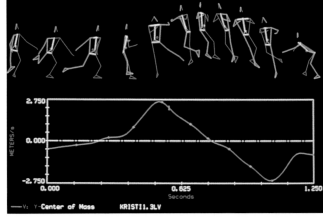

Thanks to a device called the "Leaper Beeper," developed by Florida State University sports scientist John Shea, divers can also get immediate feedback during training sessions. Electronic sensors, connected to a laptop computer, instantly gather information on the height of each dive and the force of the diver's impact on the board. Coded beeps emitted by the system give athletes information about their dives before they even hit the water.

Sports scientists have also exploited laser technology to improve training techniques. Olympic shooters, for example, now practice using a rifle or pistol mounted with a finger-sized laser that projects a light beam onto the target. The beam, recorded on video, tracks shooters' aim and the steadiness of their hold before firing. The system is now also being adapted to help archers perfect their aim.

While new training technology is enabling athletes to coax extra power and control out of their muscles, improvements in equipment are also helping Olympic-caliber competitors achieve faster, higher, and stronger performances than ever thought possible. Over the past forty years, record after record has been shattered, partly as the result of stronger, lighter, and more accurate athletic gear. To be sure, natural factors have also contributed to competitive success. With the tripling of the world's population since 1900, there are probably more talented athletes in the world today than there were a century ago. Better nutrition and medicine in many countries have also enhanced sports performance.

But scientific innovations in equipment design may play the single biggest role in helping athletes accomplish the incredible. The sport of pole vaulting is a good example. In the 1960s, the bamboo pole traditionally used in the event was replaced by a fiberglass version, borrowed from a deep-sea fishing-rod design. After elite athletes switched to the new poles—and, more recently, to poles made of carbon composite materials—they vaulted 30 percent higher than ever before, raising the world record from fifteen feet to more than twenty feet.

Records also fell fast—frighteningly so—after the javelin was redesigned. In the 1950s, an American engineer, Dick Held, constructed a streamlined aluminum javelin for his brother

LASER AIMING

Olympic shooters improve their scores with the help of training lasers mounted on their guns. The laser projects a light beam onto the target. The beam is then captured on video and used to analyze an athlete's steadiness and aim.

Photo: © Duomo, William Sallaz.

Cross-country ski boot

ON-BOARD ANALYSIS

Using sensitive, on-board instrumentation and telemetry equipment, kayakers and other Olympic oarsmen are able to refine their technique with the help of immediate training feedback on their boat's acceleration and speed and the force and angle of their oars.

Photo: © Allsport.

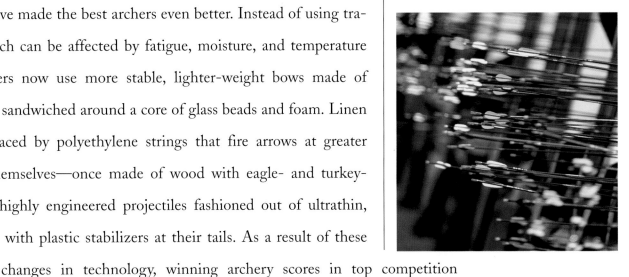

Bud, a college athlete, because traditional wooden javelins often broke and were expensive to replace. With the new, aerodynamic javelin, Bud Held was able to reach astonishing distances, shattering the previous world record by more than twenty feet. By the early 1980s, engineers had refined Held's original design so much that the newest javelins traveled even farther. In fact, they were quite capable of sailing out of the field and into the bleachers, imperiling spectators and unsuspecting athletes. Alarmed, the sport's rules committee decided to restrain scientific progress in the name of safety and, in 1986, banished these aerodynamically advanced models. As a result, the world record in the javelin throw has since plunged by thirty feet.

Hockey skate

A more successful outcome has resulted from improvements in archery equipment. Olympic-caliber archers are amazingly accurate, able to cluster most of their arrows within the top-scoring center circle of the target. But recent innovations in bow and arrow design have made the best archers even better. Instead of using traditional wooden bows, which can be affected by fatigue, moisture, and temperature changes, tournament archers now use more stable, lighter-weight bows made of fiberglass and carbon fibers sandwiched around a core of glass beads and foam. Linen bowstrings have been replaced by polyethylene strings that fire arrows at greater speeds. And the arrows themselves—once made of wood with eagle- and turkey-feather fletches—are now highly engineered projectiles fashioned out of ultrathin, carbon-wrapped aluminum with plastic stabilizers at their tails. As a result of these changes in technology, winning archery scores in top competition rounds have shot up from the 1,100s in the 1960s—out of a perfect score of 1,440—to the mid-1,300s today.

STRAIGHT ARROWS

New ultrathin aluminum arrows stabilized with plastic fletches, fired from polyethylene bowstrings, are more consistent projectiles than the old-fashioned wood-and-feather arrows, which were propelled by bowstrings made of linen.

Photo: © Duomo.

HIGH-TECH BOWS

Archers' scores are benefiting from new lightweight fiberglass bows, which are less sensitive to temperature and moisture than traditional wooden bows. Laser aim-tracking devices, used by Olympic shooters, are being adapted to help archers improve their accuracy.

Photo: © Duomo, Steven E. Sutton.

U.S. Olympic rifle and pistol shooters have benefited from a big improvement in the .22-caliber ammunition that they use. For years, the U.S. team purchased their ammunition from European manufacturers, who were widely recognized as producing the best-quality .22-caliber bullets. U.S. shooters remained at a disadvantage, however, because the top-of-the-line bullets were usually reserved for the European shooting teams. To level the playing field, U.S. Olympic Committee (USOC) sports scientists analyzed the characteristics of the best-performing, straightest-flying bullets. They then teamed up with a U.S. manufacturer to produce new ammunition called UltraMatch, which is made to exacting specifications with highly refined gunpowder. Armed with UltraMatch, U.S. shooters improved their standing and scored medals in Barcelona—Launi Meili's gold in the women's three-position rifle competition, the first for an American woman, and Bob Foth's silver in the men's.

A BETTER BULLET

U.S. sports scientists analyzed the qualities of the world's best .22-caliber bullets, then teamed with a manufacturer to produce super-high-quality UltraMatch ammunition. The new bullets helped U.S. shooters successfully target Olympic medals in Barcelona.

Photo: © Allsport, Powell.

Changes in equipment have also helped speed skaters smash racing records. In February 1962, Canadian skater Paul Enoch astonished spectators at an international racing meet in Hamar, Norway—not just by his performance, which beat the world record by three seconds—but also by his unusual attire. At a time when speed skaters still wore flapping woolen clothing, Enoch sped around the rink dressed in a pair of his wife's skintight nylon stockings. His eyebrow-raising, aerodynamic outfit reduced air drag, propelling him to a record-breaking performance and setting a new standard for speed skating apparel. A year later, the first nylon racing suit was on the market, which evolved into the head-to-toe-sheathing racing skins worn by Olympic speed skaters today. In the near future, racers may be further aided by the new Norwegian "superskate," which has not yet been worn in Olympic competition. The completely redesigned carbon-fiber and steel skate weighs 30 percent less than traditional models and has an aerodynamic covering that encases the boot and blade almost to the ice. Its designers claim that, for every one hundred meters skated, it can increase a racer's speed by a full tenth of a second.

In some instances, it is technique rather than technology that breaks performance barriers. When U.S. Olympic high jumper Dick Fosbury introduced the revolutionary "Fosbury Flop" by hurling himself backward over the bar at the Mexico City Games in 1968, he beat the previous Olympic record by two and a half inches, took home the gold, and created a new, dominant style of jumping. And in the Winter Olympic sport of ski jumping, today's jumps far outstrip those of the 1960s, thanks to the innovative technique pioneered by Swedish jumper Jan Boklov. Instead of keeping his skis close together and parallel in the air—the usual jumping position—Boklov spread his ski tips far apart in an unconventional V-shaped formation. In this position, Boklov was able to sail enormous distances. Eventually, his

Weightlifting shoe

Ski jumping boot

controversial V-jump became a standard among ski jumpers, leading to jump distances that have increased nearly 50 percent in the last twenty-five years.

Mental preparedness can be every bit as important as athletic form. In fact, for Olympic athletes, the greatest challenge may not be the physically demanding schedule of practices and competition, but the intense psychological pressure that comes from competing in the world's most intensely watched arena. To help athletes bear up—and even more importantly, muster the mental control they need to win—sports psychologists coach competitors in breathing control, relaxation, and visualization methods. These techniques can have a powerful impact on performance.

Before the 1984 Games in Los Angeles, for example, gold-medal-winning U.S. gymnast Peter Vidmar and his teammates would, right before they ended practice every day, imagine that they were tied with the People's Republic of China in the last event of the Olympic men's team finals. Vidmar would close his eyes and picture himself standing in front of 10,000 people, fantasizing that millions more were watching him on television and that his performance would determine whether his team won or lost. Worked up by the imaginary intensity of competition, his heart would begin to pound as he began his last routine of the day. "Of course," Vidmar later recalled, "it was just practice, and we never really thought we would have to confront such a situation in the Olympics."

But as it turned out, they did. Going into the last event of the 1984 Games, the U.S. and Chinese scores were very close, and Vidmar was one of two final competitors on the horizontal bar. Just before his turn, he realized how well prepared he was for the enormous pressure of that moment—because he had already lived it dozens of times in his imagination. Vidmar's mental preparation worked. Feeling relaxed and comfortable, he scored a near-perfect 9.95 on his routine, and his team brought home the Olympic gold.

THE FOSBURY FLOP

At the Mexico City Games in 1968, U.S. high jumper Dick Fosbury revolutionized the sport with his backward "Fosbury Flop" over the bar. With his new jumping technique, Fosbury hurled himself two and a half inches past the previous Olympic record.

Photo: Allsport / MSI

Track shoe

Every one of these performance-enhancing factors—scientific training, state-of-the-art equipment, and mental preparation—are being marshalled to help the U.S. cycling team gear up for the 1996 Games in Atlanta. The multidisciplinary effort, known as Project '96, involves an innovative, intense collaboration among the U.S. Cycling Federation, USOC sports scientists, and commercial sponsors including GT Bicycles, Mavic (a manufacturer of bicycle components), EDS computer technology, and Pearl Izumi (a bike-racing-wear designer).

To make sure that U.S. cyclists are at peak conditioning for the Games, scientists are monitoring each athlete's pedaling mechanics, aerodynamic positioning, power output, speed, and heart rate, as well as lactic acid measurements (high levels of lactic acid can signal that muscles are being overworked). With the data in hand, coaches are able to design highly individualized training regimens. Groundbreaking equipment will help reduce wind resistance, which can account for more than 90 percent of the forces that slow down a rider and bicycle at speeds of more than thirty miles per hour.

COMPUTERS SCORE PUNCHES

Science and technology are also having an impact on the Olympic judging process. A new computerized scoring system in boxing instantly tallies results and maintains databases that, for the first time, keep tabs on judges' scoring patterns. The system is designed to detect any potential inconsistencies or bias—a new, technological solution to a problem that's as old as sport.

Photo: © Duomo.

One of the main weapons against aerodynamic drag will be the GT Superbike—a new, wafer-thin, aluminum-frame bicycle that weighs in at less than seventeen pounds. The ultrastreamlined Superbike features a rear disk wheel, an aerodynamically spoked front wheel, a smooth profile with no protruding bolts or cables, and custom-designed aero handlebars. Positioned far over the front wheel, aero-bars force riders into the low-slung tuck position that helped U.S. cyclist Greg LeMond snatch victory in the 1989 Tour de France. In addition, bell-shaped helmets and one-piece, drag-resistant racing suits—tested, with the other equipment, in the General Motors wind tunnel—will make U.S. cyclists as "slippery" as possible in the road races and the velodrome.

WIND TUNNEL TESTS

Wind resistance is a key factor in speed sports such as cycling. To help U.S. cyclists hone their edge for the 1996 Atlanta Games, the aerodynamics of their racing gear have been tested in the General Motors wind tunnel.

Photo: © U.S. Olympic Training Center.

Every millisecond gained could make a difference. In a recent match, the world champion U.S. pursuit cycling team beat the defending Australians by less than three-hundredths of a second—well within the speed advantage made possible by advances in training and aerodynamic equipment. In cycling, as in virtually every speed sport, the focus of technique, training, and science is to bridge the often infinitesimal gap between fast and fastest, between the effort and the gold.

Improvements in equipment engineering have led to big leaps in athletic performance. Back in the 1920s, for example, bike racers couldn't cover forty-five kilometers in one hour on their wood-and-steel, fixed-speed

ADVANCES IN EQUIPMENT

bikes, and it wasn't until 1935 that this barrier fell. Even on modern racing bikes in the 1970s, cyclists couldn't break fifty kilometers in an hour. Then, riding bikes with aerodynamic disk wheels, Italy's Francesco Moser bolted more than fifty-one kilometers in an hour in 1984 and Swiss cyclist Tony Rominger topped fifty-five kilometers in 1994. Changing racket technology is also putting new spins on the sport of tennis. Until the late 1960s, all rackets were made of wood. Today, they are constructed of kevlar, graphite, and other lightweight materials. And the new wide-body rackets, stiffer and with heads almost twice as wide as traditional models, put much more speed and power in the ball. Opposite: Bobsled technology, too, has come a long way since the sport debuted in Switzerland in the late 1880s. Since the 1980s, mathematical simulations, wind-tunnel testing, computer modeling, and aerodynamic designs have helped boost Olympic bobsled speeds to new levels.

Photos: Archives, Olympic Museum Lausanne, J. Donatsch;
1996 bicycle © GT Bicycles.

1896

1937

1984

1996

1992

 1890

 1910

 1930

 1976   1992

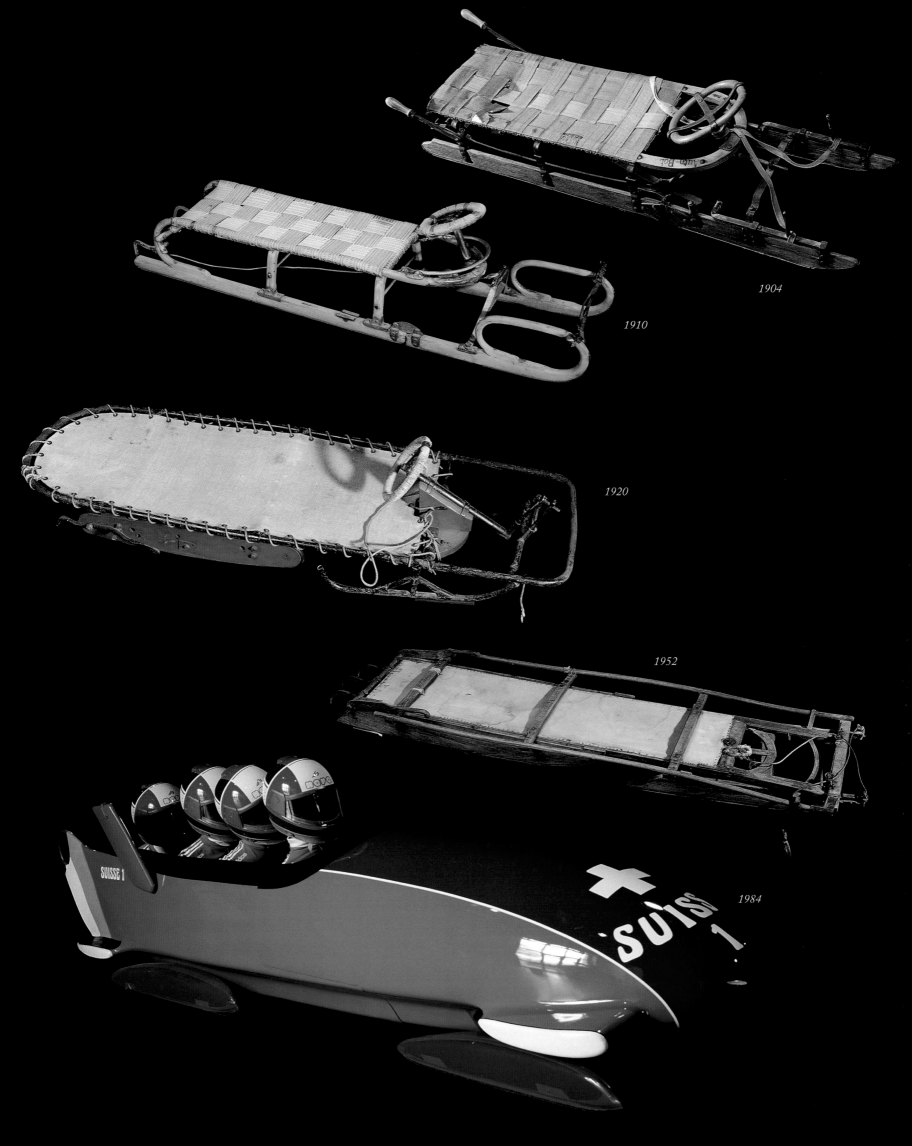

1904

1910

1920

1952

1984

FASTER, HIGHER, STRONGER

Records fall, and the greatest athletic achievements are eventually eclipsed. But, for an Olympic champion, the moment of victory is etched in the world's memory. The virtuosity and courage that drives Olympic winners to the gold earns them a place in our modern pantheon of heroes. In a contest of giants, they are the best of the best.

THE OLYMPIC CHAMPIONS

The listing of Olympic champions that follows is limited to gold-medal winners in both Summer and Winter events. Their winning scores are listed in times, distances, or points, and nationalities are indicated by country codes that have been adopted by the International Olympic Committee.

KEY

AFG Afghanistan		ISR Israel	PHI Philippines	TUN Tunisia
ALG Algeria	Armenia, Azerbaijan, Belarus,	ITA Italy	POL Poland	TUR Turkey
ARG Argentina	Georgia, Kyrghyzstan,	IVC Ivory Coast	POR Portugal	UAR United Arab Republic (Egypt
AUS Australia	Kazakhstan, Moldova, Russia,	JAM Jamaica	PRK North Korea (People's	and Syria)
AUT Austria	Tadjikistan, Turkmenistan,	JPN Japan	Republic of Korea)	UGA Uganda
BAH Bahamas	Ukraine, and Uzbekistan in	KAZ Kazakhstan	PUR Puerto Rico	UKR Ukraine (1994)
BEL Belgium	1992)	KEN Kenya	ROM Romania	URU Uruguay
BER Bermuda	FIN Finland	KOR South Korea	RUS Russia (1908-1912, and 1994)	UZB Uzbekistan
BOH Bohemia	FRA France	KUW Kuwait	SAA Saar	USA United States of America
BRA Brazil	GBR Great Britain and Northern	LAT Latvia	SAF South Africa	VEN Venezuela
BUL Bulgaria	Ireland	LEB Lebanon	SEN Senegal	VIR U.S. Virgin Islands
BWI British West Indies (Jamaica	GDR East Germany (German	LIE Liechtenstein	SIN Singapore	YUG Yugoslavia
and Trinidad)	Democratic Republic, 1956-	LIT Lithuania	SLE Sierra Leone	ZAM Zambia
CAM Cameroon	1988)	LUX Luxembourg	SMR San Marino	ZIM Zimbabwe
CAN Canada	GER Germany (1896-1936), West	MAD Madagascar	SOV Soviet Union	
CHI Chile	Germany (Federal Republic	MAL Malaysia	SPA Spain	
CHN China	of Germany, 1952-1988)	MEX Mexico	SRL Sri Lanka (Ceylon)	TERMS:
COL Colombia	GHA Ghana	MLW Malawi	SUD Sudan	* variations in types of
CON Congo	GRE Greece	MON Mongolia	SUR Surinam	matches or distances
CRC Costa Rica	GUA Guatemala	MOR Morocco	SWE Sweden	+ one-hand lift
CUB Cuba	GUY Guyana	MYA Myanmar (Burma)	SWI Switzerland	++ two-hand lift
CZE Czechoslovakia	HAI Haiti	NGR Nigeria	SYR Syria	▲ events held during Summer
DEN Denmark	HOL Holland (Netherlands)	NIG Niger	TAI Taiwan	Olympic Games, prior to
DJI Djibouti	HUN Hungary	NLA Netherland Antilles	TAN Tanzania	commencement of official
DOM Dominican Republic	ICE Iceland	NOR Norway	TCH Czech and Slovak	Winter Olympics in 1924
EGY Egypt	INA Indonesia	NZE New Zealand	Federative Republic	
EST Estonia	IND India	OMA Oman	THA Thailand	
ETH Ethiopia	INT International Team	PAK Pakistan	TOG Togo	
EUN Unified Team (represented	IRL Ireland (Eire)	PAN Panama	TON Tonga	
the former Soviet republics of	IRN Iran	PER Peru	TRI Trinidad and Tobago	
	IRQ Iraq			

TERMS:
*	variations in types of matches or distances	EOR	Equaled Olympic Record
+	one-hand lift	EWR	Equaled World Record
++	two-hand lift	ICt	Indoor court
▲	events held during Summer Olympic Games, prior to commencement of official Winter Olympics in 1924	OR	Olympic Record
		pts.	points
		T	total
		w	wind-aided
		WB	World Best
		WR	World Record

RECORD RESOURCE:
The Complete Book of the Olympics (David Wallechinsky, 1992 Edition.)
Archery, Badminton, Baseball, Basketball, Canoeing, Cycling, Equestrian, Fencing, Field Hockey, Football (Soccer), Gymnastics, Handball, Judo, Modern Pentathlon, Rowing, Shooting, Swimming and Diving, Table Tennis, Tennis, Volleyball, Weightlifting, Wrestling, Yachting. All 1924–1988 Winter Olympic Champions and Records: Alpine Skiing, Bobsledding, Biathlon, Cross-Country Skiing- Men's and Women's, Figure Skating, Luge, Ski Jumping, Speed Skating, Short Track Speed Skating

The World Almanac and Book of Facts 1994:
Boxing, Track and Field - Men's and Women's, and all 1992 and 1994 Winter Olympic Records

The U.S. Olympic Committee:
All 1992 Summer Olympic Records
Note: Some country codes were changed in 1992 and are not reflected in this listing.

Discontinued events have not been inluded in this listing.

CHAMPIONS OF THE SUMMER GAMES

SUMMER GAMES SITES

1896	Athens, Greece
1900	Paris, France
1904	St. Louis, USA
1906	Athens, Greece*
1908	London, Great Britain
1912	Stockholm, Sweden
1920	Antwerp, Belgium
1924	Paris, France
1928	Amsterdam, Holland
1932	Los Angeles, USA
1936	Berlin, Germany
1948	London, Great Britain
1952	Helsinki, Finland
1956	Melbourne, Australia
1960	Rome, Italy
1964	Tokyo, Japan
1968	Mexico City, Mexico
1972	Munich, Germany
1976	Montreal, Canada
1980	Moscow, USSR
1984	Los Angeles, USA
1988	Seoul, Korea
1992	Barcelona, Spain
1996	Atlanta, USA
2000	Sydney, Australia

*Games not recognized by International Olympic Committee.

ARCHERY

MEN'S INDIVIDUAL
1896-1968 not held
1972 John Williams, USA   WR
1976 Darrell Pace, USA   WR
1980 Tomi Poikolainen, FIN
1984 Darrell Pace, USA   OR
1988 Jay Barrs, USA
1992 Sebastian Flute, FRA
1996

MEN'S TEAM
1896-1984 not held
1988 KOR
1992 SPA
1996

WOMEN'S INDIVIDUAL
1896-1968 not held
1972 Doreen Wilber, USA   WR
1976 Luann Ryon, USA   WR
1980 Keto Lossaberidze, SOV

1984 Seo Hyang-soon, KOR   OR
1988 Kim Soo-nyung, KOR
1992 Cho Youn Jeong, KOR
1996

WOMEN'S TEAM
1896-1984 not held
1988 KOR
1992 KOR
1996

BADMINTON

MEN'S SINGLES
1896-1988 not held
1992 Alan Budi Kushuma, INA
1996

MEN'S DOUBLES
1896-1988 not held
1992 Kim Moon-Soo, Park Joo-Bong, KOR
1996

WOMEN'S SINGLES
1896-1988 not held
1992 Susy Susanti, INA
1996

WOMEN'S DOUBLES
1896-1988 not held
1992 Hwang Hye Young, Chung So-Young, KOR
1996

BASEBALL · BASKETBALL

BASEBALL
Demonstration sport eight times previously.
1992 CUB
1996

MEN'S BASKETBALL
1896-1932 not held
1936 USA
1948 USA
1952 USA
1956 USA
1960 USA
1964 USA
1968 USA

1972 SOV
1976 USA
1980 YUG
1984 USA
1988 SOV
1992 USA
1996

WOMEN'S BASKETBALL
1896-1972 not held
1976 SOV
1980 SOV
1984 USA
1988 USA
1992 EUN
1996

BOXING

LIGHT FLYWEIGHT
1896-1964 not held
1968 Francisco Rodriguez, VEN
1972 György Gedó, HUN
1976 Jorge Hernandez, CUB
1980 Shamil Sabyrov, SOV
1984 Paul Gonzalez, USA
1988 Ivailo Hristov, BUL
1992 Rogelio Marcelo, CUB
1996

FLYWEIGHT
1896-1900 not held
1904 George Finnegan, USA
1908-1912 not held
1920 William De Genaro, USA
1924 Fidel LaBarba, USA
1928 Antal Kocsis, HUN
1932 István Énekes, HUN
1936 Willi Kaiser, GER
1948 Pascual Perez, ARG
1952 Nathan Brooks, USA
1956 Terence Spinks, GBR
1960 Gyula Török, HUN
1964 Fernando Atzori, ITA
1968 Ricardo Delgado, MEX
1972 Georgi Kostadinov, BUL
1976 Leo Randolph, USA
1980 Peter Lessov, BUL
1984 Steve McCrory, USA
1988 Kim Kwang-sun, KOR
1992 Su Choi Choi, PRK
1996

BANTAMWEIGHT
1896-1900 not held
1904 Oliver Kirk, USA
1908 A. Henry Thomas, GBR
1912 not held
1920 Clarence Walker, SAF
1924 William Smith, SAF
1928 Vittorio Tamagnini, ITA
1932 Horace Gwynne, CAN
1936 Ulderico Sergo, ITA
1948 Tibor Csik, HUN
1952 Pentti Hämäläinen, FIN
1956 Wolfgang Behrendt, GDR
1960 Oleg Grigoryev, SOV
1964 Takao Sakurai, JPN

1968 Valery Sokolov, SOV
1972 Orlando Martinez, CUB
1976 Gu Yong-Jo, PRK
1980 Juan Hernandez, CUB
1984 Maurizio Stecca, ITA
1988 Kennedy McKinney, USA
1992 Joel Casamayor, CUB
1996

FEATHERWEIGHT
1896-1900 not held
1904 Oliver Kirk, USA
1908 Richard Gunn, GBR
1912 not held
1920 Paul Fritsch, FRA
1924 John Fields, USA
1928 Lambertus van
     Klaveren, HOL
1932 Carmelo Robledo, ARG
1936 Oscar Casanovas, ARG
1948 Ernesto Formenti, ITA
1952 Jan Zachara, CZE
1956 Vladimir Safronov, SOV
1960 Francesco Musso, ITA
1964 Stanislav Stepashkin, SOV
1968 Antonio Roldan, MEX
1972 Boris Kousnetsov, SOV
1976 Angel Herrera, CUB
1980 Rudi Fink, GDR
1984 Meldrick Taylor, USA
1988 Giovanni Parisi, ITA
1992 Andreas Tews, GER
1996

LIGHTWEIGHT
1896-1900 not held
1904 Harry Spanger, USA
1908 Frederick Grace, GBR
1912 not held
1920 Samuel Mosberg, USA
1924 Hans Nielsen, DEN
1928 Carlo Orlandi, ITA
1932 Lawrence Stevens, SAF
1936 Imre Harangi, HUN
1948 Gerald Dreyer, SAF
1952 Aureliano Bolognesi, ITA
1956 Richard McTaggart, GBR
1960 Kazimierz Paździor, POL
1964 Józef Grudzień, POL

1968 Ronald Harris, USA
1972 Jan Szczepański, POL
1976 Howard Davis, USA
1980 Angel Herrera, CUB
1984 Pernell Whitaker, USA
1988 Andreas Zuelow, GDR
1992 Oscar De La Hoya, USA
1996

LIGHT WELTERWEIGHT
1896-1948 not held
1952 Charles Adkins, USA
1956 Vladimir Yengibaryan, SOV
1960 Bohumil Nemeček, CZE
1964 Jerzy Kulej, POL
1968 Jerzy Kulej, POL
1972 Ray Seales, USA
1976 Ray Leonard, USA
1980 Patrizio Oliva, ITA
1984 Jerry Page, USA
1988 Vyacheslav Yanovsky, SOV
1992 Hector Vinent, CUB
1996

WELTERWEIGHT
1896-1900 not held
1904 Albert Young, USA
1908-1912 not held
1920 Albert Schneider, CAN
1924 Jean Delarge, BEL
1928 Edward Morgan, NZE
1932 Edward Flynn, USA
1936 Sten Suvio, FIN
1948 Julius Torma, CZE
1952 Zygmunt Chychla, POL
1956 Nicolae Linca, ROM
1960 Giovanni Benvenuti, ITA
1964 Marian Kasprzyk, POL
1968 Manfred Wolke, GDR
1972 Emilio Correa, CUB
1976 Jochen Bachfeld, GDR
1980 Andrés Aldama, CUB
1984 Mark Breland, USA
1988 Robert Wangila, KEN
1992 Michael Carruth, IRL
1996

LIGHT MIDDLEWEIGHT
1896-1948 not held
1952 László Papp, HUN
1956 László Papp, HUN
1960 Wilbert McClure, USA
1964 Boris Lagutin, SOV
1968 Boris Lagutin, SOV
1972 Dieter Kottysch, GER
1976 Jerzy Rybicki, POL
1980 Armando Martinez, CUB
1984 Frank Tate, USA
1988 Park Si-hun, KOR
1992 Juan Lemus, CUB
1996

MIDDLEWEIGHT
1896-1900 not held
1904 Charles Mayer, USA
1908 John Douglas, GBR
1912 not held
1920 Harry Mallin, GBR
1924 Harry Mallin, GBR
1928 Piero Toscani, ITA
1932 Carmen Barth, USA
1936 Jean Despeaux, FRA
1948 László Papp, HUN
1952 Floyd Patterson, USA
1956 Gennady Schatkov, SOV
1960 Edward Crook, USA
1964 Valery Popenchenko, SOV
1968 Christopher Finnegan, GBR
1972 Vyacheslav Lemechev, SOV
1976 Michael Spinks, USA
1980 José Gomez, CUB
1984 Shin Joon-sup, KOR
1988 Henry Maske, GDR
1992 Ariel Hernandez, CUB
1996

LIGHT HEAVYWEIGHT
1896-1912 not held
1920 Edward Eagan, USA
1924 Harry Mitchell, GBR
1928 Victor Avendaño, ARG
1932 David Carstens, SAF
1936 Roger Michelot, FRA
1948 George Hunter, SAF

1952 Norvel Lee, USA
1956 James Boyd, USA
1960 Cassius Clay, USA
1964 Cosimo Pinto, ITA
1968 Dan Poznjak, SOV
1972 Mate Parlov, YUG
1976 Leon Spinks, USA
1980 Slobodan Kacar, YUG
1984 Anton Josipović, YUG
1988 Andrew Maynard, USA
1992 Torsten May, GER
1996

HEAVYWEIGHT
1896-1980 not held
1984 Henry Tillman, USA
1988 Ray Mercer, USA
1992 Felix Savon, CUB
1996

SUPER HEAVYWEIGHT (UNLIMITED)
(known as heavyweight 1904-1980)
1904 Samuel Berger, USA
1908 Albert Oldham, GBR
1912 not held
1920 Ronald Rawson, GBR
1924 Otto von Porat, NOR
1928 Arturo Rodriguez Jurado, ARG
1932 Santiago Lovell, ARG
1936 Herbert Runge, GER
1948 Rafael Inglesias, ARG
1952 H. Edward Sanders, USA
1956 T. Peter Rademacher, USA
1960 Franco De Piccoli, ITA
1964 Joe Frazier, USA
1968 George Foreman, USA
1972 Teofilo Stevenson, CUB
1976 Teofilo Stevenson, CUB
1980 Teofilo Stevenson, CUB
1984 Tyrell Biggs, USA
1988 Lennox Lewis, CAN
1992 Roberto Balado, CUB
1996

CANOEING

MEN'S KAYAK SINGLES 500 METERS
1896–1972 not held

1976	V. Diba, ROM	1:46.41
1980	V. Parfenovich, SOV	1:43.43
1984	I. Ferguson, NZE	1:47.84
1988	Z. Gyulay, HUN	1:44.82
1992	M. Yrjoe Kolehmainen, FIN	1:40.34
1996		

MEN'S KAYAK SINGLES 1000 METERS
1896–1932 not held

1936	G. Hradetzky, AUT	4:22.90
1948	G. Fredriksson, SWE	4:33.20
1952	G. Fredriksson, SWE	4:07.90
1956	G Fredriksson, SWE	4:12.80
1960	E. Hansen, DEN	3:53.00
1964	R. Peterson, SWE	3:57.13
1968	M. Hesz, HUN	4:02.63
1972	A. Shaparenko, SOV	3:48.06
1976	R. Helm, GDR	3:48.20
1980	R. Helm, GDR	3:48.77
1984	A. Thompson, NZE	3:45.73
1988	G. Barton, USA	3:55.27
1992	C. Robinson, AUS	3:37.26
1996		

MEN'S KAYAK PAIRS 500 METERS
1896–1972 not held

1976	J. Mattern, B. Olbricht, GDR	1:35.87
1980	V. Parfenovich, S. Chukhrai, SOV	1:32.38
1984	I. Ferguson, P. MacDonald, NZE	1:34.21
1988	I. Ferguson, P. MacDonald, NZE	1:33.98
1992	K. Bluhm, T. Gutsche, GER	1:29.84
1996		

MEN'S KAYAK PAIRS 1000 METERS
1896–1932 not held

1936	A. Kainz, A. Dorfner, AUT	4:03.80
1948	H. Berglund, K. Klingström, SWE	4:07.30
1952	K. Wires, Y. Hietanen, FIN	3:51.10
1956	M. Scheuer, M. Miltenberger, GER	3:49.60
1960	G. Fredriksson, S. Sjödelius, SWE	3:34.73
1964	S. Sjödelius, N. Utterberg, SWE	3:38.54
1968	A. Shaparenko, V. Morozov, SOV	3:37.54
1972	N. Gorbachev, V. Kratassyuk, SOV	3:31.23

1976	S. Nagorny, V. Romanovsky, SOV	3:29.01
1980	V. Parfenovich, S. Chukhrai, SOV	3:26.72
1984	H. Fisher, A. Morris, CAN	3:24.22
1988	G. Barton, N. Bellingham, USA	3:32.42
1992	K. Bluhm, T. Gutsche, GER	3:16.10
1996		

MEN'S KAYAK FOURS 1000 METERS
1896–1960 not held

1964	SOV	3:14.67
1968	NOR	3:14.38
1972	SOV	3:14.02
1976	SOV	3:08.69
1980	GDR	3:13.76
1984	NZE	3:02.28
1988	HUN	3:00.20
1992	GER	2:54.18
1996		

MEN'S CANADIAN SINGLES 500 METERS
1896–1972 not held

1976	A. Rogov, SOV	1:59.23
1980	S. Postrekhin, SOV	1:53.37
1984	L. Cain, CAN	1:57.01
1988	O. Heukrodt, GDR	1:56.42
1992	N. Boukhalov, BUL	1:51.15
1996		

MEN'S CANADIAN SINGLES 1000 METERS
1896–1932 not held

1936	F. Amyot, CAN	5:32.10
1948	J. Holeček, CZE	5:42.00
1952	J. Holeček, CZE	4:56.30
1956	L. Rotman, ROM	5:05.30
1960	J. Parti, HUN	4:33.93
1964	J. Eschert, GDR	4:35.14
1968	T. Tatai, HUN	4:36.14
1972	I. Patzaichin, ROM	4:08.94
1976	M. Ljubek, YUG	4:09.51
1980	L. Lyubenov, BUL	4:12.38
1984	U. Eiche, GER	4:06.32
1988	I. Klementyev, SOV	4:12.78
1992	N. Boukhalov, BUL	4:05.92
1996		

MEN'S CANADIAN PAIRS 500 METERS
1896–1972 not held

1976	S. Petrenko, A. Vinogradov, SOV	1:45.81
1980	L. Foltán, I. Vaskuti, HUN	1:43.39
1984	M. Ljubek, M. Nišović, YUG	1:43.67
1988	V. Reneisky, N. Zhuravsky, SOV	1:41.77
1992	A. Masseikov, D. Dovgalenok, EUN	1:41.54
1996		

MEN'S CANADIAN PAIRS 1000 METERS
1896–1932 not held

1936	V. Syrovátka, J. Brzák-Felix, CZE	4:50.10
1948	J. Brzák-Felix, B. Kudrna, CZE	5:07.10
1952	B. Rasch, F. Haunstoft, DEN	4:38.30
1956	A. Dumitru, S. Ismailciuc, ROM	4:47.40
1960	L. Geischtor, S. Makarenko, SOV	4:17.94
1964	A. Khimich, S. Oschepkov, SOV	4:04.64
1968	I. Patzaichin, S. Covaliov, ROM	4:07.18
1972	V. Česiunas, Y. Lobanov, SOV	3:52.60
1976	S. Petrenko, A. Vinogradov, SOV	3:52.76
1980	I. Patzaichin, T. Siminov, ROM	3:47.65
1984	I. Patzaichin, T. Siminov, ROM	3:40.60
1988	V. Reneisky, N. Zhuravsky, SOV	3:48.36
1992	U. Papke, I. Spelly, GER	3:37.42
1996		

MEN'S KAYAK SLALOM SINGLES
1896–1968 not held

1972	S. Horn, GDR	

1976–1988 not held

1992	P. Ferrazzi, ITA	
1996		

MEN'S CANADIAN SLALOM SINGLES
1896–1968 not held

1972	R. Eiben, GDR	

1976–1988 not held

1992	L. Pollert, TCH	
1996		

MEN'S DOUBLE CANOE SLALOM
1896–1988 not held

1992	J. Jacobi, S. Strausbaugh, USA	
1996		

WOMEN'S KAYAK SINGLES 500 METERS
1896–1936 not held

1948	K. Hoff, DEN	2:31.90
1952	S. Saimo, FIN	2:18.40
1956	Y. Dementyeva, SOV	2:18.90
1960	A. Seredina, SOV	2:08.08
1964	L. Khvedosyuk, SOV	2:12.87
1968	L. Pinayeva (Khvedosyuk), SOV	2:11.09
1972	Y. Ryabchinskaya, SOV	2:03.17
1976	C. Zirzow, GDR	2:01.05
1980	B. Fischer, GDR	1:57.96
1984	A. Andersson, SWE	1:58.72
1988	V. Gesheva, BUL	1:55.19
1992	B. Schmidt, GER	1:51.60
1996		

WOMEN'S KAYAK PAIRS 500 METERS
1896–1956 not held

1960	M. Chubina, A. Seredina, SOV	1:54.76
1964	R. Esser, A. Zimmermann, GER	1:56.95
1968	R. Esser, A. Zimmermann, GER	1:56.44
1972	L. Pinayeva, E. Kuryshko, SOV	1:53.50
1976	N. Gopova, G. Kreft, SOV	1:51.15
1980	C. Genäuss, M. Bischof, GDR	1:43.88
1984	A. Andersson, A. Olsson, SWE	1:45.25
1988	B. Schmidt (Fischer), A. Nothnagel, GDR	1:43.46
1992	R. Portwich, A. vonSeck, GER	1:40.29
1996		

WOMEN'S KAYAK FOURS 500 METERS
1896–1980 not held

1984	ROM	1:38.34
1988	GDR	1:40.78
1992	HUN	1:38.32
1996		

WOMEN'S KAYAK SLALOM SINGLES
1896–1968 not held

1972	Angelika Bahmann, GDR	

1976–1988 not held

1992	Elisabeth Micheler, GER	
1996		

CYCLING

MEN'S 1000-METER SPRINT (SCRATCH)

1896	Paul Masson, FRA	
1900	Georges Taillandier, FRA	
1904 not held		
1908	Final declared void; time limit exceeded	
1912 not held		
1920	Maurice Peeters, HOL	
1924	Lucien Michard, FRA	
1928	Roger Beaufrand, FRA	
1932	Jacobus van Egmond, HOL	
1936	Toni Merkens, GER	
1948	Mario Ghella, ITA	
1952	Enzo Sacchi, ITA	
1956	Michel Rousseau, FRA	
1960	Sante Gaiardoni, ITA	
1964	Giovanni Pettenella, ITA	
1968	Daniel Morelon, FRA	
1972	Daniel Morelon, FRA	
1976	Anton Tkáč, CZE	
1980	Lutz Hesslich, GDR	
1984	Mark Gorski, USA	
1988	Lutz Hesslich, GDR	
1992	Jans Fiedler, GER	
1996		

MEN'S 1000-METER TIME TRIAL
1896–1924 not held

1928	Willy Flack Hansen, DEN	1:14.40
1932	Edgar Gray, AUS	1:13.00 OR
1936	Arie van Vliet, HOL	1:12.00 OR
1948	Jacques Dupont, FRA	1:13.50

1952	Russell Mockridge, AUS	1:11.100 OR
1956	Leandro Faggin, ITA	1:09.800 OR
1960	Sante Gaiardoni, ITA	1:07.270 WR
1964	Patrick Sercu, BEL	1:09.590
1968	Pierre Trentin, FRA	1:03.910 WR
1972	Niels Fredborg, DEN	1:06.440
1976	Klaus-Jürgen Grünke, GDR	1:05.927
1980	Lothar Thoms, GDR	1:02.955 WR
1984	Fredy Schmidtke, GER	1:06.100
1988	Aleksandr Kirichenko, SOV	1:04.499
1992	Jose Moreno, SPA	1:03.342
1996		

MEN'S 4000-METER INDIVIDUAL PURSUIT
1896–1960 not held

1964	Jiří Daler, CZE	5:04.750
1968	Daniel Rebillard, FRA	4:41.710
1972	Knut Knudsen, NOR	4:45.740
1976	Gregor Braun, GER	4:47.610
1980	Robert Dill-Bundi, SWI	4:35.660
1984	Steve Hegg, USA	4:39.350
1988	Gintautas Umaras, SOV	4:32.000
1992	Chris Boardman, GBR	3:21.649
1996		

MEN'S 4000-METER TEAM PURSUIT
1896–1904 not held

1908	GER	2:18.600
1912 not held		
1920	ITA	5:20.000
1924	ITA	5:15.000

1928	ITA	5:01.800
1932	ITA	4:53.000
1936	FRA	4:45.000
1948	FRA	4:57.800
1952	ITA	4:46.100
1956	ITA	4:37.400
1960	ITA	4:30.900
1964	GER	4:35.670
1968	DEN	4:22.440
1972	GER	4:22.140
1976	GER	4:21.060
1980	SOV	4:15.700
1984	AUS	4:25.990
1988	SOV	4:13.310
1992	GER	4:08.791
1996		

MEN'S 50-KILOMETER POINTS RACE
1896–1980 not held

1984	Roger Ilegems, BEL	
1988	Dan Frost, DEN	
1992	Giovanni Lombardi, ITA	
1996		

MEN'S INDIVIDUAL ROAD RACE

1896	(87 KM) A. Konstantinidis, GDR	3:21:10.00	
1900–1908 not held			
1912	(320 KM) R. Lewis, SAF	10:42:39.00	
1920	(175 KM) H. Stenqvist, SWE	4:40:01.80	
1924	(188 KM) A. Blanchonnet, FRA	6:20:48.00	
1928	(168 KM) H. Hansen, DEN	4:47:18.00	

1932	(100 KM) A. Pavesi, ITA	2:28:05.60
1936	(100 KM) R. Charpentier, FRA	2:33:05.00
1948	(194.63 KM) J. Beyaert, FRA	5:18:12.60
1952	(190.4 KM) A. Noyelle, BEL	5:06:03.40
1956	(187.73 KM) E. Baldini, ITA	5:21:17.00
1960	(175.38 KM) V. Kapitonov, SOV	4:20:37.00
1964	(194.83 KM) M. Zanin, ITA	4:39:51.63
1968	(196.2 KM) P. Vianelli, ITA	4:41:25.24
1972	(182.4 KM) H. Kuiper, HOL	4:14:37.00
1976	(175 KM) B. Johansson, SWE	4:46:52.00
1980	(189 KM) S. Sukhoruchenkov, SOV	4:48:28.90
1984	(190.2 KM) A. Grewal, USA	4:59:57.00
1988	(196.8 KM) O. Ludwig, GDR	4:32:22.00
1992	(194 KM) F. Casartelli, ITA	4:35:21.00
1996		

MEN'S TEAM TIME TRIAL
1896–1908 not held

1912	(320 KM) SWE	44:35:33.60
1920	(175 KM) FRA	19:16:43.20
1924	(188 KM) FRA	19:30:14.00
1928	(168 KM) DEN	15:09:14.00
1932	(100 KM) ITA	7:27:15.20
1936	(100 KM) FRA	7:39:16.20
1948	(194.63 KM) BEL	15:58:17.40
1952	(190.4 KM) BEL	15:20:46.60
1956	(187.73 KM) FRA	22 pts.
1960	(100 KM) ITA	2:14:33.53
1964	(109.89 KM) HOL	2:26:31.19
1968	(104 KM) HOL	2:07:49.06
1972	(100 KM) SOV	2:11:17.80

CYCLING

1976 (100 KM) SOV	2:08:53.00
1980 (101 KM) SOV	2:01:21.70
1984 (100 KM) ITA	1:58:28.00
1988 (100 KM) GDR	1:57:47.70
1992 (100 KM) GER	2:01:39.00
1996	

WOMEN'S 1000-METER SPRINT (SCRATCH)
1896–1984 not held
1988　E. Salumäe, SOV
1992　E. Salumäe, EST
1996

WOMEN'S 3000-METER INDIVIDUAL PURSUIT
1896–1988 not held
1992　Petra Rossner, GER
1996

WOMEN'S INDIVIDUAL ROAD RACE
1896–1980 not held
1984　(79.2 KM) C. Carpenter-Phinney, USA
　　　　　　　　　　　　　　2:11:14
1988　(82 KM) M. Knol, HOL　2:00:52
1992　Kathryn Watt, AUS　　2:04:42
1996

EQUESTRIAN

THREE-DAY EVENT, INDIVIDUAL
1896–1908 not held
1912　A. Nordlander, SWE
1920　H. Mörner, SWE
1924　A. van der Voort van Zijp, HOL
1928　C. Pahud de Mortanges, HOL
1932　C. Pahud de Mortanges, HOL
1936　L. Stubbendorff, GER
1948　B. Chevallier, FRA
1952　H. von Blixen-Finecke, Jr. SWE
1956　P. Kastenman, SWE
1960　L. Morgan, AUS
1964　M. Checcoli, ITA
1968　J. Guyon, FRA
1972　R. Meade, GBR
1976　E. Coffin, USA
1980　E. Roman, ITA
1984　M. Todd, NZE
1988　M. Todd, NZE
1992　M. Ryan, AUS
1996

THREE-DAY EVENT, TEAM
1896–1908 not held
1912　SWE
1920　SWE
1924　HOL
1928　HOL
1932　USA
1936　GER
1948　USA
1952　SWE
1956　GER
1960　AUS
1964　ITA
1968　GBR
1972　GBR
1976　USA
1980　SOV
1984　USA
1988　GER
1992　AUS
1996

JUMPING (PRIX DES NATIONS), INDIVIDUAL
1896 not held
1900　A. Haegeman, BEL
1904–1908 not held
1912　J. Cariou, FRA
1920　T. Lequio, ITA
1924　A. Gemuseus, SWI
1928　F. Ventura, CZE
1932　T. Nishi, JPN
1936　K. Hasse, GER
1948　H. Cortés, MEX
1952　P. Jonquères d'Oriola, FRA
1956　H. Winkler, GER
1960　R. D'Inzeo, ITA
1964　P. Jonquères d'Oriola, FRA
1968　W. Steinkraus, USA
1972　G. Mancinelli, ITA
1976　A. Schockemöhle, GER
1980　J. Kowalczyk, POL
1984　J. Fargis, USA
1988　P. Durand, FRA
1992　L. Beerbaum, GER
1996

JUMPING (PRIX DES NATIONS), TEAM
1896–1908 not held
1912　SWE
1920　SWE
1924　SWE
1928　SPA
1932　*No nation completed the course with three riders*
1936　GER
1948　MEX
1952　GBR
1956　GER
1960　GER
1964　GER
1968　CAN
1972　GER
1976　FRA
1980　SOV
1984　USA
1988　GER
1992　HOL
1996

DRESSAGE, INDIVIDUAL
1896–1908 not held
1912　C. Bonde, SWE
1920　J. Lundbald, SWE
1924　E. Linder, SWE
1928　C. von Langen-Parow, GER
1932　X. Lesage, FRA
1936　H. Pollay, GER
1948　H. Moser, SWI
1952　H. Saint Cyr, SWE
1956　H. Saint Cyr, SWE
1960　S. Filatov, SOV
1964　H. Chammartin, SWI
1968　I. Kizimov, SOV
1972　L. Linsenhoff, GER
1976　C. Stückelberger, SWI
1980　E. Theurer, AUT
1984　R. Klimke, GER
1988　N. Uphoff, GER
1992　N. Uphoff, GER
1996

DRESSAGE, TEAM
1896–1924 not held
1928　GER
1932　FRA
1936　GER
1948　SWE
1952　SWE
1956　SWE
1960 not held
1964　GER
1968　GER
1972　SOV
1976　GER
1980　SOV
1984　GER
1988　GER
1992　GER
1996

FENCING

MEN'S FOIL, INDIVIDUAL
1896　E. Gravelotte, FRA
1900　E. Coste, FRA
1904　R. Fonst, CUB
1908 not held
1912　N. Nadi, ITA
1920　N. Nadi, ITA
1924　R. Ducret, FRA
1928　L. Gaudin, FRA
1932　G. Marzi, ITA
1936　G. Gaudini, ITA
1948　J. Buhan, FRA
1952　C. d'Oriola, FRA
1956　C. d'Oriola, FRA
1960　V. Zhdanovich, SOV
1964　E. Franke, POL
1968　L. Drimbă, ROM
1972　W. Woyda, POL
1976　F. Dal Zotto, ITA
1980　V. Smirnov, SOV
1984　M. Numa, ITA
1988　S. Cerioni, ITA
1992　P. Omnes, FRA
1996

MEN'S FOIL, TEAM
1896–1900 not held
1904　CUB/USA
1908–1912 not held
1920　ITA
1924　FRA
1928　ITA
1932　FRA
1936　ITA
1948　FRA
1952　FRA
1956　ITA
1960　SOV
1964　SOV
1968　FRA
1972　POL
1976　GER
1980　FRA
1984　ITA
1988　SOV
1992　GER
1996

MEN'S ÉPÉE, INDIVIDUAL
1896 not held
1900　R. Fonst, CUB
1904　R. Fonst, CUB
1908　G. Alibert, FRA
1912　P. Anspach, BEL
1920　A. Massard, FRA
1924　C. Delporte, BEL
1928　L. Gaudin, FRA
1932　G. Cornaggia-Medici, ITA
1936　F. Riccardi, ITA
1948　L. Cantone, ITA
1952　E. Mangiarotti, ITA
1956　C. Pavesi, ITA
1960　G. Delfino, ITA
1964　G. Kriss, SOV
1968　G. Kulcsár, HUN
1972　C. Fenyvesi, HUN
1976　A. Pusch, GER
1980　J. Harmenberg, SWE
1984　P. Boisse, FRA
1988　A. Schmitt, GER
1992　E. Srecki, FRA
1996

MEN'S ÉPÉE, TEAM
1896–1904 not held
1908　FRA
1912　BEL
1920　ITA
1924　FRA
1928　ITA
1932　FRA
1936　ITA
1948　FRA
1952　ITA
1956　ITA
1960　ITA
1964　HUN
1968　HUN
1972　HUN
1976　SWE
1980　FRA
1984　GER
1988　FRA
1992　GER
1996

MEN'S SABRE, INDIVIDUAL
1896　I. Georgiadis, GRE
1900　G. de la Falaise, FRA
1904　M. Diaz, CUB
1908　J. Fuchs, HUN
1912　J. Fuchs, HUN
1920　N. Nadi, ITA
1924　S. Posta, HUN
1928　O. Tersztyánszky, HUN
1932　G. Piller (Jekelfalussy), HUN
1936　E. Kabos, HUN
1948　A. Gerevich, HUN
1952　P. Kovács, HUN
1956　R. Kárpáti, HUN
1960　R. Kárpáti, HUN
1964　T. Pézsa, HUN
1968　J. Pawlowski, POL
1972　V. Sidiak, SOV
1976　V. Krovopuskov, SOV
1980　V. Krovopuskov, SOV
1984　J. Lamour, FRA
1988　J. Lamour, FRA
1992　B. Szabo, HUN
1996

MEN'S SABRE, TEAM
1896–1904 not held
1908　HUN
1912　HUN
1920　ITA
1924　ITA
1928　HUN
1932　HUN
1936　HUN
1948　HUN
1952　HUN
1956　HUN
1960　HUN
1964　SOV
1968　SOV
1972　ITA
1976　SOV
1980　SOV
1984　ITA
1988　HUN
1992　EUN
1996

WOMEN'S FOIL, INDIVIDUAL
1896–1920 not held
1924　E. Osiier, DEN
1928　H. Mayer, GER
1932　E. Preis, AUT
1936　I. Schacherer-Elek, HUN
1948　I. Elek, HUN
1952　I. Camber, ITA
1956　G. Sheen, GBR
1960　H. Schmid, GER
1964　I. Ujlaki-Rejtö, HUN
1968　Y. Novikova, SOV
1972　A. Ragno-Lonzi, ITA
1976　I. Schwarczenberger, HUN
1980　P. Trinquet, FRA
1984　L. Jujie, CHN
1988　A. Fichtel, GER
1992　G. Trillini, ITA
1996

WOMEN'S FOIL, TEAM
1896–1956 not held
1960　SOV
1964　HUN
1968　SOV
1972　SOV
1976　SOV
1980　FRA
1984　GER
1988　GER
1992　ITA
1996

FIELD HOCKEY

MEN'S FIELD HOCKEY
1896–1904 not held
1908　GBR
1912 not held
1920　GBR
1924 not held
1928　IND
1932　IND
1936　IND
1948　IND
1952　IND
1956　IND
1960　PAK
1964　IND
1968　PAK
1972　GER
1976　NZE
1980　IND
1984　PAK
1988　GBR
1992　GER
1996

WOMEN'S FIELD HOCKEY
1896–1976 not held
1980　ZIM
1984　HOL
1988　AUS
1992　SPA
1996

FOOTBALL (SOCCER)

1896 not held	*1932 not held*	1972 POL
1900 GBR	1936 ITA	1976 GDR
1904 CAN	1948 SWE	1980 CZE
1908 GBR	1952 HUN	1984 FRA
1912 GBR	1956 SOV	1988 SOV
1920 BEL	1960 YUG	1992 SPA
1924 URU	1964 HUN	1996
1928 URU	1968 HUN	

GYMNASTICS

MEN'S INDIVIDUAL ALL-AROUND
1896 not held
1900 G. Sandras, FRA
1904 J. Lenhart, AUT
1908 A. Braglia, ITA
1912 A. Braglia, ITA
1920 G. Zampori, ITA
1924 L. Štukelj, YUG
1928 G. Miez, SWI
1932 R. Neri, ITA
1936 A. Schwarzmann, GER
1948 V. Huhtanen, FIN
1952 V. Chukarin, SOV
1956 V. Chukarin, SOV
1960 B. Shakhlin, SOV
1964 Y. Endo, JPN
1968 S. Kato, JPN
1972 S. Kato, JPN
1976 N. Andrianov, SOV
1980 A. Dityatin, SOV
1984 K. Gushiken, JPN
1988 V. Artemov, SOV
1992 V. Scherbo, EUN
1996

MEN'S HORIZONTAL BAR
1896 H. Weingärtner, GER
1900 not held
1904 A. Heida, USA
1908–1920 not held
1924 L. Štukelj, YUG
1928 G. Miez, SWI
1932 D. Bixler, USA
1936 A. Saarvala, FIN
1948 J. Stalder, SWI
1952 J. Günthard, SWI
1956 T. Ono, JPN
1960 T. Ono, JPN
1964 B. Shakhlin, SOV
1968 A. Nakayama, JPN
1972 M. Tsukahara, JPN
1976 M. Tsukahara, JPN
1980 S. Deltchev, BUL
1984 S. Morisue, JPN
1988 V. Artemov, SOV
1992 T. Dimas, USA
1996

MEN'S PARALLEL BARS
1896 A. Flatow, GER
1900 not held
1904 G. Eyser, USA
1908–1920 not held
1924 A. Güttinger, SWI
1928 L. Vácha, CZE
1932 R. Neri, ITA
1936 K. Frey, GER
1948 M. Reusch, SWI
1952 H. Eugster, SWI
1956 V. Chukarin, SOV
1960 B. Shakhlin, SOV
1964 Y. Endo, JPN
1968 A. Nakayama, JPN
1972 S. Kato, JPN
1976 S. Kato, JPN
1980 A. Tkachyov, SOV
1984 B. Conner, USA
1988 V. Artemov, SOV
1992 V. Scherbo, EUN
1996

MEN'S LONG HORSE VAULT
1896 K. Schumann, GER
1900 not held
1904 G. Eyser, USA
1908–1920 not held
1924 F. Kriz, USA
1928 E. Mack, SWI
1932 S. Guglielmetti, ITA
1936 A. Schwarzmann, GER
1948 P. Aaltonen, FIN
1952 V. Chukarin, SOV
1956 H. Bantz, GER
1960 T. Ono, JPN
1964 H. Yamashita, JPN
1968 M. Voronin, SOV
1972 K. Köste, GDR
1976 N. Andrianov, SOV
1980 N. Andrianov, SOV
1984 L. Yun, CHN
1988 L. Yun, CHN
1992 V. Scherbo, EUN
1996

MEN'S SIDE HORSE (POMMELED HORSE)
1896 L. Zutter, SWI
1900 not held
1904 A. Heida, USA
1908–1920 not held
1924 J. Wilhelm, SWI
1928 H. Hänggi, SWI
1932 I. Pelle, HUN
1936 K. Frey, GER
1948 P. Aaltonen, FIN
1952 V. Chukarin, SOV
1956 B. Shakhlin, SOV
1960 E. Ekman, FIN
1964 M. Cerar, YUG
1972 V. Klimenko, SOV
1976 Z. Magyar, HUN
1980 Z. Magyar, HUN
1984 L. Ning, CHN
1988 D. Bilozerchev, SOV
1992 V. Scherbo, EUN
    Pae Gil-Su, PRK (tie)
1996

MEN'S RINGS
1896 I. Mitropoulos, GRE
1900 not held
1904 H. Glass, USA
1908–1920 not held
1924 F. Martino, ITA
1928 L. Štukelj, YUG
1932 G. Gulack, USA
1936 A. Hudec, CZE
1948 K. Frei, SWI
1952 G. Shaginyan, SOV
1956 A. Azaryan, SOV
1960 A. Azaryan, SOV
1964 T. Haytta, JPN
1968 A. Nakayama, JPN
1972 A. Nakayama, JPN
1976 N. Andrianov, SOV
1980 A. Dityatin, SOV
1984 K. Gushiken, JPN
1988 H. Behrendt, GDR
1992 V. Scherbo, EUN
1996

MEN'S FLOOR EXERCISE
1896–1928 not held
1932 I. Pelle, HUN
1936 G. Miez, SWI
1948 F. Pataki, HUN
1952 K. W. Thoresson, SWI
1956 V. Muratov, SOV
1960 N. Aihara, JPN
1964 F. Menichelli, ITA
1968 S. Kato, JPN
1972 N. Andrianov, SOV
1976 N. Andrianov, SOV
1980 R. Brückner, GDR
1984 L. Ning. CHN
1988 S. Kharkov, SOV
1992 L. Xiaosahuang, CHN
1996

MEN'S TEAM COMBINED EXERCISES
1896–1900 not held
1904 T. Philadelphia
1908 SWE
1912 ITA
1920 ITA
1924 ITA
1928 SWI
1932 ITA
1936 GER
1948 FIN
1952 SOV
1956 SOV
1960 JPN
1964 JPN
1968 JPN
1972 JPN
1976 JPN
1980 SOV
1984 USA
1988 SOV
1992 EUN
1996

WOMEN'S ALL-AROUND
1896–1948 not held
1952 M. Gorokhovskaya, SOV
1956 L. Latynina, SOV
1960 L. Latynina, SOV
1964 V. Čáslavská, CZE
1968 V. Čáslavská, CZE
1972 L. Tourischeva, SOV
1976 N. Comaneci, ROM
1980 Y. Davydova, SOV
1984 M. Retton, USA
1988 Y. Shushunova, SOV
1992 T. Goutsou, EUN
1996

WOMEN'S SIDE HORSE VAULT
1896–1948 not held
1952 Y. Kalinchuk, SOV
1956 L. Latynina, SOV
1960 M. Nikolayeva, SOV
1964 V. Čáslavská, CZE
1968 V. Čáslavská, CZE
1972 K. Janz, GDR
1976 N. Kim, SOV
1980 N. Shaposhnikova, SOV
1984 E. Szabó, ROM
1988 S. Boginskaya, SOV
1992 H. Onodi, HUN
    L. C. Milosovici, ROM (tie)
1996

WOMEN'S ASYMMETRICAL (UNEVEN) BARS
1896–1948 not held
1952 M. Korondi, HUN
1956 Á. Keleti, HUN
1960 P. Astakhova, SOV
1964 P. Astakhova, SOV
1968 V. Čáslavská, CZE
1972 K. Janz, GDR
1976 N. Comaneci, ROM
1980 M. Gnauck, GDR
1984 M. Yanhong, CHN
1988 D. Silivas, ROM
1992 L. Li, CHN
1996

WOMEN'S BALANCE BEAM
1896–1948 not held
1952 N. Bocharova, SOV
1956 Á. Keleti, HUN
1960 E. Bosáková, CZE
1964 V. Čáslavská, CZE
1968 N. Kuchinskaya, SOV
1972 O. Korbut, SOV
1976 N. Comaneci, ROM
1980 N. Comaneci, ROM
1984 S. Pauca, ROM
1988 D. Silivas, ROM

WOMEN'S FLOOR EXERCISES
1896–1948 not held
1952 Á. Keleti, HUN
1956 Á. Keleti, HUN
1960 L. Latynina, SOV
1964 L. Latynina, SOV
1968 V. Čáslavská, CZE
1972 O. Korbut, SOV
1976 N. Kim, SOV
1980 N. Comaneci, ROM
1984 E. Szabó, ROM
1988 D. Silivas, ROM
1992 L. C. Milosovici, ROM
1996

WOMEN'S TEAM COMBINED EXERCISES
1896–1924 not held
1928 HOL
1932 not held
1936 GER
1948 CZE
1952 SOV
1956 SOV
1960 SOV
1964 SOV
1968 SOV
1972 SOV
1976 SOV
1980 SOV
1984 ROM
1988 SOV
1992 EUN
1996

RHYTHMIC ALL-AROUND
1896–1980 not held
1984 L. Fung, CAN
1988 M. Lobach, SOV
1992 A. Timoshenko, EUN
1996

HANDBALL

MEN'S TEAM HANDBALL
1896–1932 not held
1936 GER
1948–1968 not held
1972 YUG
1976 SOV
1980 GDR
1984 YUG
1988 SOV
1992 EUN
1996

WOMEN'S TEAM HANDBALL
1896–1972 not held
1976 SOV
1980 SOV
1984 YUG
1988 KOR
1992 KOR
1996

JUDO

MEN'S EXTRA-LIGHTWEIGHT
1896–1976 not held
1980 T. Rey, FRA
1984 S. Hosokawa, JPN
1988 K. Jae-yup, KOR
1992 N. Gousseinov, EUN
1996

MEN'S HALF-LIGHTWEIGHT
1896–1976 not held
1980 N. Solodukhin, SOV
1984 Y. Matsuoka, JPN
1988 L. Kyung-keun, KOR
1992 R. Sampaio Cardoso, BRA
1996

MEN'S LIGHTWEIGHT
1896–1960 not held
1964 T. Nakatani, JPN
1968 not held
1972 T. Kawaguchi, JPN
1976 H. Rodriguez Torres, CUB
1980 E. Gamba, ITA
1984 A. Byeong-keun, KOR
1988 M. Alexandre, FRA
1992 T. Koga, JPN
1996

MEN'S HALF-MIDDLEWEIGHT
1896–1968 not held
1972 T. Nomura, JPN
1976 V. Nevzorov, SOV
1980 S. Khabareli, SOV
1984 F. Wieneke, GER
1988 W. Legień, POL
1992 H. Yosida, JPN
1996

MEN'S MIDDLEWEIGHT
1896–1960 not held
1964 I. Okano, JPN
1968 not held
1972 S. Sekine, JPN
1976 I. Sonoda, JPN
1980 J. Röthlisberger, SWI
1984 P. Seisenbacher, AUT
1988 P. Seisenbacher, AUT
1992 W. Legien, POL
1996

MEN'S HALF-HEAVYWEIGHT
1896–1968 not held
1972 S. Chochoshvili, SOV
1976 K. Ninomiya, JPN
1980 R. Van de Walle, BEL
1984 H. Hyoung-zoo, KOR
1988 A. Miguel, BRA
1992 A. Kovacs, HUN
1996

MEN'S HEAVYWEIGHT
1896–1960 not held
1964 I. Inokuma, JPN
1968 not held
1972 W. Ruska, HOL
1976 S. Novikov, SOV
1980 A. Parisi, FRA
1984 H. Saito, JPN
1988 H. Saito, JPN
1992 D. Khakhaleichvili, EUN
1996

WOMEN'S EXTRA-LIGHTWEIGHT
1896–1988 not held
1992 C. Nowak, FRA
1996

WOMEN'S HALF-LIGHTWEIGHT
1896–1988 not held
1992 A. Munoz Martinez, SPA
1996

WOMEN'S LIGHTWEIGHT
1896–1988 not held
1992 M. Blasco Soto, SPA
1996

WOMEN'S HALF-MIDDLEWEIGHT
1896–1988 not held
1992 C. Fleury, FRA
1996

WOMEN'S MIDDLEWEIGHT
1896–1988 not held
1992 O. Reve Jimenez, CUB
1996

WOMEN'S HALF-HEAVYWEIGHT
1896–1988 not held
1992 K. M. Jung, KOR
1996

WOMEN'S HEAVYWEIGHT
1896–1988 not held
1992 Z. Xiaoyan, CHN
1996

MODERN PENTATHLON

INDIVIDUAL
1896–1908 not held
1912 Gösta Lilliehöök, SWE
1920 Gustaf Dyrssen, SWE
1924 Bo Lindman, SWE
1928 Sven Thofelt, SWE
1932 Johan Oxenstierna, SWE
1936 Gotthardt Handrick, GER
1948 William Grut, SWE
1952 Lars Hall, SWE
1956 Lars Hall, SWE
1960 Férenc Németh, HUN
1964 Ferenc Török, HUN
1968 Björn Ferm, SWE
1972 András Balczó, HUN
1976 Janusz Pyciak-Peciak, POL
1980 Anatoly Starostin, SOV
1984 Daniele Masala, ITA
1988 János Martinek, HUN
1992 A. Skrzypaszek, POL
1996

TEAM
1896–1948 not held
1952 HUN
1956 SOV
1960 HUN
1964 SOV
1968 HUN
1972 SOV
1976 GBR
1980 SOV
1984 ITA
1988 HUN
1992 POL
1996

ROWING

MEN'S SINGLE SCULLS
1896 not held
1900 Henri Barrelet, FRA 7:35.60
1904 Frank Greer, USA 10:08.50
1908 Harry Blackstaffe, GBR 9:26.00
1912 William Kinnear, GBR 7:47.60
1920 John Kelly, Sr., USA 7:35.00
1924 Jack Beresford, GBR 7:49.20
1928 Henry Pearce, AUS 7:11.00
1932 Henry Pearce, AUS 7:44.40
1936 Gustav Schäfer, GER 8:21.50
1948 Mervyn Wood, AUS 7:24.40
1952 Yuri Tyukalov, SOV 8:12.80
1956 Vyacheslav Ivanov, SOV 8:02.50
1960 Vyacheslav Ivanov, SOV 7:13.96
1964 Vyacheslav Ivanov, SOV 8:22.51
1968 Henri Jan Wienese, HOL 7:47.80
1972 Yuri Malishev, SOV 7:10.12
1976 Pertti Karppinen, FIN 7:29.03
1980 Pertti Karppinen, FIN 7:09.61
1984 Pertti Karppinen, FIN 7:00.24
1988 Thomas Lange, GDR 6:49.86
1992 Thomas Lange, GER 6:51.40
1996

MEN'S DOUBLE SCULLS
1896–1900 not held
1904 USA 10:03.20
1908–1912 not held
1920 USA 7:09.00
1924 USA 6:34.00
1928 USA 6:41.40
1932 USA 7:17.40
1936 GBR 7:20.80
1948 GBR 6:51.30
1952 ARG 7:32.20
1956 SOV 7:24.00
1960 CZE 6:47.50
1964 SOV 7:10.66
1968 SOV 6:51.82
1972 SOV 7:01.77
1976 NOR 7:13.20
1980 GDR 6:24.33
1984 USA 6:36.87
1988 HOL 6:21.13
1992 AUS 6:17.32
1996

MEN'S QUADRUPLE SCULLS
1896–1972 not held
1976 GDR 6:18.65
1980 GDR 5:49.81
1984 GER 5:57.55
1988 ITA 5:53.37
1992 GER 5:45.17
1996

MEN'S PAIR-OARED SHELL WITHOUT COXSWAIN
1896–1900 not held
1904 USA 10:57.00
1908 GBR 9:41.00
1912–1920 not held
1924 HOL 8:19.40
1928 GER 7:06.40
1932 GBR 8:00.00
1936 GER 8:16.10
1948 GBR 7:21.10
1952 USA 8:20.70
1956 USA 7:55.40
1960 SOV 7:02.01
1964 CAN 7:32.94
1968 GDR 7:26.56
1972 GDR 6:53.16
1976 GDR 7:23.31
1980 GDR 6:48.01
1984 ROM 6:45.39
1988 GBR 6:36.84
1992 GBR 6:27.72
1996

MEN'S PAIR-OARED SHELL WITH COXSWAIN
1896 not held
1900 HOL 7:34.20
1904–1912 not held
1920 ITA 7:56.00
1924 SWI 8:39.00
1928 SWI 7:42.60
1932 USA 8:25.80
1936 GER 8:36.90
1948 DEN 8:00.50
1952 FRA 8:28.60
1956 USA 8:26.10
1960 GER 7:29.14
1964 USA 8:21.23
1968 ITA 8:04.81
1972 GDR 7:17.25
1976 GDR 7:58.99
1980 GDR 7:02.54
1984 ITA 7:05.99
1988 ITA 6:58.79
1992 GBR 6:49.83
1996

MEN'S FOUR-OARED SHELL WITHOUT COXSWAIN
1896–1900 not held
1904 USA 9:05.80
1908 GBR 8:34.00
1912–1920 not held
1924 GBR 7:08.60
1928 GBR 6:36.00
1932 GBR 6:58.20
1936 GER 7:01.80
1948 ITA 6:39.00
1952 YUG 7:16.00
1956 CAN 7:08.80
1960 USA 6:26.26
1964 DEN 6:59.30
1968 GDR 6:39.18
1972 GDR 6:24.27
1976 GDR 6:37.42
1980 GDR 6:08.17
1984 NZE 6:03.48
1988 GDR 6:03.11
1992 AUS 5:55.04
1996

MEN'S FOUR-OARED SHELL WITH COXSWAIN
1896 not held
1900 1st Final FRA 7:11.00
     2nd Final GER 5:59.00
1904–1908 not held
1912 GER 6:59.40
1920 SWI 6:54.00
1924 SWI 7:18.40
1928 ITA 6:47.80
1932 GER 7:19.00
1936 GER 7:16.20
1948 USA 6:50.30
1952 CZE 7:33.40
1956 ITA 7:19.40
1960 GER 6:39.12
1964 GER 7:00.44
1968 NZE 6:45.62
1972 GER 6:31.85
1976 SOV 6:40.22
1980 GDR 6:14.51
1984 GBR 6:18.64
1988 GDR 6:10.74
1992 ROM 5:59.37
1996

MEN'S EIGHT-OARED SHELL WITH COXSWAIN
1896 not held
1900 USA 6:09.80
1904 USA 7:50.00
1908 GBR 7:52.00
1912 GBR 6:15.00
1920 USA 6:02.60
1924 USA 6:33.40
1928 USA 6:03.20
1932 USA 6:37.60
1936 USA 6:25.40
1948 USA 5:56.70
1952 USA 6:25.90
1956 USA 6:35.20
1960 GER 5:57.18
1964 USA 6:18.23
1968 GER 6:07.00
1972 NZE 6:08.94
1976 GDR 5:58.29
1980 GDR 5:49.05
1984 CAN 5:41.32
1988 GER 5:46.05
1992 CAN 5:29.53
1996

WOMEN'S SINGLE SCULLS
1896–1972 not held
1976 C. Scheiblich, GDR 4:05.56
1980 S. Toma, ROM 3:40.69
1984 V. Račilá, ROM 3:40.68
1988 J. Behrendt, GDR 7:47.19
1992 E. Lipa, ROM 7:25.54
1996

WOMEN'S DOUBLE SCULLS
1896–1972 not held
1976 BUL 3:44.36
1980 SOV 3:16.27
1984 ROM 3:26.75
1988 GDR 7:00.48
1992 GER 6:49.00
1996

WOMEN'S QUADRUPLE SCULLS
1896–1984 not held
1988 GDR 6:21.06
1992 GER 6:20.18
1996

WOMEN'S PAIR-OARED SHELL WITHOUT COXSWAIN
1896–1972 not held
1976 BUL 4:01.22
1980 GDR 3:30.49
1984 ROM 3:32.60
1988 ROM 7:28.13
1992 CAN 7:06.22
1996

WOMEN'S FOUR-OARED SHELL WITHOUT COXSWAIN
1896–1988 not held
1992 CAN 6:30.85
1996

WOMEN'S EIGHT-OARED SHELL WITH COXSWAIN
1896–1972 not held
1976 GDR 3:33.32
1980 GDR 3:03.32
1984 USA 2:59.80
1988 GDR 6:15.17
1992 CAN 6:02.62
1996

SHOOTING

MEN'S RAPID-FIRE PISTOL
1896 Ioannis Phrangoudis, GRE
1900 Maurice Larrouy, FRA
1904 not held
1908 Paul van Asbroeck, BEL
1912 Alfred Lane, USA
1920 Guilherme Paraense, BRA
1924 Henry Bailey, USA
1928 not held
1932 Renzo Morigi, ITA
1936 Cornelius van Oyen, GER
1948 Károly Takács, HUN WR
1952 Károly Takács, HUN
1956 Stefan Petrescu, ROM
1960 William McMillan, USA EOR
1964 Pentti Linnosvuo, FIN OR
1968 Józef Zapedzki, POL OR
1972 Józef Zapedzki, POL OR
1976 Norbert Klaar, GDR OR
1980 Corneliu Ion, ROM
1984 Takeo Kamachi, JPN
1988 Afanasi Kuzmin, SOV WR
1992 Ralf Schumann, GER OR
1996

MEN'S FREE PISTOL
1896 Sumner Paine, USA
1900 Conrad Karl Röderer, SWI
1904–1908 not held
1912 Alfred Lane, USA
1920 Karl Frederick, USA
1924–1932 not held
1936 Torsten Ullman, SWE WR
1948 Edwin Vasquez Cam, PER
1952 Huelet Benner, USA OR
1956 Pentti Linnosvuo, FIN OR
1960 Aleksei Gustchin, SOV OR
1964 Väinö Markkanen, FIN OR
1968 Grigory Kossykh, SOV OR
1972 Ragnar Skanåker, SWE OR
1976 Uwe Potteck, GDR WR
1980 Aleksandr Melentev, SOV WR
1984 Xu Haifeng, CHN
1988 Sorin Babii, ROM
1992 Konstantine Loukachik, EUN
1996

MEN'S AIR PISTOL
1896–1984 not held
1988 Tanue Kiriakov, BUL

MEN'S SMALL-BORE RIFLE, PRONE
1896–1904 not held
1908 A. A. Carnell, GBR
1912 Frederick Hird, USA
1920 not held
1924 Pierre Coquelin de Lisle, FRA
1928 not held
1932 Bertil Rönnmark, SWE
1936 Willy Rögeberg, NOR WR
1948 Arthur Cook, USA WR
1952 Iosif Sirbu, ROM EWR
1956 Gerald Ouellette, CAN
1960 Peter Kohnke, GER
1964 László Hammerl, HUN WR
1968 Jan Kurka, CZE EWR
1972 Li Ho-jun, PRK WR
1976 Karlheinz Smieszek, GER EWR
1980 Károly Varga, HUN EWR
1984 Edward Etzel, USA EOR
1988 Miroslav Varga, CZE
1992 Lee Eun-Chul, KOR EOR
1996

1992 Wang Yifu, CHN
1996

MEN'S SMALL-BORE RIFLE, 3 POSITIONS
1896–1948 not held
1952 Erling Kongshaug, NOR
1956 Anatoly Bogdanov, SOV OR
1960 Viktor Shamburkin, SOV EWR
1964 Lones Wigger, USA WR
1968 Bernd Klingner, GER
1972 John Writer, USA WR
1976 Lanny Bassham, USA
1980 Viktor Vlasov, SOV WR
1984 Malcolm Cooper, GBR EWR
1988 Malcolm Cooper, GBR
1992 Gracha Petikiane, EUN OR
1996

MEN'S AIR RIFLE
1896–1980 not held
1984 Philippe Heberle, FRA
1988 Goran Maksimović, YUG
1992 Iouri Fedkine, EUN
1996

MEN'S MOVING TARGET
1896 not held
1900 Louis Debray, FRA
1904–1968 not held
1972 Lakov Zhelezniak, SOV WR
1976 Aleksandr Gazov, SOV WR
1980 Igor Sokolov, SOV WR
1984 Li Yuwei, CHN
1988 Tor Heiestad, NOR
1992 Michael Jakosits, GER OR
1996

WOMEN'S SPORT PISTOL
1896–1980 not held
1984 Linda Thom, CAN
1988 Nino Salukvadze, SOV
1992 Marina Logvinenko, EUN
1996

WOMEN'S AIR PISTOL
1896–1984 not held
1988 Jasna Šekarić, YUG WR
1992 Marina Logvinenko, EUN OR
1996

SHOOTING

WOMEN'S SMALL-BORE RIFLE, 3 POSITIONS
1896–1980 not held
1984 Wu Xiaoxuan, CHN
1988 Sylvia Sperber, GER
1992 Launi Meili, USA
1996

WOMEN'S AIR RIFLE
1896–1980 not held
1984 Pat Spurgin, USA
1988 Irina Shilova, SOV
1992 Yeo Kab-Soon, KOR
1996

MIXED TRAP SHOOTING
1896 not held
1900 Roger de Barbarin, FRA
1904 not held
1908 Walter Ewing, CAN
1912 James Graham, USA
1920 Mark Arie, USA
1924 Gyula Halasy, HUN   OR
1928–1948 not held
1952 George Généreux, CAN
1956 Galliano Rossini, ITA   OR
1960 Ion Dumitrescu, ROM
1964 Ennio Mattarelli, ITA   OR
1968 John Braithwaite, GBR   EWR
1972 Angelo Scalzone, ITA   WR
1976 Donald Haldeman, USA
1980 Luciano Giovannetti, ITA
1984 Luciano Giovannetti, ITA
1988 Dmitri Monakov, SOV
1992 Petr Hrdlicka, TCH   OR
1996

SKEET SHOOTING
1896–1964 not held
1968 Yevgeny Petrov, SOV   EWR
1972 Konrad Wirnhier, GER
1976 Josef Panaček, CZE   EOR
1980 Hans Kjeld Rasmussen, DEN
1984 Matthew Dryke, USA   EOR
1988 Axel Wegner, GDR
1992 Zhang Shan, CHN   OR
1996

SWIMMING AND DIVING

MEN'S 50-METER FREESTYLE
1896–1900 not held
1904 Zoltán Halmay, HUN   0:28.00
1908–1984 not held
1988 Matthew Biondi, USA   0:22.14 WR
1992 Aleksandr Popov, EUN   0:21.91 OR
1996

MEN'S 100-METER FREESTYLE
1896 Alfréd Hajós, HUN   1:22.20 OR
1900 not held
1904 Zoltán Halmay, HUN   1:02.80
1908 Charles Daniels, USA   1:05.60 WR
1912 Duke Paoa Kahanamoku, USA   1:03.40
1920 Duke Paoa Kahanamoku, USA   1:00.40 WR
1924 Johnny Weissmuller, USA   0:59.00 OR
1928 Johnny Weissmuller, USA   0:58.60 OR
1932 Yasuji Miyazaki, JPN   0:58.20
1936 Ferenc Csík, HUN   0:57.60
1948 Walter Ris, USA   0:57.30 OR
1952 Clarke Scholes, USA   0:57.40
1956 Jon Henricks, AUS   0:55.40 OR
1960 John Devitt, AUS   0:55.20 OR
1964 Donald Schollander, USA   0:53.40 OR
1968 Michael Wenden, AUS   0:52.20 WR
1972 Mark Spitz, USA   0:51.22 WR
1976 Jim Montgomery, USA   0:49.99 WR
1980 Jörg Woithe, GDR   0:50.40
1984 Ambrose Gaines, USA   0:49.80 OR
1988 Matthew Biondi, USA   0:48.63 OR
1992 Aleksandr Popov, EUN   0:49.02
1996

MEN'S 200-METER FREESTYLE
1896 not held
1900 Frederick Lane, AUS   1:25.20 OR
1904 Charles Daniels, USA   2:44.20
1908–1964 not held
1968 Michael Wenden, AUS   1:55.20 OR
1972 Mark Spitz, USA   1:52.78 WR
1976 Bruce Furniss, USA   1:50.29 WR
1980 Sergei Kopliakov, SOV   1:49.81 OR
1984 Michael Gross, GER   1:47.44 WR ·
1988 Duncan Armstrong, AUS   1:47.25 OR
1992 Evgueni Sadovyi, EUN   1:46.70 OR
1996

MEN'S 400-METER FREESTYLE
1896 Paul Neumann, AUT   8:12.60
1900 not held
1904 Charles Daniels, USA   6:16.20
1908 Henry Taylor, GBR   5:36.80
1912 George Hodgson, CAN   5:24.40
1920 Norman Ross, USA   5:26.80
1924 Johnny Weissmuller, USA 5:04.20 OR
1928 Alberto Zorilla, ARG   5:01.60 OR
1932 Clarence Crabbe, USA   4:48.40 OR
1936 Jack Medica, USA   4:44.50 OR
1948 William Smith, USA   4:41.00 OR
1952 Jean Boiteux, FRA   4:30.70 OR
1956 Murray Rose, AUS   4:27.30 OR
1960 Murray Rose, AUS   4:18.30 OR
1964 Donald Schollander, USA 4:12.20 WR
1968 Michael Burton, USA   4:09.00 OR
1972 Bradford Cooper, AUS   4:00.27 OR
1976 Brian Goodell, USA   3:51.93 WR
1980 Vladimir Salnikov, SOV 3:51.31 OR
1984 George DiCarlo, USA   3:51.23 OR
1988 Uwe Dassler, GDR   3:46.95 WR
1992 Evgueni Sadovyi, EUN   3:45.00 WR
1996

MEN'S 1500-METER FREESTYLE
1896 Alfréd Hajós, HUN   18:22.20*
1900 John Arthur Jarvis, GBR 13:40.20*
1904 Emil Rausch, GER   27:18.20*
1908 Henry Taylor, GBR   22:48.40 WR
1912 George Hodgson, CAN   22:00.00 WR
1920 Norman Ross, USA   22:23.20
1924 Andrew Charlton, AUS   20:06.60 WR
1928 Arne Borg, SWE   19:51.80 WR
1932 Kusuo Kitamura, JPN   19:12.40 OR
1936 Noboru Terada, JPN   19:13.70
1948 James McLane, USA   19:18.50
1952 Ford Konno, USA   18:30.30 OR
1956 Murray Rose, AUS   17:58.90
1960 Jon Konrads, AUS   17:19.60 OR
1964 Robert Windle, AUS   17:01.70 OR
1968 Michael Burton, USA   16:38.90 OR
1972 Michael Burton, USA   15:52.58 WR
1976 Brian Goodell, USA   15:02.40 WR
1980 Vladimir Salnikov, SOV 14:58.27 WR
1984 Michael O'Brien, USA   15:05.20
1988 Vladimir Salnikov, SOV 15:00.40
1992 Kieren Perkins, AUS   14:43.48 WR
1996

MEN'S 100-METER BACKSTROKE
1896–1900 not held
1904 Walter Brack, GER   1:16.80*
1908 Arno Bieberstein, GER   1:24.60 WR
1912 Harry Hebner, USA   1:21.20
1920 Warren Paoa Kealoha, USA 1:15.20
1924 Warren Paoa Kealoha, USA 1:13.20 OR
1928 George Kojac, USA   1:08.20
1932 Masaji Kiyokawa, JPN   1:08.60
1936 Adolf Kiefer, USA   1:05.90 OR
1948 Allen Stack, USA   1:06.40
1952 Yoshinobu Oyakawa, USA   1:05.40 OR
1956 David Theile, AUS   1:02.20 OR
1960 David Theile, AUS   1:01.90 OR
1964 not held
1968 Roland Matthes, GDR   0:58.70 OR
1972 Roland Matthes, GDR   0:56.58 OR
1976 John Naber, USA   0:55.49 WR
1980 Bengt Baron, SWE   0:56.33
1984 Richard Carey, USA   0:55.79
1988 Daichi Suzuki, JPN   0:55.05
1992 Mark Tewksburg, CAN   0:53.98 OR
1996

MEN'S 200-METER BACKSTROKE
1896 not held
1900 Ernst Hoppenberg, GER   2:47.00
1904–1960 not held
1964 Jed Graef, USA   2:10.30 WR
1968 Roland Matthes, GDR   2:09.60 OR
1972 Roland Matthes, GDR   2:02.82 EWR
1976 John Naber, USA   1:59.19 WR
1980 Sándor Wladár, HUN   2:01.93
1984 Richard Carey, USA   2:00.23
1988 Igor Poliansky, SOV   1:59.37
1992 Martin Lopez-Zubero, SPA 1:58.47 OR
1996

MEN'S 100-METER BREASTSTROKE
1896–1964 not held
1968 Donald McKenzie, USA   1:07.70 OR
1972 Nobutaka Taguchi, JPN   1:04.94 WR
1976 John Hencken, USA   1:03.11 WR
1980 Duncan Goodhew, GBR   1:03.44
1984 Steve Lundquist, USA   1:01.65 WR
1988 Adrian Moorhouse, GBR   1:02.04
1992 Nelson Diebel, USA   1:01.50 OR
1996

MEN'S 200-METER BREASTSTROKE
1896–1904 not held
1908 Frederick Holman, GBR   3:09.20 WR
1912 Walter Bathe, GER   3:01.80 OR
1920 Håkan Malmroth, SWE   3:04.40
1924 Robert Skelton, USA   2:56.60
1928 Yoshiyuki Tsuruta, JPN   2:48.80 OR
1932 Yoshiyuki Tsuruta, JPN   2:45.40
1936 Tetsuo Hamuro, JPN   2:41.50 OR
1948 Joseph Verdeur, USA   2:39.30 OR
1952 John Davies, AUS   2:34.40 OR
1956 Masaru Furukawa, JPN   2:34.70 OR
1960 William Mulliken, USA   2:37.40
1964 Ian O'Brien, AUS   2:27.80 WR
1968 Felipe Múñoz, MEX   2:28.70
1972 John Hencken, USA   2:21.55 WR
1976 David Wilkie, GBR   2:15.11 WR
1980 Robertas Zhulpa, SOV   2:15.85
1984 Victor Davis, CAN   2:13.34 WR
1988 József Szabó, HUN   2:13.52
1992 Mike Barrowman, USA   2:10.16 WR
1996

MEN'S 100-METER BUTTERFLY
1896–1964 not held
1968 Douglas Russell, USA   0:55.90 OR
1972 Mark Spitz, USA   0:54.27 WR
1976 Matt Vogel, USA   0:54.35
1980 Pär Arvidsson, SWE   0:54.92
1984 Michael Gross, GER   0:53.08 WR
1988 Anthony Nesty, SUR   0:53.00 OR
1992 Pablo Morales, USA   0:53.32
1996

MEN'S 200-METER BUTTERFLY
1896–1952 not held
1956 William Yorzyk, USA   2:19.30 OR
1960 Michael Troy, USA   2:12.80 WR
1964 Kevin Berry, AUS   2:06.60 WR
1968 Carl Robie, USA   2:08.70
1972 Mark Spitz, USA   2:00.70 WR
1976 Mike Bruner, USA   1:59.23 WR
1980 Sergei Fesenko, SOV   1:59.76
1984 Jon Sieben, AUS   1:57.04 WR
1988 Michael Gross, GER   1:56.94 OR
1992 Melvin Stewart, USA   1:56.26 WR
1996

MEN'S 200-METER INDIVIDUAL MEDLEY
1896–1964 not held
1968 Charles Hickcox, USA   2:12.00 OR
1972 Gunnar Larsson, SWE   2:07.17 WR
1976–1980 not held
1984 Alex Baumann, CAN   2:01.42 WR
1988 Tamás Darnyi, HUN   2:00.17 WR
1992 Tamás Darnyi, HUN   2:00.76
1996

MEN'S 400-METER INDIVIDUAL MEDLEY
1896–1960 not held
1964 Richard Roth, USA   4:45.40 WR
1968 Charles Hickcox, USA   4:48.40
1972 Gunnar Larsson, SWE   4:31.98 OR
1976 Rod Strachan, USA   4:23.68 WR
1980 Aleksandr Sidorenko, SOV 4:22.89 OR
1984 Alex Baumann, CAN   4:17.41 WR
1988 Tamás Darnyi, HUN   4:14.75 WR
1992 Tamás Darnyi, HUN   4:14.23 OR
1996

MEN'S 4 X 100-METER FREESTYLE RELAY
1896–1960 not held
1964 USA   3:32.20 WR
1968 USA   3:31.70 WR
1972 USA   3:26.42 WR
1976–1980 not held
1984 USA   3:19.03 WR
1988 USA   3:16.53 WR
1992 USA   3:16.74
1996

MEN'S 4 X 200-METER FREESTYLE RELAY
*1896–1904 not held (*distances varried)*
1908 GBR   10:55.60 WR
1912 AUS/NZE   10:11.60 WR
1920 USA   10:04.40 WR
1924 USA   9:53.40   WR
1928 USA   9:36.20   WR
1932 JPN   8:58.40   WR
1936 JPN   8:51.50   WR
1948 USA   8:46.00   WR
1952 USA   8:31.10   OR
1956 AUS   8:23.60   WR
1960 USA   8:10.20   WR
1964 USA   7:52.10   WR
1968 USA   7:52.33
1972 USA   7:35.78   WR
1976 USA   7:23.22   WR
1980 SOV   7:23.50
1984 USA   7:15.69   WR
1988 USA   7:12.51   WR
1992 EUN   7:11.95   WR
1996

MEN'S 4 X 100-METER MEDLEY RELAY
1896–1956 not held
1960 USA   4:05.40   WR
1964 USA   3:58.40   WR
1968 USA   3:54.90   WR
1972 USA   3:48.16   WR
1976 USA   3:42.22   WR
1980 AUS   3:45.70
1984 USA   3:39.30   WR
1988 USA   3:36.93   WR
1992 USA   3:36.93   EWR
1996

SWIMMING AND DIVING

MEN'S SPRINGBOARD DIVING
1896–1904 not held

1908	Albert Zürner, GER	
1912	Paul Günther, GER	
1920	Louis Kuehn, USA	
1924	Albert White, USA	
1928	Ulise Desjardins, USA	
1932	Michael Galitzen (Riley), USA	
1936	Richard Degener, USA	
1948	Bruce Harlan, USA	
1952	David Browning, USA	
1956	Robert Clotworthy, USA	
1960	Gary Tobian, USA	
1964	Kenneth Sitzberger, USA	
1968	Bernard Wrightson, USA	
1972	Vladimir Vasin, SOV	
1976	Philip Boggs, USA	
1980	Aleksandr Portnov, SOV	
1984	Gregory Louganis, USA	
1988	Gregory Louganis, USA	
1992	Mark Lenzi, USA	
1996		

MEN'S PLATFORM DIVING
1896–1900 not held

1904	George Sheldon, USA	
1908	Hjalmar Johansson, SWE	
1912	Erik Adlerz, SWE	
1920	Clarence Pinkston, USA	
1924	Albert White, USA	
1928	Ulise Desjardins, USA	
1932	Harold Smith, USA	
1936	Marshall Wayne, USA	
1948	Samuel Lee, USA	
1952	Samuel Lee, USA	
1956	Joaquin Capilla Pérez, MEX	
1960	Robert Webster, USA	
1964	Robert Webster, USA	
1968	Klaus Dibiasi, ITA	
1972	Klaus Dibiasi, ITA	
1976	Klaus Dibiasi, ITA	
1980	Falk Hoffmann, GDR	
1984	Gregory Louganis, USA	
1988	Gregory Louganis, USA	
1992	Sun Shuwei, CHN	
1996		

WATER POLO
1896 not held

1900	GBR	1952	HUN
1904	USA	1956	HUN
1908	GBR	1960	ITA
1912	GBR	1964	HUN
1920	GBR/IRL	1968	YUG
1924	FRA	1972	SOV
1928	GER	1976	HUN
1932	HUN	1980	SOV
1936	HUN	1984	YUG
1948	ITA	1988	YUG
		1992	ITA
		1996	

WOMEN'S 50-METER FREESTYLE
1896–1984 not held

1988	Kristin Otto, GDR	0:25.49	OR
1992	Yang Wenyi, CHN	0:24.79	WR
1996			

WOMEN'S 100-METER FREESTYLE
1896–1908 not held

1912	Fanny Durack, AUS	1:22.20	
1920	Ethelda Bleibtrey, USA	1:13.60	WR
1924	Ethel Lackie, USA	1:12.40	
1928	Albina Osipowich, USA	1:11.00	OR
1932	Helene Madison, USA	1:06.80	OR
1936	Hendrika Mastenbroek, HOL	1:05.90	OR
1948	Greta Andersen, DEN	1:06.30	
1952	Katalin Szöke, HUN	1:06.80	
1956	Dawn Fraser, AUS	1:02.00	WR
1960	Dawn Fraser, AUS	1:01.20	OR
1964	Dawn Fraser, AUS	0:59.50	OR
1968	Jan Henne, USA	1:00.00	
1972	Sandra Neilson, USA	0:58.59	OR

1976	Kornelia Ender, GDR	0:55.65	WR
1980	Barbara Krause, GDR	0:54.79	WR
1984	Nancy Hogshead, USA	0:55.92	
1988	Kristin Otto, GDR	0:54.93	
1992	Zhuang Yong, CHN	0:54.65	OR
1996			

WOMEN'S 200-METER FREESTYLE
1896–1964 not held

1968	Deborah Meyer, USA	2:10.50	OR
1972	Shane Gould, AUS	2:03.56	WR
1976	Kornelia Ender, GDR	1:59.26	WR
1980	Barbara Krause, GDR	1:58.33	OR
1984	Mary Wayte, USA	1:59.23	
1988	Heike Friedrich, GDR	1:57.65	OR
1992	Nicole Haislett, USA	1:57.90	
1996			

WOMEN'S 400-METER FREESTYLE
1896–1912 not held

1920	Ethelda Bleibtrey, USA	4:34.00	WR
1924	Martha Norelius, USA	6:02.20	
1928	Martha Norelius, USA	5:42.80	WR
1932	Helene Madison, USA	5:28.50	WR
1936	Hendrika Mastenbroek, HOL	5:26.40	OR
1948	Ann Curtis, USA	5:17.80	OR
1952	Valéria Gyenge, HUN	5:12.10	OR
1956	Lorraine Crapp, AUS	4:54.60	OR
1960	S. Christine Von Saltza, USA	4:50.60	OR
1964	Virginia Duenkel, USA	4:43.30	OR
1968	Debbie Meyer, USA	4:31.80	OR
1972	Shane Gould, AUS	4:19.44	WR
1976	Petra Thümer, GDR	4:09.89	WR
1980	Ines Diers, GDR	4:08.76	OR
1984	Tiffany Cohen, USA	4:07.10	OR
1988	Janet Evans, USA	4:03.85	WR
1992	Dagmar Hase, GER	4:07.18	
1996			

WOMEN'S 800-METER FREESTYLE
1896–1964 not held

1968	Deborah Meyer, USA	9:24.00	OR
1972	Keena Rothhammer, USA	8:53.68	WR
1976	Petra Thümer, GDR	8:37.14	WR
1980	Michelle Ford, AUS	8:28.90	OR
1984	Tiffany Cohen, USA	8:24.95	OR
1988	Janet Evans, USA	8:20.20	OR
1992	Janet Evans, USA	8:25.52	
1996			

WOMEN'S 100-METER BACKSTROKE
1896–1920 not held

1924	Sybil Bauer, USA	1:23.20	OR
1928	Maria Braun, HOL	1:22.00	
1932	Eleanor Holm, USA	1:19.40	
1936	Dina Senff, HOL	1:18.90	
1948	Karen-Margrete Harup, DEN	1:14.40	OR
1952	Joan Harrison, SAF	1:14.30	
1956	Judith Grinham, GBR	1:12.90	OR
1960	Lynn Burke, USA	1:09.30	OR
1964	Cathy Ferguson, USA	1:07.70	WR
1968	Kaye Hall, USA	1:06.20	WR
1972	Melissa Belote, USA	1:05.78	OR
1976	Ulrike Richter, GDR	1:01.83	OR
1980	Rica Reinisch, GDR	1:00.86	WR
1984	Theresa Andrews, USA	1:02.55	
1988	Kristin Otto, GDR	1:00.89	
1992	Krisztina Egerszegi, HUN	1:00.68	OR
1996			

WOMEN'S 200-METER BACKSTROKE
1896–1964 not held

1968	Lillian Watson, USA	2:24.80	OR
1972	Melissa Belote, USA	2:19.19	WR
1976	Ulrike Richter, GDR	2:13.43	OR
1980	Rica Reinisch, GDR	2:11.77	WR
1984	Jolanda de Rover, HOL	2:12.38	
1988	Krisztina Egerszegi, HUN	2:09.29	OR
1992	Krisztina Egerszegi, HUN	2:07.06	OR
1996			

WOMEN'S 100-METER BREASTSTROKE
1896–1964 not held

1968	Djurdjica Bjedov, YUG	1:15.80	OR
1972	Catherine Carr, USA	1:13.58	WR
1976	Hannelore Anke, GDR	1:11.16	
1980	Ute Geweniger, GDR	1:10.22	
1984	Petra van Staveren, HOL	1:09.88	OR
1988	Tania Dangalakova (Bogomilova), BUL	1:07.95	OR
1992	Elena Roudkovskaia, EUN	1:08.00	
1996			

WOMEN'S 200-METER BREASTSTROKE
1896–1920 not held

1924	Lucy Morton, GBR	3:33.20	OR
1928	Hildegard Schrader, GER	3:12.60	
1932	Clare Dennis, AUS	3:06.30	OR
1936	Hideko Maehata, JPN	3:03.60	
1948	Petronella van Vliet, HOL	2:57.20	
1952	Êva Székely, HUN	2:51.70	OR
1956	Ursula Happe, GER	2:53.10	OR
1960	Anita Lonsbrough, GBR	2:49.50	WR
1964	Galina Prozumenshikova, SOV	2:46.40	OR
1968	Sharon Wichman, USA	2:44.40	OR
1972	Beverley Whitfield, AUS	2:41.71	OR
1976	Marina Koshevaia, SOV	2:33.35	WR
1980	Lina Kačiušte, SOV	2:29.54	OR
1984	Anne Ottenbrite, CAN	2:30.38	
1988	Silke Hörner, GDR	2:26.71	WR
1992	Kyoko Iwasaki, JPN	2:26.65	OR
1996			

WOMEN'S 100-METER BUTTERFLY
1896–1952 not held

1956	Shelly Mann, USA	1:11.00	OR
1960	Carolyn Schuler, USA	1:09.50	OR
1964	Sharon Stouder, USA	1:04.70	WR
1968	Lynette McClements, AUS	1:05.50	
1972	Mayumi Aoki, JPN	1:03.34	WR
1976	Kornelia Ender, GDR	1:00.13	EWR
1980	Caren Metschuck, GDR	1:00.42	
1984	Mary T. Meagher, USA	0:59.26	
1988	Kristin Otto, GDR	0:59.00	
1992	Qian Hong, CHN	0:58.62	OR
1996			

WOMEN'S 200-METER BUTTERFLY
1896–1964 not held

1968	Ada Kok, HOL	2:24.70	OR
1972	Karen Moe, USA	2:15.57	WR
1976	Andrea Pollack, GDR	2:11.41	OR
1980	Ines Geissler, GDR	2:10.44	OR
1984	Mary T. Meagher, USA	2:06.90	OR
1988	Kathleen Nord, GDR	2:09.51	
1992	Summer Sanders, USA	2:08.67	
1996			

WOMEN'S 200-METER INDIVIDUAL MEDLEY
1896–1964 not held

1968	Claudia Kolb, USA	2:24.70	OR
1972	Shane Gould, AUS	2:23.07	WR
1976–1980 not held			
1984	Tracy Caulkins, USA	2:12.64	OR
1988	Daniela Hunger, GDR	2:12.59	OR
1992	Lin Li, CHN	2:11.65	OR
1996			

WOMEN'S 400-METER INDIVIDUAL MEDLEY
1896–1960 not held

1964	Donna De Varona, USA	5:18.70	OR
1968	Claudia Kolb, USA	5:08.50	OR
1972	Gail Neall, AUS	5:02.97	WR
1976	Ulrike Tauber, GDR	4:42.77	WR
1980	Petra Schneider, GDR	4:36.29	WR
1984	Tracy Caulkins, USA	4:39.24	
1988	Janet Evans, USA	4:37.76	
1992	Krisztina Egerszegi, HUN	4:36.54	
1996			

WOMEN'S 4 X 100-METER FREESTYLE RELAY
1896–1908 not held

1912	GBR	5:52.80	WR
1920	USA	5:11.60	WR
1924	USA	4:58.80	WR
1928	USA	4:47.60	WR
1932	USA	4:38.00	WR
1936	HOL	4:36.00	OR
1948	USA	4:29.20	OR
1952	HUN	4:24.40	WR
1956	AUS	4:17.10	WR
1960	USA	4:08.90	WR
1964	USA	4:03.80	WR
1968	USA	4:02.50	WR
1972	USA	3:55.19	WR
1976	USA	3:44.82	WR
1980	GDR	3:42.71	WR
1984	USA	3:43.43	
1988	GDR	3:40.63	OR
1992	USA	3:39.46	WR
1996			

WOMEN'S 4 X 100-METER MEDLEY RELAY
1896–1956 not held

1960	USA	4:41.10	WR
1964	USA	4:33.90	WR
1968	USA	4:28.30	OR
1972	USA	4:20.75	WR
1976	GDR	4:07.95	WR
1980	GDR	4:06.67	WR
1984	USA	4:08.34	
1988	GDR	4:03.74	OR
1992	USA	4:02.54	OR
1996			

WOMEN'S SYNCHRONIZED SWIMMING: SOLO
1896–1980 not held

1984	Tracie Ruiz, USA
1988	Carolyn Waldo, CAN
1992	Kristen Babb-Sprague, USA
1996	

WOMEN'S SYNCHRONIZED SWIMMING: DUET
1896–1980 not held

1984	Candy Costie, Tracie Ruiz, USA
1988	Michelle Cameron, Carolyn Waldo, CAN
1992	Karen Josephson, Sarah Josephson, USA
1996	

WOMEN'S SPRINGBOARD DIVING
1896–1912 not held

1920	Aileen Riggin, USA
1924	Elizabeth Becker, USA
1928	Helen Meany, USA
1932	Georgia Coleman, USA
1936	Marjorie Gestring, USA
1948	Victoria Draves, USA
1952	Patricia McCormick, USA
1956	Patricia McCormick, USA
1960	Ingrid Krämer, GDR
1964	Ingrid Engel-Krämer, GDR
1968	Sue Gossick, USA
1972	Maxine King, USA
1976	Jennifer Chandler, USA
1980	Irina Kalinina, SOV
1984	Sylvie Bernie, CAN
1988	Gao Min, CHN
1992	Gao Min, CHN
1996	

WOMEN'S PLATFORM DIVING
1896–1908 not held

1912	Greta Johansson, SWE
1920	Stefani Fryland-Clausen, DEN
1924	Caroline Smith, USA
1928	Elizabeth Becker Pinkston, USA
1932	Dorothy Poynton, USA
1936	Dorothy Poynton Hill, USA
1948	Victoria Draves, USA
1952	Patricia McCormick, USA
1956	Patricia McCormick, USA
1960	Ingrid Krämer, GDR
1964	Lesley Bush, USA

SWIMMING AND DIVING

1968	Milena Duchková, CZE	1984	Zhou Jihong, CHN
1972	Ulrika Knape, SWE	1988	Xu Yanmei, CHN
1976	Elena Vaytsekhovskaya, SOV	1992	Fu Mingxia, CHN
1980	Martina Jäschke, GDR	1996	

TABLE TENNIS

MEN'S SINGLES
1896-1984 not held
1988 Yoo Nam-kyu, KOR
1992 Jan Waldner, SWE
1996

WOMEN'S TABLE TENNIS SINGLES
1896-1984 not held
1988 Chen Jing, CHN
1992 Deng Yaping, CHN
1996

MEN'S TABLE TENNIS DOUBLES
1896-1984 not held
1988 C. Longcan, W. Qingguang, CHN
1992 L. Lin, Wong Tao, CHN
1996

WOMEN'S TENNIS DOUBLES
1896-1984 not held
1988 H. Jung-hwa, Y. Young-ja, KOR
1992 Deng Yaping, Qiao Hong, CHN
1996

TENNIS

MEN'S TENNIS SINGLES
1896 John Boland, GBR/IRL
1900 Hugh Doherty, GBR
1904 Beals Wright, USA
1908 Josiah Ritchie, GBR
1908 Arthur Gore, GBR (ICt)
1912 Charles Winslow, SAF
1912 André Gobert, FRA (ICt)
1920 Louis Raymond, SAF
1924 Vincent Richards, USA
1928-1984 not held
1988 Miloslav Mečíř, CZE
1992 Marc Rosset, SWI
1996

MEN'S TENNIS DOUBLES
1896 J. Borland, F. Traun, GBR/IRL
1900 R. Doherty, H. Doherty, GBR
1904 E. Leonard, B. Wright, USA

1908 G. Hillyard, R. Doherty, GBR
1908 A. Gore, H. Barrett, GBR (ICt)
1912 C. Winslow, H. Kitson, SAF
1912 A. Gobert, M. Germot, FRA (ICt)
1920 O. Turnbull, M. Woosnam, GBR
1924 V. Richards, F. Hunter, USA
1928-1984 not held
1988 K. Flach, R. Seguso, USA
1992 B. Becker, M. Stich, GER
1996

WOMEN'S TENNIS SINGLES
1896 not held
1900 Charlotte Cooper, GBR
1904 not held
1908 Gwendoline Eastlake-Smith, GBR (ICt)
1912 Marguerite Broquedis, FRA
1912 Edith Hannam, GBR (ICt)

1920 Suzanne Lenglen, FRA
1924 Helen Wills, USA
1928-1984 not held
1988 Stefanie Graf, GER
1992 Jennifer Capriati, USA
1996

WOMEN'S TENNIS DOUBLES
1896-1912 not held
1920 W. McNair, K. McKane, GBR
1924 H. Wightman, H. Willis, USA
1928-1984 not held
1988 P. Shriver, Z. Garrison, USA
1992 G. Fernandez, M. J. Fernandez, USA
1996

TRACK AND FIELD · MEN

100-METER RUN

1896	Thomas Burke, USA	12.00	
1900	Frank W. Jarvis, USA	11.00	
1904	Archie Hahn, USA	11.00	
1908	Reginald Walker, SAF	10.80	EOR
1912	Ralph Craig, USA	10.80	
1920	Charles Paddock, USA	10.80	
1924	Harold Abrahams, GBR	10.60	EOR
1928	Percy Williams, CAN	10.80	
1932	Eddie Tolan, USA	10.30	OR
1936	Jesse Owens, USA	10.30	
1948	Harrison Dillard, USA	10.30	EOR
1952	Lindy Remigino, USA	10.40	
1956	Bobby Morrow, USA	10.50	
1960	Armin Hary, GER	10.20	OR
1964	Hayes, USA	10.00	EWR
1968	Jim Hines, USA	9.95	WR
1972	Valery Borzov, SOV	10.14	
1976	Hasely Crawford, TRI	10.06	
1980	Allan Wells, GBR	10.25	
1984	Carl Lewis, USA	9.99	
1988	Carl Lewis, USA	9.92	OR
1992	Linford Christie, GBR	9.96	
1996			

200-METER RUN
1896 not held

1900	Walter Tewksbury, USA	22.20	
1904	Archie Hahn, USA	21.60	OR
1908	Robert Kerr, CAN	22.60	
1912	Ralph Craig, USA	21.70	
1920	Allen Woodring, USA	22.00	
1924	Jackson Scholz, USA	21.60	
1928	Percy Williams, CAN	21.80	
1932	Eddie Tolan, USA	21.20	OR
1936	Jesse Owens, USA	20.70	OR
1948	Mel Patton, USA	21.10	
1952	Andrew Stanfield, USA	20.70	
1956	Bobby Morrow, USA	20.60	OR
1960	Livio Berruti, ITA	20.50	EWR
1964	Henry Carr, USA	20.30	OR
1968	Tommie Smith, USA	19.83	WR
1972	Valery Borzov, SOV	20.00	
1976	Donald Quarrie, JAM	20.23	
1980	Pietro Mennea, ITA	20.19	
1984	Carl Lewis, USA	19.80	OR
1988	Joe DeLoach, USA	19.75	OR
1992	Mike Marsh, USA	20.01	
1996			

400-METER RUN

1896	Thomas Burke, USA	54.20	
1900	Maxey Long, USA	49.40	OR
1904	Harry Hillman, USA	49.20	OR
1908	Wyndham Halswelle, GBR,	50.00	
1912	Charles Reidpath, USA	48.20	OR
1920	Bevil Rudd, SAF	49.60	
1924	Eric Liddell, GBR	47.60	OR

1928	Ray Barbuti, USA	47.80	
1932	William Carr, USA	46.20	WR
1936	Archie Williams, USA	46.50	
1948	Arthur Wint, JAM	46.20	
1952	George Rhoden, JAM	45.90	OR
1956	Charles Jenkins, USA	46.70	
1960	Otis Davis, USA	44.90	WR
1964	Michael Larrabee, USA	45.10	
1968	Lee Evans, USA	43.80	WR
1972	Vincent Matthews, USA	44.66	
1976	Alberto Juantorena, CUB	44.26	
1980	Viktor Markin, SOV	44.60	
1984	Alonzo Babers, USA	44.27	
1988	Steven Lewis, USA	43.87	
1992	Quincy Watts, USA	44.21	
1996			

800-METER RUN

1896	Edwin Flack, AUS	2:11.00	
1900	Alfred Tysoe, GBR	2:01.20	
1904	James Lightbody, USA	1:56.00	OR
1908	Mel Sheppard, USA	1:52.80	WR
1912	James Meredith, USA	1:51.90	WR
1920	Albert Hill, GBR	1:53.40	
1924	Douglas Lowe, GBR	1:52.40	
1928	Douglas Lowe, GBR	1:51.80	OR
1932	Thomas Hampson, GBR	1:49.70	WR
1936	John Woodruff, USA	1:52.90	
1948	Mal Whitfield, USA	1:49.20	OR
1952	Mal Whitfield, USA	1:49.20	EOR
1956	Thomas Courtney, USA	1:47.70	OR
1960	Peter Snell, NZE	1:46.30	OR
1964	Peter Snell, NZE	1:45.10	OR
1968	Ralph Doubell, AUS	1:44.30	EWR
1972	Dave Wottle, USA	1:45.90	
1976	Alberto Juantorena, CUB	1:43.50	WR
1980	Steve Ovett, GBR	1:45.40	
1984	Joaquim Cruz, BRA	1:43.00	OR
1988	Paul Ereng, KEN	1:43.45	
1992	William Tanui, KEN	1:43.66	
1996			

1500-METER RUN

1896	Edwin Flack, AUS	4:33.20	
1900	Charles Bennett, GBR	4:06.20	WR
1904	James Lightbody, USA	4:05.40	WR
1908	Mel Sheppard, USA	4:03.40	OR
1912	Arnold Jackson, GBR	3:56.80	OR
1920	Albert Hill, GBR	4:01.80	
1924	Paavo Nurmi, FIN	3:53.60	OR
1928	Harry Larva, FIN	3:53.20	
1932	Luigi Beccali, ITA	3:51.20	OR
1936	Jack Lovelock, NZE	3:47.80	WR
1948	Henri Eriksson, SWE	3:49.80	
1952	Josef Barthel, LUX	3:45.10	OR
1956	Ron Delany, IRL	3:41.20	OR
1960	Herbert Elliott, AUS	3:35.60	WR
1964	Peter Snell, NZE	3:38.10	

1968	Kipchoge Keino, KEN	3:34.90	OR
1972	Pekka Vasala, FIN	3:36.30	
1976	John Walker, NZE	3:39.17	
1980	Sebastian Coe, GBR	3:38.40	
1984	Sebastian Coe, GBR	3:32.53	OR
1988	Peter Rono, KEN	3:35.96	
1992	Fermin Cacho Ruiz, SPA	3:40.12	
1996			

3000-METER STEEPLECHASE
1896 not held

1900	George Orton, CAN	7:34.40	
1904	James Lightbody, USA	7:39.60	
1908	Arthur Russell, GBR	10:47.80	
1912 not held			
1920	Percy Hodge, GBR	10:00.40	OR
1924	Vilho Ritola, FIN	9:33.60	OR
1928	Toivo Loukola, FIN	9:21.80	WR
1932	Volmari Iso-Hollo, FIN	10:33.40	
	(About 3,450 mtrs. extra lap by error)		
1936	Volmari Iso-Hollo, FIN	9:03.80	WR
1948	Thore Sjöstrand, SWE	9:04.60	
1952	Horace Ashenfelter, USA	8:45.40	WR
1956	Chris Brasher, GBR	8:41.20	OR
1960	Zdzislaw Krzyszkowiak, POL	8:34.20	OR
1964	Gaston Roelants, BEL	8:30.80	OR
1968	Amos Biwott, KEN	8:51.00	
1972	Kipchoge Keino, KEN	8:23.60	OR
1976	Anders Gärderud, SWE	8:08.20	WR
1980	Bronisław Malinowski, POL	8:09.70	
1984	Julius Korir, KEN	8:11.80	
1988	Julius Kariuki, KEN	8:05.51	OR
1992	Matthew Birer, KEN	8:08.84	
1996			

5000-METER RUN
1896-1908 not held

1912	Hannes Kolehmainen, FIN	14:36.60	WR
1920	Joseph Guillemot, FRA	14:55.60	
1924	Paavo Nurmi, FIN	14:31.20	OR
1928	Vilho Ritola, FIN	14:38.00	
1932	Lauri Lehtinen, FIN	14:30.00	OR
1936	Gunnar Höckert, FIN	14:22.20	OR
1948	Gaston Reiff, BEL	14:17.60	OR
1952	Emil Zátopek, CZE	14:06.60	OR
1956	Vladimir Kuts, SOV	13:39.60	OR
1960	Murray Halberg, NZE	13:43.40	
1964	Bob Schul, USA	13:48.80	
1968	Mohamed Gammoudi, TUN	14:05.00	
1972	Lasse Viren, FIN	13:26.40	OR
1976	Lasse Viren, FIN	13:24.76	
1980	Miruts Yifter, ETH	13:21.00	
1984	Said Aouita, MOR	13:05.59	OR
1988	John Ngugi, KEN	13:11.70	
1992	Dieter Baumann, GER	13:12.52	
1996			

10000-METER RUN
1896-1908 not held

1912	Hannes Kolehmainen, FIN	31:20.80	
1920	Paavo Nurmi, FIN	31:45.80	
1924	Vilho Ritola, FIN	30:23.20	WR
1928	Paavo Nurmi, FIN	30:18.80	OR
1932	Janusz Kusociński, POL	30:11.40	OR
1936	Ilmari Salminen, FIN	30:15.40	
1948	Emil Zátopek, CZE	29:59.60	OR
1952	Emil Zátopek, CZE	29:17.00	OR
1956	Vladimir Kuts, SOV	28:45.60	OR
1960	Pyotr Bolotnikov, SOV	28:32.20	OR
1964	Billy Mills, USA	28:24.40	OR
1968	Naftali Temu, KEN	29:27.40	
1972	Lasse Viren, FIN	27:38.40	WR
1976	Lasse Viren, FIN	27:40.38	
1980	Miruts Yifter, ETH	27:42.70	
1984	Alberto Cova, ITA	27:47.54	
1988	Brahim Boutaib, MOR	27:21.46	OR
1992	Khalid Skah, MOR	27:46.70	
1996			

MARATHON

1896	Spiridon Loues, GRE	2:58:50.0	
1900	Michel Théato, FRA	2:59:45.0	
1904	Thomas Hicks, USA	3:28:53.0	
1908	John J. Hayes, USA	2:55:18.4	OR
1912	Kenneth McArthur, SAF	2:36:54.8	
1920	Hannes Kolehmainen, FIN	2:32:35.8	WB
1924	Albin Stenroos, FIN	2:41:22.6	
1928	A. B. El Ouafi, FRA	2:32:57.0	
1932	Juan Zabala, ARG	2:31:36.0	OR
1936	Sohn Kee-chung, KOR	2:29:19.2	OR
1948	Delfo Cabrera, ARG	2:34:51.6	
1952	Emil Zátopek, CZE	2:23:03.2	OR
1956	Alain Mimoun, FRA	2:25:00.0	
1960	Abebe Bikila, ETH	2:15:16.2	WB
1964	Abebe Bikila, ETH	2:12:11.2	WB
1968	Mamo Wolde, ETH	2:20:26.4	
1972	Frank Shorter, USA	2:12:19.8	
1976	Waldemar Cierpinski, GDR	2:09:55.0	OR
1980	Waldemar Cierpinski, GDR	2:11:03.0	
1984	Carlos Lopes, POR	2:09:21.0	OR
1988	Gelindo Bordin, ITA	2:10:32.0	
1992	Hwang Young-Cho, KOR	2:13:23.0	
1996			

20-KILOMETER WALK
1896-1952 not held

1956	Leonid Spirin, SOV	1:31:27.4	
1960	Vladimir Golubnichiy, SOV	1:34:07.2	
1964	Kenneth Mathews, GBR	1:29:34.0	OR
1968	Vladimir Golubnichiy, SOV	1:33:58.4	
1972	Peter Frenkel, GDR	1:26:42.4	OR
1976	Daniel Bautista, MEX	1:24:40.6	OR
1980	Maurizio Damilano, ITA	1:23:35.5	OR
1984	Ernesto Canto, MEX	1:23:13.0	OR
1988	Josef Pribilinec, CZE	1:19:57.0	OR

TRACK AND FIELD • MEN

1992	Daniel Plaza Montero, SPA	1:21:45.0	
1996			

50-KILOMETER WALK

1896–1928 not held

1932	Thomas W. Green, GBR	4:50:10.0	
1936	Harold Whitlock, GBR	4:30:41.4	OR
1948	John Ljunggren, SWE	4:41:52.0	
1952	Giuseppe Dordoni, ITA	4:28:07.8	OR
1956	Norman Read, NZE	4:30:42.8	
1960	Donald Thompson, GBR	4:25:30.0	OR
1964	Abdon Pamich, ITA	4:11:12.4	OR
1968	Christoph Höhne, GDR	4:20:13.6	
1972	Bernd Kannenberg, GER	3:56:11.6	OR
1976 not held			
1980	Hartwig Gauder, GDR	3:49:24.0	OR
1984	Raúl González, MEX	3:47:26.0	OR
1988	Vyacheslav Ivanenko, SOV	3:38:29.0	OR
1992	Andrei Perlov, EUN	3:50:13.0	
1996			

110-METER HURDLES

1896	Thomas Curtis, USA	17.60	
1900	Alvin Kraenzlein, USA	15.40	OR
1904	Frederick Schule, USA	16.00	
1908	Forrest Smithson, USA	15.00	WR
1912	Frederick Kelly, USA	15.10	
1920	Earl Thomson, CAN	14.80	WR
1924	Daniel Kinsey, USA	15.00	
1928	Sydney Atkinson, SAF	14.80	
1932	George Saling, USA	14.60	
1936	Forrest Towns, USA	14.20	
1948	William Porter, USA	13.90	OR
1952	Harrison Dillard, USA	13.70	OR
1956	Lee Calhoun, USA	13.50	OR
1960	Lee Calhoun, USA	13.80	
1964	Hayes Jones, USA	13.60	
1968	Willie Davenport, USA	13.33	OR
1972	Rod Milburn, USA	13.24	EWR
1976	Guy Drut, FRA	13.30	
1980	Thomas Munkelt, GDR	13.39	
1984	Roger Kingdom, USA	13.20	OR
1988	Roger Kingdom, USA	12.98	OR
1992	Mark McCoy, CAN	13.12	
1996			

400-METER HURDLES

1896 not held

1900	J. W. Tewksbury, USA	57.60	
1904	Harry Hillman, USA	53.00	
1908	Charles Bacon, USA	55.00	WR
1920	Frank Loomis, USA	54.00	WR
1924	F. Morgan Taylor, USA	52.60	
1928	David Burghley, GBR	53.40	OR
1932	Robert Tisdall, IRL	51.70	
1936	Glenn Hardin, USA	52.40	
1948	Roy Cochran, USA	51.10	OR
1952	Charles Moore, USA	50.80	OR
1956	Glenn Davis, USA	50.10	EOR
1960	Glenn Davis, USA	49.30	OR
1964	Rex Cawley, USA	49.60	
1968	Dave Hemery, GBR	48.12	WR
1972	John Akii-Bua, UGA	47.82	WR
1976	Edwin Moses, USA	47.64	WR
1980	Volker Beck, GDR	48.70	
1984	Edwin Moses, USA	47.75	
1988	Andre Phillips, USA	47.19	OR
1992	Kevin Young, USA	46.78	OR
1996			

HIGH JUMP

1896	Ellery Clark, USA	5ft. 11 1/4in.	
1900	Irving Baxter, USA	6ft. 2 3/4 in.	OR
1904	Samuel Jones, USA	5ft. 11 in.	
1908	Harry Porter, USA	6ft. 3 in.	OR
1912	Alma Richards, USA	6ft. 4 in.	OR
1920	Richmond Landon, USA	6ft. 4 in.	EOR
1924	Harold Osborn, USA	6ft. 6 in.	OR
1928	Robert W. King, USA	6ft. 4 1/2 in.	
1932	Duncan McNaughton, CAN	6ft. 5 1/2 in.	
1936	Cornelius Johnson, USA	6ft. 8 in.	OR
1948	John L. Winter, AUS	6ft. 6 in.	
1952	Walter Davis, USA	6ft. 8 1/2 in.	OR
1956	Charles Dumas, USA	6ft. 11 1/2 in.	OR
1960	Robert Shavlakadze, SOV	7ft. 1 in.	OR
1964	Valery Brumel, SOV	7ft. 1 3/4 in.	OR
1968	Dick Fosbury, USA	7ft. 4 1/4 in.	OR
1972	Jüri Tarmak, SOV	7ft. 3 3/4 in.	
1976	Jacek Wszola, POL	7ft. 4 1/2 in.	OR
1980	Gerd Wessig, GDR	7ft. 8 3/4 in.	WR
1984	Dietmar Mögenburg, GER	7ft. 8 1/2 in.	
1988	Gennady Avdeyenko, SOV	7ft. 9 3/4 in.	OR
1992	Javier Sotomayor, CUB	7ft. 8 in.	
1996			

LONG JUMP

1896	Ellery Clark, USA	20ft. 10 in.	
1900	Alvin Kraenzlein, USA	23ft. 6 3/4 in.	OR
1904	Meyer Prinstein, USA	24ft. 1 in.	OR
1908	Frank Irons, USA	24ft. 6 1/2 in.	OR
1912	Albert Gutterson, USA	24ft. 11 1/4 in.	OR
1920	William Pettersson, SWE	23ft. 5 1/2 in.	
1924	DeHart Hubbard, USA	24ft. 5 in.	
1928	Edward B. Hamm, USA	25ft. 4 1/2 in.	OR
1932	Edward Gordon, USA	25ft. 3/4 in.	
1936	Jesse Owens, USA	26ft. 5 1/2 in.	OR
1948	William Steele, USA	25ft. 8 in.	
1952	Jerome Biffle, USA	24ft. 10 in.	
1956	Gregory Bell, USA	25ft. 8 1/4 in.	
1960	Ralph Boston, USA	26ft. 7 3/4 in.	OR
1964	Lynn Davies, GBR	26ft. 5 3/4 in.	
1968	Bob Beamon, USA	29ft. 2 1/2 in.	WR
1972	Randy Williams, USA	27ft. 1/2 in.	
1976	Arnie Robinson, USA	27ft. 4 3/4 in.	
1980	Lutz Dombrowski, GDR	28ft. 1/4 in.	
1984	Carl Lewis, USA	28ft. 1/4 in.	
1988	Carl Lewis, USA	28ft. 7 1/4 in.	
1992	Carl Lewis, USA	28ft. 5 1/2 in.	
1996			

400-METER RELAY

1896–1908 not held

1912	GBR	42.40	
1920	USA	42.20	WR
1924	USA	41.00	EWR
1928	USA	41.00	EWR
1932	USA	40.00	WR
1936	USA	39.80	WR
1948	USA	40.60	
1952	USA	40.10	
1956	USA	39.50	WR
1960	GER (USA disqualified)	39.50	EWR
1964	USA	39.00	WR
1968	USA	38.23	WR
1972	USA	38.19	WR
1976	USA	38.33	
1980	SOV	38.26	
1984	USA	37.83	WR
1988	SOV (USA disqualified)	38.19	
1992	USA	37.40	OR
1996			

1600-METER RELAY

1896–1904 not held

1908	USA	3:29.40	
1912	USA	3:16.60	WR
1920	GBR	3:22.20	
1924	USA	3:16.00	WR
1928	USA	3:14.20	WR
1932	USA	3:08.20	WR
1936	GBR	3:09.00	
1948	USA	3:10.40	
1952	JAM	3:03.90	WR
1956	USA	3:04.80	
1960	USA	3:02.20	WR
1964	USA	3:00.70	WR
1968	USA	2:56.16	WR
1972	KEN	2:59.80	
1976	USA	2:58.65	
1980	SOV	3:01.10	
1984	USA	2:57.91	
1988	USA	2:56.16	EWR
1992	USA	2:55.74	OR
1996			

POLE VAULT

1896	William Hoyt, USA	10ft. 10 in.	
1900	Irving Baxter, USA	10ft. 10 in.	
1904	Charles Dvorak, USA	11ft. 5 3/4 in.	
1908	A. C. Gilbert, USA		
	Edward Cooke, USA	12ft. 2 in.	OR
1912	Harry Babcock, USA	12ft. 11 1/2 in.	OR
1920	Frank Foss, USA	13ft. 5 in.	WR
1924	Lee Barnes, USA	12ft. 11 1/2 in.	
1928	Sabin W. Carr, USA	13ft. 9 1/4 in.	OR
1932	William Miller, USA	14ft. 1 3/4 in.	OR
1936	Earle Meadows, USA	14ft. 3 1/4 in.	OR
1948	Guinn Smith, USA	14ft. 1 1/4 in.	
1952	Robert Richards, USA	14ft. 11 in.	OR
1956	Robert Richards, USA	14ft. 11 1/2 in.	OR
1960	Don Bragg, USA	15ft. 5 in.	OR
1964	Fred Hansen, USA	16ft. 8 3/4 in.	OR
1968	Bob Seagren, USA	17ft. 8 1/2 in.	OR
1972	Wolfgang Nordwig, GDR	18ft. 1/2 in.	OR
1976	Tadeusz Slusarski, POL	18ft. 1/2 in.	EOR
1980	Wladyslaw Kozakiewicz, POL	18ft. 11 1/2 in.	WR
1984	Pierre Quinon, FRA	18ft. 10 1/4 in.	
1988	Sergei Bubka, SOV	19ft. 9 1/4 in.	OR
1992	Maksim Tarasov, EUN	19ft. 1/4 in.	
1996			

HAMMER THROW

1896 not held

1900	John Flanagan, USA	163ft. 1 in.	
1904	John Flanagan, USA	168ft. 1 in.	OR
1908	John Flanagan, USA	170ft. 4 1/4 in.	OR
1912	Matt McGrath, USA	179ft. 7 1/8 in.	OR
1920	Pat Ryan, USA	173ft. 5 5/8 in.	
1924	Fred Tootell, USA	174ft. 10 1/8 in.	
1928	Patrick O'Callaghan, IRL	168ft. 7 1/2 in.	
1932	Patrick O'Callaghan, IRL	176ft. 11 1/8 in.	
1936	Karl Hein, GER	185ft. 4 in.	OR
1948	Imre Németh, HUN	183ft. 11 1/2 in.	
1952	József Csermák, HUN	197ft. 11 9/16 in.	WR
1956	Harold Connolly, USA	207ft. 3 1/2 in.	OR
1960	Vasily Rudenkov, SOV	220ft. 1 5/8 in.	OR
1964	Romuald Klim, SOV	228ft. 9 1/2 in.	OR
1968	Gyula Zsivótsky, HUN	240ft. 8 in.	OR
1972	Anatol Bondarchuk, SOV	247ft. 8 in.	OR
1976	Yuri Sedykh, SOV	254ft. 4 in.	OR
1980	Yuri Sedykh, SOV	268ft. 4 1/2 in.	WR
1984	Juha Tiainen, FIN	256ft. 2 in.	
1988	Sergei Litinov, SOV	278ft. 2 1/2 in.	OR
1992	Andrei Abduvaliyev, EUN	270ft. 9 in.	
1996			

DISCUS THROW

1896	Robert Garrett, USA	95ft. 7 1/2 in.	
1900	Rudolf Bauer, HUN	118ft. 3 in.	OR
1904	Martin Sheridan, USA	128ft. 10 1/2 in.	OR
1908	Martin Sheridan, USA	134ft. 2 in.	OR
1912	Armas Taipale, FIN	148ft. 3 in.	OR
	Both hands–		
	Armas Taipale, FIN	271ft. 10 1/4 in.	
1920	Elmer Niklander, FIN	146ft. 7 in.	
1924	Clarence Houser, USA	151ft. 4 in.	OR
1928	Clarence Houser, USA	155ft. 3 in.	OR
1932	John Anderson, USA	162ft. 4 in.	OR
1936	Ken Carpenter, USA	165ft. 7 in.	OR
1948	Adolfo Consolini, ITA	173ft. 2 in.	OR
1952	Sim Iness, USA	180ft. 6.85 in.	OR
1956	Al Oerter, USA	184ft. 10 1/2 in.	OR
1960	Al Oerter, USA	194ft. 2 in.	OR
1964	Al Oerter, USA	200ft. 1 1/2 in.	OR
1968	Al Oerter, USA	212ft. 6 1/2 in.	OR
1972	Ludvik Daněk, CZE	211ft. 3 in.	
1976	Mac Wilkins, USA	221ft. 5 1/4 in.	
1980	Viktor Rashchupkin, SOV	218ft. 8 in.	
1984	Rolf Danneberg, GER	218ft. 6 in.	
1988	Jurgen Schult, GDR	225ft. 9 1/4 in.	OR
1992	Romas Ubartas, LIT	213ft. 8 in.	
1996			

TRIPLE JUMP

1896	James Connolly, USA	44ft. 11 3/4 in.	
1900	Meyer Prinstein, USA	47ft. 5 3/4 in.	OR
1904	Meyer Prinstein, USA	47 ft. 1 in.	
1908	Timothy Ahearne, GBR/IRL	48ft. 11 1/4 in.	OR
1912	Gustaf Lindblom, SWE	48ft. 5 1/4 in.	
1920	Vilho Tuulos, FIN	47ft. 7 in.	
1924	Anthony Winter, AUS	50ft. 11 1/4 in.	WR
1928	Mikio Oda, JPN	49ft. 11 in.	
1932	Chuhei Nambu, JPN	51ft. 7 in.	WR
1936	Naoto Tajima, JPN	52ft. 6 in.	WR
1948	Arne Åhman, SWE	50ft. 6 1/4 in.	
1952	Adhemar da Silva, BRA	53ft. 2 3/4 in.	WR
1956	Adhemar da Silva, BRA	53ft. 7 3/4 in.	OR
1960	Józef Schmidt, POL	55ft. 2 in.	
1964	Józef Schmidt, POL	55ft. 3 1/2 in.	OR
1968	Viktor Saneyev, SOV	57ft. 3/4 in.	WR
1972	Viktor Saneyev, SOV	56ft. 11 in.	
1976	Viktor Saneyev, SOV	56ft. 8 3/4 in.	
1980	Jaak Uudmäe, SOV	56ft. 11 1/4 in.	
1984	Al Joyner, USA	56ft. 7 1/2 in.	
1988	Hristo Markov, BUL	57ft. 9 1/4 in.	OR
1992	Mike Conley, USA	59ft. 7 1/2 in.	OR
1996			

16-LB. SHOT PUT

1896	Robert Garrett, USA	36ft. 9 3/4 in.	
1900	Richard Sheldon, USA	46ft. 3 1/4 in.	OR
1904	Ralph Rose, USA	48ft. 7 in.	WR
1908	Ralph Rose, USA	46ft. 7 1/2 in.	
1912	Pat McDonald, USA	50ft. 4 in.	OR
	Both hands–		
	Ralph Rose, USA	90ft. 5 1/2 in.	
1920	Ville Pörhöla, FIN	48ft. 7 1/4 in.	
1924	Clarence Houser, USA	49ft. 2 1/4 in.	
1928	John Kuck, USA	52ft. 3/4 in.	WR
1932	Leo Sexton, USA	52ft. 6 in.	OR
1936	Hans Woellke, GER	53ft. 1 3/4 in.	OR
1948	Wilbur Thompson, USA	56ft. 2 in.	OR
1952	Parry O'Brien, USA	57ft. 1 1/2 in.	OR
1956	Parry O'Brien, USA	60ft. 11 1/4 in.	OR
1960	William Nieder, USA	64ft. 6 3/4 in.	OR
1964	Dallas Long, USA	66ft. 8 1/2 in.	OR
1968	Randy Matson, USA	67ft. 4 3/4 in.	
1972	Wladyslaw Komar, POL	69ft. 6 in.	OR
1976	Udo Beyer, GDR	69ft. 3/4 in.	
1980	Vladimir Kiselyov, SOV	70ft. 1/2 in.	OR
1984	Alessandro Andrei, ITA	69ft. 9 in.	
1988	Ulf Timmermann, GDR	73ft. 8 3/4 in.	OR
1992	Michael Stulce, USA	71ft. 2 1/2 in.	OR
1996			

JAVELIN

1896–1904 not held

1908	Erik Lemming, SWE	178ft. 7 1/2 in.	
	Held in middle–		
	Erik Lemming, SWE	179ft. 10 1/2in.	WR
1912	Erik Lemming, SWE	198ft. 11 1/4 in.	WR
	Both hands,		
	Julius Saaristo, FIN	358ft. 11 7/8 in.	
1920	Jonni Myyrä, FIN	215ft. 9 3/4 in.	OR
1924	Jonni Myyrä, FIN	206ft. 6 3/4 in.	
1928	Lundkvist, SWE	218ft. 6 1/8 in.	OR
1932	Matti Järvinen, FIN	238ft. 6 in.	OR
1936	Gerhard Stoeck, GER	235ft. 8 5/16 in.	
1948	Tapio Rautavaara, FIN	228ft. 10 1/2 in.	
1952	Cy Young, USA	242ft. 0.79 in.	OR
1956	Egil Danielson, NOR	281ft. 2 1/4 in.	WR
1960	Viktor Tsibulenko, SOV	277ft. 8 3/8 in.	
1964	Pauli Nevala, FIN	271ft. 2 1/2 in.	
1968	Jānis Lūsis, SOV	295ft. 7 1/4 in.	OR
1972	Klaus Wolfermann, GDR	296ft. 10 in.	OR
1976	Miklos Németh, HUN	310ft. 4 in.	WR
1980	Dainis Kūla, SOV	299ft. 2 3/8 in.	
1984	Arto Härkönen, FIN	284ft. 8 in.	
1988	Tapio Korjus, FIN	276ft. 6 in.	
1992	Jan Zelezny, TCH	294ft. 2 in.	OR
1996			

TRACK AND FIELD · MEN

DECATHLON

1886-1900 not held

1904	Thomas Kiely, IRL	6,036.00 pts.	
1908 not held			
1912	Hugo Wieslander, SWE	7,724.49 pts.	(a)
1920	Helge Lövland, NOR	6,804.35 pts.	
1924	Harold Osborn, USA	7,710.77 pts.	WR
1928	Paavo Yrjölä, FIN	8,053.29 pts.	WR
1932	James Bausch, USA	8,462.23 pts.	WR
1936	Glenn Morris, USA	7,900.00 pts.	WR
1948	Robert Mathias, USA	7,139.00 pts.	
1952	Robert Mathias, USA	7,887.00 pts.	WR
1956	Milton Campbell, USA	7,937.00 pts.	OR
1960	Rafer Johnson, USA	8,392.00 pts.	OR
1964	Willi Holdorf, GER	7,887.00 pts.	(c)
1968	Bill Toomey, USA	8,193.00 pts.	OR
1972	Nikolai Avilov, SOV	8,454.00 pts.	WR
1976	Bruce Jenner, USA	8,617.00 pts.	WR
1980	Daley Thompson, GBR	8,495.00 pts.	
1984	Daley Thompson, GBR	8,798.00 pts. EWR	(b)
1988	Christian Schenk, GDR	8,488.00 pts.	
1992	Robert Zmelik, CZE	8,611.00 pts.	
1996			

TRACK AND FIELD · WOMEN

100-METER RUN

1896-1924 not held

Year	Athlete	Time
1928	Elizabeth Robinson, USA	12.02 EWR
1932	Stella Walsh, POL	11.09 EWR
1936	Helen Stephens, USA	11.05w
1948	Francina Blankers-Koen, HOL	11.09
1952	Marjorie Jackson, AUS	11.05 EWR
1956	Betty Cuthbert, AUS	11.05
1960	Wilma Rudolph, USA	11.00w
1964	Wyomia Tyus, USA	11.04
1968	Wyomia Tyus, USA	11.00 WR
1972	Renate Stecher, GDR	11.07 WR
1976	Annegret Richter, GDR	11.08
1980	Lyudmila Kondratyeva, SOV	11.06
1984	Evelyn Ashford, USA	10.97 OR
1988	Florence Griffith Joyner, USA	10.54w
1992	Gail Devers, USA	10.82
1996		

200-METER RUN

1896-1936 not held

Year	Athlete	Time
1948	Francina Blankers-Koen, HOL	24.04
1952	Marjorie Jackson, AUS	23.07
1956	Betty Cuthbert, AUS	23.04 EOR
1960	Wilma Rudolph, USA	24.00
1964	Edith McGuire, USA	23.00 OR
1968	Irena Szewińska, POL	22.05 WR
1972	Renate Stecher, GDR	22.40 EWR
1976	Bärbel Eckert, GDR	22.37 OR
1980	Bärbel Wockel, GDR	22.03 OR
1984	Valerie Brisco-Hooks, USA	21.81 OR
1988	Florence Griffith Joyner, USA	21.34 WR
1992	Gwen Torrence, USA	21.81 EOR
1996		

400-METER RUN

1896-1960 not held

Year	Athlete	Time
1964	Betty Cuthbert, AUS	52.00 OR
1968	Colette Besson, FRA	52.00 EOR
1972	Monika Zehrt, GDR	51.08 OR
1976	Irena Szewińska, POL	49.29 WR
1980	Marita Koch, GDR	48.88 OR
1984	Valerie Brisco-Hooks, USA	48.83 OR
1988	Olga Bryzgina, SOV	48.65 OR
1992	Marie-Jose Perec, FRA	48.83
1996		

800-METER RUN

1896-1924 not held

Year	Athlete	Time
1928·	Lina Radke, GER	2:16.08 WR
1932-1956 not held		
1960	Ludmila Shevtsova, SOV	2:04.03 EWR
1964	Ann Packer, GBR	2:01.01 WR
1968	Madeline Manning, USA	2:00.09 OR
1972	Hildegard Falck, GDR	1:58.06 OR
1976	Tatyana Kazankina, SOV	1:54.94 WR
1980	Nadezhda Olizarenko, SOV	1:53.05 WR
1984	Doina Melinte, ROM	1:57.06
1988	Sigrun Wodars, GDR	1:56.10
1992	Ellen Van Langenm, HOL	1:55.54
1996		

1500-METER RUN

1896-1968 not held

Year	Athlete	Time
1972	Lyudmila Bragina, SOV	4:01.04 WR
1976	Tatyana Kazankina, SOV	4:05.48
1980	Tatyana Kazankina, SOV	3:56.06 OR
1984	Gabriella Dorio, ITA	4:03.25
1988	Paula Ivan, ROM	3:53.96 OR
1992	Hassiba Boulmerka, ALG	3:55.30
1996		

3000-METER RUN

1896-1980 not held

Year	Athlete	Time
1984	Maricica Puică, ROM	8:35.96 OR
1988	Tatyana Samolenko, SOV	8:26.53 OR
1992	Elena Romanova, EUN	8:46.04
1996		

10000-METER RUN

1896-1984 not held

Year	Athlete	Time
1988	Olga Boldarenko, SOV	31:44.69 OR
1992	Derartu Tulu, ETH	31:06.02 OR
1996		

400-METER RELAY

1896-1924 not held

Year	Country	Time
1928	CAN	48.04 WR
1932	USA	46.09 WR
1936	USA	46.09
1948	HOL	47.05
1952	USA	45.09 WR
1956	AUS	44.05 WR
1960	USA	44.05
1964	POL	43.06
1968	USA	42.08 WR
1972	GER	42.81 WR
1976	GDR	42.55 OR
1980	GDR	41.60 WR
1984	USA	41.65
1988	USA	41.98
1992	USA	42.11
1996		

1600-METER RELAY

1896-1968 not held

Year	Country	Time
1972	GDR	3:23.00 WR
1976	GDR	3:19.23 WR
1980	SOV	3:20.02
1984	USA	3:18.29 OR
1988	SOV	3:15.18 WR
1992	EUN	3:20.20
1996		

10-KILOMETER WALK

1896-1988 not held

Year	Athlete	Time
1992	Chen Yueling, CHN	44.32 OR
1996		

100-METER HURDLES

1896-1928 not held

Year	Athlete	Time
1932	Mildred Didriksen, USA	11.70 WR
1936	Trebisonda Valla, ITA	11.70
1948	Francina Blankers-Koen, HOL	11.20 OR
1952	Shirley Strickland, AUS	10.90 WR
1956	Shirley Strickland, AUS	10.70 OR
1960	Ivina Press, SOV	10.80
1964	Karin Balzer, GDR	10.50w
1968	Maureen Caird, AUS	10.30 OR
1972	Annelie Ehrhardt, GDR	12.59 WR
1976	Johanna Schaller, GDR	12.77
1980	Vera Komisova, SOV	12.56 OR
1984	Benita Brown-Fitzgerald, USA	12.84
1988	Jordanka Donkova, BUL	12.38 OR
1992	Paraskevi Patoulidou, GRE	12.64
1996		

400-METER HURDLES

1896-1980 not held

Year	Athlete	Time
1984	Nawal el Moutawakel, MOR	54.61 OR
1988	Debra Flintoff-King, AUS	53.17 OR
1992	Sally Gunnell, GBR	53.23
1996		

HEPTATHLON

1896-1984 not held

1984	Glynis Nunn, AUS	6,390 pts.
1988	Jackie Joyner Kersee, USA	7,215 pts. WR
1992	Jackie Joyner Kersee, USA	7,044 pts.
1996		

HIGH JUMP

1896-1924 not held

1928	Ethel Catherwood, CAN	5ft. 2 1/2 in.	
1932	Jean Shiley, USA	5ft. 5 1/4 in.	WR
1936	Ibolya Csák, HUN	5ft. 3 in.	
1948	Alice Coachman, USA	5ft. 6 1/8 in.	OR
1952	Esther Brand, SAF	5ft. 5 3/4in.	
1956	Mildred L. McDaniel, USA	5ft. 9 1/4 in.	WR
1960	Iolanda Balas, ROM	6ft. 3/4 in.	OR
1964	Iolanda Balas, ROM	6ft. 2 3/4 in.	OR
1968	Miloslava Režková, CZE	5ft. 11 1/2 in.	
1972	Ulrike Meyfarth, GDR	6ft. 4 in.	EWR
1976	Rosemarie Ackermann, GDR	6ft. 3 3/4 in.	OR
1980	Sara Simeoni, ITA	6ft. 5 1/2 in.	OR
1984	Ulrike Meyfarth, GDR	6ft. 7 1/2 in.	OR
1988	Louise Ritter, USA	6ft. 8 in.	OR
1992	Heike Henkel, GER	6ft. 7 1/2 in.	
1996			

DISCUS THROW

1896-1924 not held

1928	Helena Konopacka, POL	129ft. 11 3/4 in.	WR
1932	Lillian Copeland, USA	133ft. 2 in.	OR
1936	Gisela Mauermayer, GER	156ft. 3 in.	OR
1948	Micheline Ostermeyer, FRA	137ft. 6 1/2 in.	
1952	Nina Romaschkova, SOV	168ft. 8 in.	OR
1956	Olga Fikotová, CZE	176ft. 1 in.	OR
1960	Nina Ponomaryeva, SOV	180ft. 8 1/4 in.	OR
1964	Tamara Press, SOV	187ft. 10 in.	OR
1968	Lia Manoliu, ROM	191ft. 2 in.	OR
1972	Faina Melnik, SOV	218ft. 7 in.	OR
1976	Evelin Schlaak, GDR	226ft. 4 in.	OR
1980	Evelin Jahl, GDR	229ft. 6 in.	OR
1984	Ria Stalman, NLA	214ft. 5 in.	
1988	Martina Hellmann, GDR	237ft. 2 1/4 in.	OR

(continued) 1992 Maritz Marten Garcia, CUB 229ft. 10 in.
1996

JAVELIN THROW

1896-1928 not held

1932	Mildred Didriksen, USA	143ft. 4 in.	OR
1936	Tilly Fleischer, GER	148ft. 2 3/4 in.	OR
1948	Herma Bauma, AUT	149ft. 6 in.	
1952	Dana Zatopkova, CZE	165ft. 7 in.	
1956	Inese Jaunzeme, SOV	76ft. 8 in.	
1960	Elvira Ozolina, SOV	183ft. 8 in.	OR
1964	Mihaela Penes, ROM	98ft. 7 1/2 in.	
1968	Angela Nemeth, HUN	198ft. 1/2 in.	
1972	Ruth Fuchs, GDR	209ft. 7 in.	OR
1976	Ruth Fuchs, GDR	216ft. 4 in.	OR
1980	Maria Colon, CUB	224ft. 5 in.	OR
1984	Tessa Sanderson, GBR	228ft. 2 in.	OR
1988	Petra Felke, GDR	245ft.*	OR
1992	Silke Renk, GER	224ft. 2 in.	
1996			

SHOT PUT (8LB., 13OZ.)

1896-1936 not held

1948	Micheline Ostermeyer, FRA	45ft. 1 1/2 in.	
1952	Galina Zybina, SOV	50ft. 1 3/4 in.	WR
1956	Tamara Tishkyevich, SOV	54ft. 5 in.	OR
1960	Tamara Press, SOV	56ft. 10 in.	OR
1964	Tamara Press, SOV	59ft. 6 1/4 in.	OR
1968	Margitta Gummel, GDR	64ft. 4 in.	WR
1972	Nadezhda Chizova, SOV	69ft.	WR
1976	Ivanka Hristova, BUL	69ft. 5 1/4 in.	OR
1980	Ilona Slupianek, GDR	73ft. 6 1/4 in.*	
1984	Claudia Losch, GDR	67ft. 2 1/4 in.	
1988	Natalya Lisovskaya, SOV	72ft. 11 1/2 in.	
1992	Svetlana Krivaleva, EUN	69ft. 1 1/4 in.	
1996			

LONG JUMP

1896-1936 not held

1948	Olga Gyarmati, HUN	18ft. 8 1/4 in.	
1952	Yvette Williams, NZE	20ft. 5 3/4 in.	OR
1956	Elzbieta Krzesińska, POL	20ft. 9 3/4 in.	EWR
1960	Vyera Krepkina, SOV	20ft. 10 3/4 in.	OR
1964	Mary Rand, GBR	22ft. 2 1/4 in.	WR
1968	Viorica Viscopoleanu, ROM	22ft. 4 1/2 in.	WR
1972	Heidemarie Rosendahl, GDR	22ft. 3 in.	
1976	Angela Voigt, GDR	22ft. 3/4 in.	
1980	Tatyana Kolpakova, SOV	23ft. 2 in.	OR
1984	Anisoara Stanciu, ROM	22ft. 10 in.	
1988	Jackie Joyner-Kersee, USA	24ft. 3 1/2 in.	OR
1992	Heike Drechsler, GER	23ft. 5 1/4 in.	
1996			

MARATHON

1896-1980 not held

Year	Athlete	Time
1984	Joan Benoit, USA	2:24:52
1988	Rosa Mota, POR	2:25:40
1992	Valentina Yegorova, EUN	2:32:41
1996		

VOLLEYBALL

MEN'S VOLLEYBALL		WOMEN'S VOLLEYBALL	
1896-1960 not held		*1896-1960 not held*	
1964	SOV	1964	JPN
1968	SOV	1968	SOV
1972	JPN	1972	SOV
1976	POL	1976	JPN
1980	SOV	1980	SOV
1984	USA	1984	CHN
1988	USA	1988	SOV
1992	BRA	1992	CUB
1996		1996	

WEIGHTLIFTING

FLYWEIGHT

1896-1968 not held

1972	Zygmunt Smalcerz, POL	337.5 kg	
1976	Aleksandr Voronin, SOV	242.5 kg	EWR
1980	Kanybek Osmanoliev, SOV	245.0 kg	OR
1984	Zeng Guoqiang, CHN	235.0 kg	
1988	Sevdalin Marinov, BUL	270.0 kg	WR
1992	Ivan Ivanov, BUL	265.0 KG	
1996			

BANTAMWEIGHT

1896-1936 not held

1948	Joseph Di Pietro, USA	307.5 kg	WR
1952	Ivan Udodov, SOV	315.0 kg	OR

(a) Jim Thorpe of the USA won the 1912 Decathlon with 8,413 pts.(WR) but was disqualified and had to return his medals because he had played professional baseball prior to the Olympic games. The medals were restored posthumously in 1982. (b) Scoring change effective Apr. 1985. (c) Former point systems used prior to 1964.

WEIGHTLIFTING

1956 Charles Vinci, USA 342.5 kg WR
1960 Charles Vinci, USA 345.0 kg EWR
1964 Aleksei Vakhonin, SOV 357.5 kg WR
1968 Mohammad Nassiri, IRN 367.5 kg EWR
1972 Imre Földi, HUN 377.5 kg WR
1976 Norair Nurikian, BUL 262.5 kg WR
1980 Daniel Núñez Aguiar, CUB 275.0 kg WR
1984 Wu Shude, CHN 267.5 kg
1988 Oksen Mirzoyan, SOV 292.5 kg OR
1992 Chun Byung-Kwan, KOR 287.5 kg
1996

FEATHERWEIGHT
1896–1912 not held
1920 Francois de Haes, BEL 220.0 kg
1924 Pierino Gabetti, ITA 402.5 kg
1928 Franz Andrysek, AUT 287.5 kg OR
1932 Raymond Suvigny, FRA 287.5 kg EOR
1936 Anthony Terlazzo, USA 312.5 kg WR
1948 Mahmoud Fayad, EGY 332.5 kg WR
1952 Rafael Chimishkyan, SOV 337.5 kg WR
1956 Isaac Berger, USA 352.5 kg WR
1960 Yevgeny Minayev, SOV 372.5 kg EWR
1964 Yoshinobu Miyake, JPN 397.5 kg WR
1968 Yoshinobu Miyake, JPN 392.5 kg
1972 Norair Nurikian, BUL 402.5 kg EWR
1976 Nikolai Kolesnikov, SOV 285.0 kg EWR
1980 Viktor Mazin, SOV 290.0 kg OR
1984 Chen Weiqiang, CHN 282.5 kg
1988 Naim Suleymanoğlü, TUR 342.5 kg WR
1992 Naim Suleymanoğlü, TUR 320.0 kg
1996

LIGHTWEIGHT
1896–1912 not held
1920 Alfred Neuland, EST 257.5 kg
1924 Edmond Décottignies, FRA 440.0 kg
1928 Hans Haas, GER 322.5 kg
1932 René Duverger, FRA 325.0 kg EWR
1936 Robert Fein, AUT 342.5 kg WR
1948 Ibrahim Shams, EGY 360.0 kg OR
1952 Tamio Kono, USA 362.5 kg OR
1956 Igor Rybak, SOV 380.0 kg OR
1960 Viktor Bushuyev, SOV 397.5 kg WR
1964 Waldemar Baszanowski, POL 432.5 kg WR
1968 Waldemar Baszanowski, POL 437.5 kg OR
1972 Mukharby Kirzhinov, SOV 460.0 kg WR
1976 Pyotr Korol, SOV 305.0 kg OR
1980 Yanko Roussev, BUL 342.5 kg WR
1984 Yao Jingyuan, CHN 320.0 kg
1988 Joachim Kunz, GDR 340.0 kg
1992 Israel Militossian, EUN 337.5 kg
1996

MIDDLEWEIGHT
1896–1912 not held
1920 Henri Gance, FRA 245.0 kg
1924 Carlo Galimberti, ITA 492.5 kg
1928 Roger Francois, FRA 335.0 kg WR
1932 Rudolf Ismayr, GER 345.0 kg WR
1936 Khadr Sayed El Tourni, EGY 387.5 kg WR
1948 Frank Spellman, USA 390.0 kg OR
1952 Peter George, USA 400.0 kg OR
1956 Fyodor Bogdanovsky, SOV 420.0 kg WR
1960 Aleksandr Kurynov, SOV 437.5 kg WR
1964 Hans Zdražila, CZE 445.0 kg EWR
1968 Viktor Kurentsov, SOV 475.0 kg OR
1972 Yordan Bikov, BUL 485.0 kg WR
1976 Yordan Mitkov, BUL 335.0 kg OR
1980 Assen Zlatev, BUL 360.0 kg WR
1984 Karl-Heinz Radschinsky, GER 340.0 kg
1988 Borislav Gidikov, BUL 375.0 kg OR
1992 Fedor Kassapu, EUN 357.5 kg
1996

LIGHT HEAVYWEIGHT
1896–1912 not held
1920 Ernest Cadine, FRA 295.0 kg
1924 Charles Rigoulot, FRA 502.5 kg
1928 El Sayed Mohammed Nosseir, EGY 355.0 kg WR
1932 Louis Hostin, FRA 365.0 kg EWR
1936 Louis Hostin, FRA 372.5 kg OR
1948 Stanley Stanczyk, USA 417.5 kg OR
1952 Trofim Lomakin, SOV 417.5 kg EOR
1956 Tamio Kono, USA 447.5 kg WR
1960 Ireneusz Paliński, POL 442.5 kg
1964 Rudolf Plukfelder, SOV 475.0 kg OR
1968 Boris Selitsky, SOV 485.0 kg EWR
1972 Leif Jenssen, NOR 507.5 kg OR
1976 Valery Shary, SOV 365.0 kg OR
1980 Yurik Vardanyan, SOV 400.0 kg WR
1984 Petre Becheru, ROM 355.0 kg
1988 Israil Arsamakov, SOV 377.5 kg
1992 Pyrros Dimas, GRE 370.0 kg
1996

MIDDLE HEAVYWEIGHT
1896–1948 not held
1952 Norbert Schemansky, USA 445.0 kg WR
1956 Arkady Vorobyov, SOV 462.5 kg WR
1960 Arkady Vorobyov, SOV 472.5 kg WR
1964 Vladimir Golovanov, SOV 487.5 kg WR
1968 Kaarlo Kangasniemi, FIN 517.5 kg OR
1972 Andon Nikolov, BUL 525.0 kg OR
1976 David Rigert, SOV 382.5 kg OR
1980 Péter Baczakó, HUN 377.5 kg
1984 Nicu Vlad, ROM 392.5 kg OR
1988 Anatoly Khrapaty, SOV 412.5 kg OR
1992 Kakhi Kakhiachvili, EUN 412.5 kg EOR
1996

100 KG
1896–1976 not held
1980 Ota Zaremba, CZE 395.0 kg OR
1984 Rolf Milser, GER 385.0 kg
1988 Pavel Kuznetsov, SOV 425.0 kg OR
1992 Victor Tregoubov, EUN 410.0 kg OR
1996

HEAVYWEIGHT
1896–1968 not held
1972 Jaan Talts, SOV 580.0 kg OR
1976 Yuri Zaitsev, SOV 385.0 kg
1980 Leonid Taranenko, SOV 422.5 kg WR
1984 Norberto Oberburger, ITA 390.0 kg
1988 Yuri Zakharevich, SOV 455.0 kg WR
1992 Ronny Weller, GER 432.5 kg
1996

SUPER HEAVYWEIGHT
1896 Launceston Elliot, GBR 71.0 kg +
1896 Viggo Jensen, DEN 111.5 kg ++
1900 not held
1904 Perikles Kakousis, GRE 111.7 kg ++
1904 Oscar Osthoff, USA 48.0 pts
(all-around Dumbbell contest)
1908–1912 not held
1920 Filippo Bottino, ITA 265.0 kg
1924 Giuseppe Tonani, ITA 517.5 kg T
1928 Josef Strassberger, GER 372.5 kg T WR
1932 Jaroslav Skobla, CZE 380.0 kg T OR
1936 Josef Manger, GER 410.0 kg T WR
1948 John Davis, USA 452.5 kg T OR
1952 John Davis, USA 460.0 kg T OR
1956 Paul Anderson, USA 500.0 kg T OR
1960 Yuri Vlasov, SOV 537.5 kg T WR
1964 Leonid Zhabotinsky, SOV 572.5 kg T OR
1968 Leonid Zhabotinsky, SOV 572.5 kg T EOR
1972 Vassily Alexeyev, SOV 640.0 kg T OR
1976 Vassily Alexeyev, SOV 440.0 kg T
1980 Sultan Rakhmanov, SOV 440.0 kg T EOR
1984 Dean Lukin, AUS 412.5 kg T
1988 Alexandre Kourlovitch, SOV 462.5 kg T OR
1992 Alexandre Kourlovitch, EUN 450.0 kg
1996

WRESTLING

FREESTYLE WRESTLING
LIGHT FLYWEIGHT
1896–1900 not held
1904 Robert Curry, USA
1908–1968 not held
1972 Roman Dmitriev, SOV
1976 Hasan Isaev, BUL
1980 Claudio Pollio, ITA
1984 Robert Weaver, USA
1988 Takashi Kobayashi, JPN
1992 Kim Il, PRK
1996

FLYWEIGHT
1896–1900 not held
1904 George Mehnert, USA
1908–1936 not held
1948 Lennart Viitala, FIN
1952 Hasan Gemici, TUR
1956 Mirian Tsalkalamanidze, SOV
1960 Ahmet Bilek, TUR
1964 Yoshikatsu Yoshida, JPN
1968 Shigeo Nakata, JPN
1972 Kiyomi Kato, JPN
1976 Yuji Takada, JPN
1980 Anatoly Beloglazov, SOV
1984 Šaban Trstena, YUG
1988 Mitsuru Sato, JPN
1992 Li Hak Son, KOR
1996

BANTAMWEIGHT
1896–1900 not held
1904 Isidor Niflot, USA
1908 George Mehnert, USA
1912–1920 not held
1924 Kustaa Pihlajamäki, FIN
1928 Kaarlo Mäkinen, FIN
1932 Robert Pearce, USA
1936 Ödön Zombori, HUN
1948 Nasuh Akar, TUR
1952 Shohachi Ishii, JPN
1956 Mustafa Dağistanli, TUR
1960 Terrence McCann, USA
1964 Yojiro Uetake, JPN
1968 Yojiro Uetake, JPN
1972 Hideaki Yanagida, JPN
1976 Vladimir Umin, SOV
1980 Sergei Beloglazov, SOV
1984 Hideaki Tomiyama, JPN
1988 Sergei Beloglazov, SOV
1992 Alejandro Puerto Diaz, CUB
1996

FEATHERWEIGHT
1896–1900 not held
1904 Benjamin Bradshaw, USA
1908 George Dole, USA
1912 not held
1920 Charles Ackerly, USA
1924 Robin Reed, USA
1928 Allie Morrison, USA
1932 Hermanni Pihlajamäki, FIN
1936 Kustaa Pihlajamäki, FIN
1948 Gazanfer Bilge, TUR
1952 Bayram Sit, TUR
1956 Shozo Sasahara, JPN
1960 Mustafa Dağistanli, TUR
1964 Osamu Watanabe, JPN
1968 Masaaki Kaneko, JPN
1972 Zagalav Abdulbekov, SOV
1976 Yang Jung-mo, KOR
1980 Magomedgasan Abushev, SOV
1984 Randy Lewis, USA
1988 John Smith, USA
1992 John Smith, USA
1996

LIGHTWEIGHT
1896–1900 not held
1904 Otto Roehm, USA
1908 George de Relwyskow, GBR
1912 not held
1920 Kaarlo Anttila, FIN
1924 Russell Vis, USA
1928 Osvald Käpp, EST
1932 Charles Pacome, FRA
1936 Károly Kárpáti, HUN
1948 Celal Atik, TUR
1952 Olle Anderberg, SWE
1956 Emamali Habibi, IRN
1960 Shelby Wilson, USA
1964 Enyu Vulchev (Dimov), BUL
1968 Abdollah Movahhed, IRN
1972 Dan Gable, USA
1976 Pavel Pinigin, SOV
1980 Saipulla Absaidov, SOV
1984 You In-Tak, KOR
1988 Arsen Fadzayev, SOV
1992 Arsen Fadzayev, EUN
1996

WELTERWEIGHT
1896–1900 not held
1904 Charles Erickson, USA
1908–1920 not held
1924 Hermann Gehri, SWI
1928 Arvo Haavisto, FIN
1932 Jack Van Bebber, USA
1936 Frank Lewis, USA
1948 Yasar Doğu, TUR
1952 William Smith, USA
1956 Mitsuo Ikeda, JPN
1960 Douglas Blubaugh, USA
1964 Ismail Ogan, TUR
1968 Mahmut Atalay, TUR
1972 Wayne Wells, USA
1976 Jiichiro Date, JPN
1980 Valentin Angelov, BUL
1984 David Schultz, USA
1988 Kenneth Monday, USA
1992 Park Jang Soon, KOR
1996

MIDDLEWEIGHT
1896–1904 not held
1908 Stanley Bacon, GBR
1912 not held
1920 Eino Leino, FIN
1924 Fritz Hagmann, SWI
1928 Ernst Kyburz, SWI
1932 Ivar Johansson, SWE
1936 Emile Poilvé, FRA
1948 Glen Brand, USA
1952 David Tsimakuridze, SOV
1956 Nikola Stanchev, BUL
1960 Hasan Güngör, TUR
1964 Prodan Gardzhev, BUL
1968 Boris Gurevich, SOV
1972 Levan Tediashvili, SOV
1976 John Peterson, USA
1980 Ismail Abilov, BUL
1984 Mark Schultz, USA
1988 Han Myung-woo, KOR
1992 Kevin Jackson, USA
1996

LIGHT HEAVYWEIGHT
1896–1912 not held
1920 Anders Larsson, SWE
1924 John Spellman, USA
1928 Thure Sjöstedt, SWE
1932 Peter Mehringer, USA
1936 Knut Fridell, SWE
1948 Henry Wittenberg, USA
1952 Wiking Palm, SWE
1956 Gholam Reza Takhti, IRN
1960 Ismet Atli, TUR
1964 Aleksandr Medved, SOV
1968 Ahmet Ayik, TUR
1972 Benjamin Peterson, USA
1976 Levan Tediashvili, SOV
1980 Sanasar Oganesyan, SOV
1984 Ed Banach, USA
1988 Makharbek Khadartsev, SOV
1992 Makharbek Khadartsev, EUN
1996

HEAVYWEIGHT
1896–1968 not held
1972 Ivan Yarygin, SOV
1976 Ivan Yarygin, SOV
1980 Ilya Mate, SOV
1984 Lou Banach, USA
1988 Vasile Puscasu, ROM
1992 Leri Khabelov, EUN
1996

SUPER HEAVYWEIGHT
1896–1900 not held
1904 Bernhuff Hansen, USA
1908 George Con O'Kelly, GBR/IRL
1912 not held
1920 Robert Roth, SWI

WRESTLING

1924 Harry Steel, USA
1928 Johan Richthoff, SWE
1932 Johan Richthoff, SWE
1936 Kristjan Palusalu, EST
1948 Gyula Bóbis, HUN
1952 Arsen Mekokishvili, SOV
1956 Hamit Kaplan, TUR
1960 Wilfried Dietrich, GER
1964 Aleksandr Ivanitsky, SOV
1968 Aleksandr Medved, SOV
1972 Aleksandr Medved, SOV
1976 Soslan Andiev, SOV
1980 Soslan Andiev, SOV
1984 Bruce Baumgartner, USA
1988 David Gobezhishvili, SOV
1992 Bruce Baumgartner, USA
1996

GRECO-ROMAN WRESTLING
LIGHT FLYWEIGHT
1896-1968 not held
1972 Gheorghe Berceanu, ROM
1976 Alexei Shumakov, SOV
1980 Zaksylik Ushkempirov, SOV
1984 Vincenzo Maenza, ITA
1988 Vincenzo Maenza, ITA
1992 Oleg Koutcherenko, EUN
1996

FLYWEIGHT
1896-1936 not held
1948 Pietro Lombardi, ITA
1952 Boris Gurevitch, SOV
1956 Nikolai Solovyov, SOV
1960 Dumitru Pirvulescu, ROM
1964 Tsutomu Hanahara, JPN
1968 Peter Kirov, BUL
1972 Peter Kirov, BUL
1976 Vitaly Konstantinov, SOV
1980 Vakhtang Blagidze, SOV
1984 Atsuji Miyahara, JPN
1988 Jon Ronningen, NOR

1992 Jon Ronningen, NOR
1996

BANTAMWEIGHT
1896-1920 not held
1924 Eduardo Pütsep, EST
1928 Kurt Leucht, GER
1932 Jakob Brendel, GER
1936 Márton Lörincz, HUN
1948 Kurt Pettersén, SWE
1952 Imre Hódos, HUN
1956 Konstantin Vyrupayev, SOV
1960 Oleg Karavayev, SOV
1964 Masamitsu Ichiguchi, JPN
1968 János Varga, HUN
1972 Rustem Kazakov, SOV
1976 Pertti Ukkola, FIN
1980 Shamil Serikov, SOV
1984 Pasquale Passarelli, GER
1988 András Sike, HUN
1992 An Han-Bong, KOR
1996

FEATHERWEIGHT
1896-1908 not held
1912 Kaarlo Koskelo, FIN
1920 Oskar Friman, FIN
1924 Kaarlo Anttila, FIN
1928 Voldemar Väli, EST
1932 Giovanni Gozzi, ITA
1936 Yasar Erkan, TUR
1948 Mehmet Oktav, TUR
1952 Yakov Punkin, SOV
1956 Rauno Mäkinen, FIN
1960 Müzahir Sille, TUR
1964 Imre Polyák, HUN
1968 Roman Rurua, SOV
1972 Georgi Markov, BUL
1976 Kazimierz Lipień, POL
1980 Stylianos Mygiakis, GRE
1984 Kim Weon-kee, KOR
1988 Kamandar Madzhidov, SOV

1992 M. Akif Pirim, TUR
1996

LIGHTWEIGHT
1896-1904 not held
1908 Enrico Porro, ITA
1912 Eemil Wäre, FIN
1920 Eemil Wäre, FIN
1924 Oskar Friman, FIN
1928 Lajos Keresztes, HUN
1932 Erik Malmberg, SWE
1936 Lauri Koskela, FIN
1948 Gustav Freij, SWE
1952 Schazam Safin, SOV
1956 Kyösti Lehtonen, FIN
1960 Avtandil Koridze, SOV
1964 Kazim Ayvaz, TUR
1968 Munji Mumemura, JPN
1972 Shamil Khisamutdinov, SOV
1976 Suren Nalbandyan, SOV
1980 Stefan Rusu, ROM
1984 Vlado Lisjak, YUG
1988 Levon Dzhulfalakyan, SOV
1992 Attila Repka, HUN
1996

WELTERWEIGHT
1896-1928 not held
1932 Ivar Johansson, SWE
1936 Rudolf Svedberg, SWE
1948 Gösta Andersson, SWE
1952 Miklós Szilvási, HUN
1956 Mithat Bayrak, TUR
1960 Mithat Bayrak, TUR
1964 Anatoly Kolesov, SOV
1968 Rudolf Vesper, GDR
1972 Vítězslav Mácha, CZE
1976 Anatoly Bykov, SOV
1980 Ferenc Kocsis, HUN
1984 Jouko Salomäki, FIN
1988 Kim Young-nam, KOR
1992 Mnatsakan Iskandarian, EUN
1996

MIDDLEWEIGHT
1896-1904 not held
1908 Frithiof Mårtensson, SWE
1912 Claes Johanson, SWE
1920 Carl Westergren, SWE
1924 Edvard Westerlund, FIN
1928 Väinö Kokkinen, FIN
1932 Väinö Kokkinen, FIN
1936 Ivar Johansson, SWE
1948 Axel Grönberg, SWE
1952 Axel Grönberg, SWE
1956 Givy Kartoziya, SOV
1960 Dimiter Dobrev, BUL
1964 Branislav Simič, YUG
1968 Lothar Metz, GDR
1972 Csaba Hegedüs, HUN
1976 Momir Petkovič, YUG
1980 Gennady Korban, SOV
1984 Ion Draica, ROM
1988 Mikhail Mamiashvili, SOV
1992 Peter Farkas, HUN
1996

LIGHT HEAVYWEIGHT
1896-1904 not held
1908 Verner Weckman, FIN
1912 *no gold awarded* 2-Silver
   A. Ahlgren, SWE; I. Böhling, FIN
1920 Claes Johanson, SWE
1924 Carl Westergren, SWE
1928 Ibrahim Moustafa, EGY
1932 Rudolf Svensson, SWE
1936 Axel Cardier, SWE
1948 Karl-Erik Nilsson, SWE
1952 Kaelpo Gröndahl, FIN
1956 Valentin Nikolayev, SOV
1960 Tevfik Kis, TUR
1964 Boyan Radev, BUL
1968 Boyan Radev, BUL
1972 Valery Rezantsev, SOV
1976 Valery Rezantsev, SOV
1980 Norbert Növényi, HUN
1984 Steven Fraser, USA

1988 Atanas Komchev, BUL
1992 Maik Bullmann, GER
1996

HEAVYWEIGHT
1896-1968 not held
1972 Nicolae Martinescu, ROM
1976 Nikolai Balboshin, SOV
1980 Georgi Raikov, BUL
1984 Vasile Andrei, ROM
1988 Andrzej Wrónski, POL
1992 Hector Milian Perez, CUB
1996

SUPER HEAVYWEIGHT
1896 Karl Schumann, GER
1900-1904 not held
1908 Richárd Weisz, HUN
1912 Yrjö Saarela, FIN
1920 Adolf Lindfors, FIN
1924 Henri Deglane, FRA
1928 Rudolf Svensson, SWE
1932 Carl Westergren, SWE
1936 Kristjan Palusalu, EST
1948 Ahmet Kirecci, TUR
1952 Johannes Kotkas, SOV
1956 Anatoly Parfenov, SOV
1960 Ivan Bogdan, SOV
1964 István Kozma, HUN
1968 István Kozma, HUN
1972 Anatoly Roshin, SOV
1976 Aleksandr Kolchinsky, SOV
1980 Aleksandr Kolchinsky, SOV
1984 Jeffrey Blatnick, USA
1988 Alexandre Kareline, SOV
1992 Alexandre Kareline, EUN
1996

YACHTING

MEN'S BOARDSAILING
1986-1980 not held
1984 (Windglider)
   Stephan van den Berg, HOL
1988 (Div. II) Bruce Kendall, NZE
1992 Franck David, FRA
1996

FINN
1896-1912 not held
1920 (12 ft. Dinghy) HOL
1920 (18 ft. Dinghy) GBR
1924 Léon Huybrechts, BEL
1928 Sven Thorell, SWE
1932 Jacques Lebrun, FRA
1936 Daniel Kagchelland, HOL
1948 Paul Elvström, DEN
1952 Paul Elvström, DEN
1956 Paul Elvström, DEN
1960 Paul Elvström, DEN
1964 Wilhelm Kuhweide, GER
1968 Valentin Mankin, SOV

1972 Serge Maury, FRA
1976 Jochen Schümann, GDR
1980 Esko Rechardt, FIN
1984 Russell Coutts, NZE
1988 José Luis Doreste, SPA
1992 José van der Ploeg, SPA
1996

470
1896-1972 not held
1976 F. Hübner, H. Bode, GER
1980 M. Soares, E. Penido, BRA
1984 L. Doreste, R. Molina, SPA
1988 T. Peponnet, L. Pillot, FRA
1992 J. Calafat, F. Sanchez, SPA
1996

WOMEN'S BOARDSAILING
1896-1988 not held
1992 Barbara Kendall, NZE
1996

EUROPE
1896-1988 not held
1992 Linda Andersen, NOR
1996

470
1896-1984 not held
1988 A. Jolly, L. Jewell, USA
1992 T. Zabella, P. Guerra, SPA
1996

MIXED STAR
1896-1928 not held
1932 G. Gray, A. Libano, USA
1936 P. Bischoff, H. Weise, GER
1948 H. Smart, P. Smart, USA
1952 A. Straulino, N. Rode, ITA
1956 H. Williams, L. Low, USA
1960 T. Pinegin, F. Shutkov, SOV
1964 D. Knowles, C. Cooke, BAH
1968 L. North, P. Barrett, USA
1972 D. Forbes, J. Anderson, AUS

1980 V. Mankin, A. Muzötšenko, SOV
1984 W. Buchan, S. Erickson, USA
1988 M. McIntyre, B. Vaile, GBR
1992 M. Reynolds, H. Haenel, USA
1996

MIXED FLYING DUTCHMAN
1896-1956 not held
1960 P. Lunde, Jr., B. Bergvall, NOR
1964 H. Pedersen, E. Wells, NZE
1968 R. Pattison, I. Macdonald-Smith, GBR
1972 J. Diesch, E. Diesch, GER
1980 A. Abascal, M. Noguer, SPA
1984 J. McKee, W. Buchan, USA
1988 J. Bojsen-Möller, C. Grönborg, DEN
1992 L. Doreste, D. Manrique, SPA
1996

MIXED TORNADO
1896-1972 not held
1976 R. White, J. Osborn, GBR
1980 A. Welter, L. Björkström, BRA
1984 R. Sellers, C. Timms, NZE
1988 J. Le Déroff, N. Hénard, FRA
1992 Y. Loday, N. Henard, FRA
1996

MIXED SOLING
1896-1968 not held
1972 USA
1976 DEN
1980 DEN
1984 USA
1988 GDR
1992 DEN
1996

CHAMPIONS OF THE WINTER GAMES

WINTER GAME SITES

1924 Chamonix, France
1928 St. Moritz, Switzerland
1932 Lake Placid, USA
1936 Garmisch-Partenkirchen, Germany
1948 St. Moritz, Switzerland
1952 Oslo, Norway
1956 Cortina d'Ampezzo, Italy
1960 Squaw Valley, USA
1964 Innsbruck, Austria
1968 Grenoble, France
1972 Sapporo, Japan
1976 Innsbruck, Austria
1980 Lake Placid, USA
1984 Sarajevo, Yugoslavia
1988 Calgary, Canada
1992 Albertville, France
1994 Lillehammer, Norway
1998 Nagano, Japan
2002 Salt Lake City, USA

BIATHLON

MEN'S 10 KILOMETERS
1924–1976 not held
1980 Frank Ullrich, GDR   0:32:10.69
1984 Eirik Kvalfoss, NOR   0:30:53.80
1988 Frank-Peter Roetsch, GDR   0:25:08.10
1992 Mark Kirchner, GER   0:26:02.30
1994 Sergei Tchepikov, RUS   0:28:07.00
1998

MEN'S 20 KILOMETERS
1924–1956 not held
1960 Klas Lestander, SWE   1:33:21.60
1964 Vladimir Melanin, SOV   1:20:26.80
1968 Magnar Solberg, NOR   1:13:45.90
1972 Magnar Solberg, NOR   1:15:55.50
1976 Nikolai Kruglov, SOV   1:14:12.26
1980 Anatoly Alyabyev, SOV   1:08:16.31
1984 Peter Angerer, GER   1:11:52.70
1988 Frank-Peter Roetsch, GDR   0:56:33.33
1992 Yevgeny Redkine, EUN   0:57:34.40
1994 Sergei Tarasov, RUS   0:57:25.30
1998

MEN'S 30-KILOMETER RELAY
1924–1964 not held
1968 SOV (40 km)   2:13:02.40
1972 SOV (40 km)   1:51:44.92
1976 SOV (40 km)   1:57:55.64
1980 SOV   1:34:03.27

1984 SOV   1:38:51.70
1988 SOV   1:22:30.00
1992 GER   1:24:43.50
1994 GER   1:30:22.10
1998

WOMEN'S 7.5 KILOMETERS
1924–1988 not held
1992 Anfissa Restsova, EUN   0:24:29.20
1994 Myriam Bedard, CAN   0:26:08.80
1998

WOMEN'S 15 KILOMETERS
1924–1988 not held
1992 Antje Misersky, GER   0:51:47.20
1994 Myriam Bedard, CAN   0:52:06.60
1998

WOMEN'S 22.5-KILOMETER RELAY
1924–1988 not held
1992 FRA   1:15:55.60
1994
1998

WOMEN'S 30-KILOMETER RELAY
1924–1992 not held
1994 RUS   1:47:19.50
1998

BOBSLEDDING

4-MAN BOB
(Driver in parentheses)
1924 SWI (Eduard Scherrer)   5:45.54
1928 USA (William Fiske) (5-man)   3:20.50
1932 USA (William Fiske)   7:53.68
1936 SWI (Pierre Musy)   5:19.85
1948 USA (Francis Tyler)   5:20.10
1952 GER (Andreas Ostler)   5:07.84
1956 SWI (Franz Kapus)   5:10.44
1960 not held
1964 CAN (Victor Emery)   4:14.46
1968 ITA (Eugenio Monti) (2 races) 2:17.39
1972 SWI (Jean Wicki)   4:43.07
1976 GDR (Meinhard Nehmer)   3:40.43
1980 GDR (Meinhard Nehmer)   3:59.92
1984 GDR (Wolfgang Hoppe)   3:20.22
1988 SWI (Ekkehard Fasser)   3:47.51
1992 AUT (Ingo Appelt)   3:53.90
1994 GER (Wolfgang Hoppe)   3:27.28
1998

2-MAN BOB
1924–1928 not held
1932 USA (Hubert Stevens)   8:14.74
1936 USA (Ivan Brown)   5:29.29
1948 SWI (Felix Endrich)   5:29.20
1952 GER (Andreas Ostler)   5:24.54
1956 ITA (Lamberto Dalla Costa)   5:30.14
1960 not held
1964 GBR (Anthony Nash)   4:21.90
1968 ITA (Eugenio Monti)   4:41.54
1972 GER (Wolfgang Zimmerer)   4:57.07
1976 GDR (Meinhard Nehmer)   3:44.42
1980 SWI (Erich Schärer)   4:09.36
1984 GDR (Wolfgang Hoppe)   3:25.56
1988 SOV (Jānis Kipours)   3:53.48
1992 SWI (Gustav Weber)   4:03.26
1994 SWI (Gustav Weber)   3:30.81
1998

LUGE

MEN'S SINGLES
1924–1960 not held
1964 Thomas Köhler, GDR   3:26.770
1968 Manfred Schmid, AUT   2:52.480
1972 Wolfgang Scheidel, GDR   3:27.580
1976 Dettlef Günther, GDR   3:27.688
1980 Bernhard Glass, GDR   2:54.796
1984 Paul Hildgartner, ITA   3:04.258
1988 Jens Müller, GDR   3:05.548
1992 Georg Hackl, GER   3:02.363
1994 Georg Hackl, GER   3:21.571
1998

MEN'S PAIRS
1924–1960 not held
1964 AUT   1:41.620
1968 GDR   1:35.850
1972 ITA, GDR (tie)   1:28.350
1976 GDR   1:25.604
1980 GDR   1:19.331
1984 GER   1:23.620
1988 GDR   1:31.940
1992 GER   1:32.053
1994 ITA   1:36.720
1998

WOMEN'S SINGLES
1924–1960 not held
1964 Ortrun Enderlein, GER   3:24.670
1968 Erica Lechner, ITA   2:28.660
1972 Anna-Maria Müller, GDR   2:59.180
1976 Margit Schumann, GDR   2:50.621
1980 Vera Zozulya, SOV   2:36.537
1984 Steffi Martin, GDR   2:46.570
1988 Steffi Walter, GDR   3:03.973
1992 Doris Neuner, AUT   3:06.696
1994 Gerda Weissensteiner, ITA   3:15.517
1998

FIGURE SKATING

MEN'S SINGLES
1908 Ulrich Salchow, SWE▲
1912 not held
1920 Gillis Grafström, SWE▲
1924 Gillis Grafström, SWE
1928 Gillis Grafström, SWE
1932 Karl Schäfer, AUT
1936 Karl Schäfer, AUT
1948 Richard Button, USA
1952 Richard Button, USA
1956 Hayes Alan Jenkins, USA
1960 David W. Jenkins, USA
1964 Manfred Schnelldorfer, GER
1968 Wolfgang Schwarz, AUT
1972 Ondrej Nepela, CZE
1976 John Curry, GBR
1980 Robin Cousins, GBR
1984 Scott Hamilton, USA
1988 Brian Boitano, USA
1992 Viktor Petrenko, EUN
1994 Aleksei Urmanov, RUS
1998

WOMEN'S SINGLES
1908 Madge Syers, GBR▲
1912 not held
1920 Magda Julin-Mauroy, SWE▲
1924 Herma Planck-Szabó, AUT
1928 Sonja Henie, NOR
1932 Sonja Henie, NOR
1936 Sonja Henie, NOR
1948 Barbara Ann Scott, CAN
1952 Jeanette Altwegg, GBR
1956 Tenley Albright, USA
1960 Carol Heiss, USA
1964 Sjoukje Dijkstra, HOL
1968 Peggy Fleming, USA
1972 Beatrix Schuba, AUT
1976 Dorothy Hamill, USA
1980 Anett Pötzsch, GDR
1984 Katarina Witt, GDR
1988 Katarina Witt, GDR
1992 Kristi Yamaguchi, USA
1994 Oksana Baiul, UKR
1998

PAIRS
1908 Anna Hübler & Heinrich Burger, GER▲
1912 not held
1920 Ludovika & Walter Jakobsson, FIN▲
1924 Helene Engelman & Alfred Berger, AUT
1928 Andrée Joly & Pierre Brunet, FRA
1932 Andrée Joly & Pierre Brunet, FRA
1936 Maxi Herber & Ernst Baier, GER
1948 Micheline Lannoy & Pierre Baugniet, BEL
1952 Ria & Paul Falk, GER
1956 Elisabeth Schwartz & Kurt Oppelt, AUT
1960 Barbara Wagner & Robert Paul, CAN
1964 Ludmila Beloussova & Oleg Protopopov, SOV
1968 Ludmila Beloussova & Oleg Protopopov, SOV
1972 Irina Rodnina & Alexei Ulanov, SOV
1976 Irina Rodnina & Aleksandr Zaitzev, SOV
1980 Irina Rodnina & Aleksandr Zaitzev, SOV
1984 Elena Valova & Oleg Vassiliev, SOV
1988 Ekaterina Gordeeva & Sergei Grinkov, SOV
1992 Natalia Mishkutienok & Artur Dimitriev, EUN
1994 Ekaterina Gordeeva & Sergei Grinkov, RUS
1998

ICE DANCING
1924–1972 not held
1976 Ludmila Pakhomova & Aleksandr Gorschkov, SOV
1980 Natalya Linichuk & Gennadi Karponosov, SOV
1984 Jayne Torvill & Christopher Dean, GBR
1988 Natalia Bestemianova & Andrei Bukin, SOV
1992 Marina Klimova & Sergei Ponomarenko, EUN
1994 Oksana Grichtchuk & Yevgeny Platov, RUS
1998

ICE HOCKEY

1920	CAN▲	1948	CAN	1968	SOV	1988	SOV
1924	CAN	1952	CAN	1972	SOV	1992	EUN
1928	CAN	1956	SOV	1976	SOV	1994	SWE
1932	CAN	1960	USA	1980	USA	1998	
1936	GBR	1964	SOV	1984	SOV		

SPEED SKATING

MEN'S 500 METERS
1924	Charles Jewtraw, USA	44.00
1928	Clas Thunberg, FIN	OR
	Bernt Evensen, NOR (tie)	43.40 OR
1932	John Shea, USA	43.40 EOR
1936	Ivar Ballangrud, NOR	43.40 EOR
1948	Finn Helgesen, NOR	43.10 OR
1952	Kenneth Henry, USA	43.20
1956	Yevgeny Grishin, SOV	40.20 EWR
1960	Yevgeny Grishin, SOV	40.20 EWR
1964	Terry McDermott, USA	40.10 OR
1968	Erhard Keller, GER	40.30
1972	Erhard Keller, GER	39.44 OR
1976	Yevgeny Kulikov, SOV	39.17 OR
1980	Eric Heiden, USA	38.03 OR
1984	Sergei Fokichev, SOV	38.19
1988	Uwe-Jens Mey, GDR	36.45 WR
1992	Uwe-Jens Mey, GER	37.14
1994	Aleksandr Golubev, RUS	36.33 OR
1998		

MEN'S 1000 METERS
1924–1972 not held
1976	Peter Mueller, USA	1:19.32
1980	Eric Heiden, USA	1:15.18 OR
1984	Gaétan Boucher, CAN	1:15.80
1988	Nikolai Gulyaev, SOV	1:13.03 OR
1992	Olaf Zinke, GER	1:14.85
1994	Dan Jansen, USA	1:12.43 WR
1998		

MEN'S 1500 METERS
1924	Clas Thunberg, FIN	2:20.80
1928	Clas Thunberg, FIN	2:21.10
1932	John Shea, USA	2:57.50
1936	Charles Mathisen, NOR	2:19.20 OR
1948	Sverre Farstad, NOR	2:17.60 OR
1952	Hjalmar Andersen, NOR	2:20.40
1956	Yevgeny Grishin, SOV	WR
	Yuri Mikhailov, SOV (tie)	2:08.60 WR
1960	Roald Aas, NOR	
	Yevgeny Grishin, SOV (tie)	2:10.40
1964	Ants Anston, SOV	2:10.30
1968	Cornelis Verkerk, HOL	2:03.40 OR
1972	Ard Schenk, HOL	2:02.96 OR
1976	Jan Egil Storholt, NOR	1:59.38 OR
1980	Eric Heiden, USA	1:55.44 OR
1984	Gaétan Boucher, CAN	1:58.36
1988	André Hoffmann, GDR	1:52.06 WR
1992	Johann Koss, NOR	1:54.81
1994	Johann Koss, NOR	1:51.29 OR
1998		

MEN'S 5000 METERS
1924	Clas Thunberg, FIN	8:39.00
1928	Ivar Ballangrud, NOR	8:50.50
1932	Irving Jaffee, USA	9:40.80
1936	Ivar Ballangrud, NOR	8:19.60 OR
1948	Reidar Liaklev, NOR	8:29.40
1952	Hjalmar Andersen, NOR	8:10.60 OR
1956	Boris Shilkov, SOV	7:48.70 OR
1960	Viktor Kosichkin, SOV	7:51.30
1964	Knut Johannesen, NOR	7:38.40 OR
1968	Anton Maier, NOR	7:22.40 WR
1972	Ard Schenk, HOL	7:23.61
1976	Sten Stensen, NOR	7:24.48
1980	Eric Heiden, USA	7:02.29 OR
1984	Tomas Gustafson, SWE	7:12.28
1988	Tomas Gustafson, SWE	6:44.63 OR
1992	Geir Karlstad, NOR	6:59.97
1994	Johann Koss, NOR	6:34.96 OR
1998		

MEN'S 10000 METERS
1924	Julius Skutnabb, FIN	18:04.80
1928	*Event not held, thawing of ice*	
1932	Irving Jaffee, USA	19:13.60
1936	Ivar Ballangrud, NOR	17:24.30 OR
1948	Åke Seyffarth, SWE	17:26.30
1952	Hjalmar Andersen, NOR	16:45.80 OR
1956	Sigvard Ericsson, SWE	16:35.90 OR
1960	Knut Johannesen, NOR	15:46.60 WR
1964	Jonny Nilsson, SWE	15:50.10
1968	Johnny Höglin, SWE	15:23.60 OR
1972	Ard Schenk, HOL	15:01.35 OR
1976	Piet Kleine, HOL	14:50.59 OR
1980	Eric Heiden, USA	14:28.13
1984	Igor Malkov, SOV	14:39.90
1988	Tomas Gustafson, SWE	13:48.20 WR
1992	Bart Veldkamp, HOL	14:12.12
1994	Johann Koss, NOR	13:30.55 OR
1998		

WOMEN'S 500 METERS
1924–1956 not held
1960	Helga Haase, GDR	45.90
1964	Lydia Skoblikova, SOV	45.00 OR
1968	Ludmila Titova, SOV	46.10
1972	Anne Henning, USA	43.33 OR
1976	Sheila Young, USA	42.76 OR
1980	Karin Enke, GDR	41.78 OR
1984	Christa Rothenburger, GDR	41.02 OR
1988	Bonnie Blair, USA	39.10 WR
1992	Bonnie Blair, USA	40.33
1994	Bonnie Blair, USA	39.25
1998		

WOMEN'S 1000 METERS
1924–1956 not held
1960	Klara Guseva, SOV	1:34.10
1964	Lydia Skoblikova, SOV	1:33.20 OR
1968	Carolina Geijssen, HOL	1:32.60 OR
1972	Monika Pflug, GER	1:31.40 OR
1976	Tatiana Averina, SOV	1:28.43 OR
1980	Natalya Petruseva, SOV	1:24.10 OR
1984	Karin Enke, GDR	1:21.61 OR
1988	Christa Rothenburger, GDR	1:17.65 WR
1992	Bonnie Blair, USA	1:21.90
1994	Bonnie Blair, USA	1:18.74
1998		

WOMEN'S 1500 METERS
1924–1956 not held
1960	Lydia Skoblikova, SOV	2:52.20 WR
1964	Lydia Skoblikova, SOV	2:22.60 OR
1968	Kaija Mustonen, FIN	2:22.40 OR
1972	Dianne Holum, USA	2:20.85 OR
1976	Galina Stepanskaya, SOV	2:16.58 OR
1980	Anne Borckink, HOL	2:10.95 OR
1984	Karin Enke, GDR	2:03.42 WR
1988	Yvonne van Gennip, HOL	2:00.68 OR
1992	Jacqueline Boerner, GER	2:05.87
1994	Emese Hunyady, AUS	2:02.19
1998		

WOMEN'S 3000 METERS
1924–1956 not held
1960	Lydia Skoblikova, SOV	5:14.30
1964	Lydia Skoblikova, SOV	5:14.90
1968	Johanna Schut, HOL	4:56.20 OR
1972	Christina Baas-Kaiser, HOL	4:52.14 OR
1976	Tatiana Averina, SOV	4:45.19 OR
1980	Bjorg Eva Jensen, NOR	4:32.13 OR
1984	Andrea Schöne, GDR	4:24.79 OR
1988	Yvonne van Gennip, HOL	4:11.94 WR
1992	Gunda Niemann, GER	4:19.90
1994	Svetlana Bazhanova, RUS	4:17.43
1998		

WOMEN'S 5000 METERS
1924–1984 not held
1988	Yvonne van Gennip, HOL	7:14.13 WR
1992	Gunda Niemann, GER	7:31.57
1994	Claudia Pechstein, GER	7:14.37
1998		

ALPINE SKIING

MEN'S DOWNHILL
1924–1944 not held
1948	Henri Oreiller, FRA	2:55.00
1952	Zeno Colò, ITA	2:30.80
1956	Anton Sailer, AUT	2:52.20
1960	Jean Vuarnet, FRA	2:06.00
1964	Egon Zimmermann, AUT	2:18.16
1968	Jean-Claude Killy, FRA	1:59.85
1972	Bernhard Russi, SWI	1:51.43
1976	Franz Klammer, AUT	1:45.73
1980	Leonhard Stock, AUT	1:45.50
1984	Bill Johnson, USA	1:45.59
1988	Pirmin Zurbriggen, SWI	1:59.63
1992	Patrick Ortlieb, AUT	1:50.37
1994	Tommy Moe, USA	1:45.75
1998		

MEN'S SUPER GIANT SLALOM
1924–1984 not held
1988	Franck Piccard, FRA	1:39.66
1992	Kjetil-Andre Aamodt, NOR	1:13.04
1994	Markus Wasmeier, GER	1:32.53
1998		

MEN'S GIANT SLALOM
1924–1948 not held
1952	Stein Eriksen, NOR	2:25.00
1956	Anton Sailer, AUT	3:00.10
1960	Roger Staub, SWI	1:48.30
1964	Francois Bonlieu, FRA	1:46.71
1968	Jean-Claude Killy, FRA	3:29.28
1972	Gustav Thöni, ITA	3:09.62
1976	Heini Hemmi, SWI	3:26.97
1980	Ingemar Stenmark, SWE	2:40.74
1984	Max Julen, SWI	2:41.18
1988	Alberto Tomba, ITA	2:06.37
1992	Alberto Tomba, ITA	2:06.98
1994	Markus Wasmeier, GER	2:52.46
1998		

MEN'S SLALOM
1924–1936 not held
1948	Edi Reinalter, SWI	2:10.30
1952	Othmar Schneider, AUT	2:00.00
1956	Anton Sailer, AUT	3:14.70
1960	Ernst Hinterseer, AUT	2:08.90
1964	Josef Stiegler, AUT	2:11.13
1968	Jean-Claude Killy, FRA	1:39.73
1972	Francisco Fernandez Ochoa, SPA	1:49.27
1976	Piero Gros, ITA	2:03.29
1980	Ingemar Stenmark, SWE	1:44.26
1984	Phil Mahre, USA	1:39.41
1988	Alberto Tomba, ITA	1:39.47
1992	Finn Christian Jagge, NOR	1:44.39
1994	Thomas Stangassinger, AUT	2:02.02
1998		

MEN'S COMBINED
1924–1932 not held
1936	Franz Pfnür, GER	99.25 pts.
1948	Henri Oreiller, FRA	3.27 pts.
1952–1984 not held		
1988	Hubert Strolz, AUT	36.55 pts.
1992	Josef Polig, ITA	14.58 pts.
1994	Lasse Kjus, NOR	14.58 pts.
1998		

WOMEN'S DOWNHILL
1924–1936 not held
1948	Hedi Schlunegger, SWI	2:28.30
1952	Trude Jochum-Beiser, AUT	1:47.10
1956	Madeleine Berthod, SWI	1:40.70
1960	Heidi Biebl, GER	1:37.60
1964	Christl Haas, AUT	1:55.39
1968	Olga Pall, AUT	1:40.87
1972	Marie-Theres Nadig, SWI	1:36.68
1976	Rosi Mittermaier, GER	1:46.16
1980	Annemarie Moser-Pröll, AUT	1:37.52
1984	Michela Figini, SWI	1:13.36
1988	Marina Kiehl, GER	1:25.86
1992	Kerrin Lee-Gartner, CAN	1:52.55
1994	Katja Seizinger, GER	1:35.93
1998		

WOMEN'S SUPER GIANT SLALOM
1924–1984 not held
1988	Sigrid Wolf, AUT	1:19.03
1992	Deborah Compagnoni, ITA	1:21.22
1994	Diann Roffe-Steinrotter, USA	1:22.15
1998		

WOMEN'S GIANT SLALOM
1924–1948 not held
1952	Andrea Mead Lawrence, USA	2:06.80
1956	Ossi Reichert, GER	1:56.50
1960	Yvonne Rüegg, SWI	1:39.90
1964	Marielle Goitschel, FRA	1:52.24
1968	Nancy Greene, CAN	1:51.97
1972	Marie-Theres Nadig, SWI	1:29.90
1976	Kathy Kreiner, CAN	1:29.13
1980	Hanni Wenzel, LIE (2 runs)	2:41.66
1984	Debbie Armstrong, USA	2:20.98
1988	Vreni Schneider, SWI	2:06.49
1992	Pernilla Wiberg, SWE	2:12.74
1994	Deborah Compagnoni, ITA	2:30.97
1998		

WOMEN'S SLALOM
1924–1936 not held
1948	Gretchen Fraser, USA	1:57.20
1952	Andrea Mead Lawrence, USA	2:10.60
1956	Renée Colliard, SWI	1:52.30
1960	Anne Heggtveit, CAN	1:49.60
1964	Christine Goitschel, FRA	1:29.86
1968	Marielle Goitschel, FRA	1:25.86
1972	Barbara Cochran, USA	1:31.24
1976	Rosi Mittermaier, GER	1:30.54
1980	Hanni Wenzel, LIE	1:25.09
1984	Paoletta Magoni, ITA	1:36.47
1988	Vreni Schneider, SWI	1:36.69
1992	Petra Kronberger, AUT	1:32.68
1994	Vreni Schneider, SWI	1:56.01
1998		

WOMEN'S COMBINED
1924–1932 not held
1936	Christl Cranz, GER	97.06 pts.
1948	Trude Beiser, AUT	6.58 pts.
1952–1984 not held		
1988	Anita Wachter, AUT	29.25 pts.
1992	Petra Kronberger, AUT	2.55 pts.
1994	Pernilla Wiberg, SWE	3:05.16
1998		

FREESTYLE SKIING

MEN'S MOGULS
1924–1988 not held
1992	Edgar Grospiron, FRA	
1994	Jean-Luc Brassard, CAN	
1998		

MEN'S AERIALS
1924–1992 not held
1994	Andreas Schoenbaechler, SWI	
1998		

WOMEN'S MOGULS
1924–1988 not held
1992	Donna Weinbrecht, USA	
1994	Stine Lise Hattestad, NOR	
1998		

WOMEN'S AERIALS
1924–1992 not held
1994	Lina Tcherjazova, UZB	

CROSS-COUNTRY SKIING · MENS

10 KILOMETERS
1924–1988 not held
1992 Vegard Ulvang, NOR   0:27:36.00
1994 Bjorn Daehlie, NOR   0:24:20.10
1998

15 KILOMETERS
1924 Thorleif Haug, NOR   1:14:31.00
1928 Johan Gröttumsbråten, NOR 1:37:01.00
1932 Sven Utterström, SWE   1:23:07.00
1936 Erik-August Larsson, SWE 1:14:38.00
1948 Martin Lundström, SWE   1:13:50.00
1952 Hallgeir Brenden, NOR   1:01:34.00
1956 Hallgeir Brenden, NOR   0:49:39.00
1960 Håkon Brusveen, NOR   0:51:55.50
1964 Eero Mäntyranta, FIN   0:50:54.10
1968 Harald Grönningen, NOR   0:47:54.20
1972 Sven-Ake Lundbäck, SWE   0:45:28.24
1976 Nikolai Bazhukov, SOV   0:43:58.47
1980 Thomas Wassberg, SWE   0:41:57.63
1984 Gunde Svan, SWE   0:41:25.60
1988 Mikhail Devyatyarov, SOV 0:41:18.90
1992 Bjorn Daehlie, NOR   0:38:01.90
1994 Bjorn Daehlie, NOR   0:35:48.80
1998
(Note: approx. 18-km. course 1924–1952)

30 KILOMETERS
1924–1952 not held
1956 Veikko Hakulinen, FIN   1:44:06.00
1960 Sixten Jernberg, SWE   1:51:03.90
1964 Eero Mäntyranta, FIN   1:30:50.70
1968 Franco Nones, ITA   1:35:39.20
1972 Vyacheslav Vedenine, SOV 1:36:31.15
1976 Sergei Saveliev, SOV   1:30:29.38
1980 Nikolai Zimyatov, SOV   1:27:02.80
1984 Nikolai Zimyatov, SOV   1:28:56.30
1988 Aleksei Prokurorov, SOV   1:24:26.30
1992 Vegard Ulvang, NOR   1:22:27.80
1994 Thomas Alsgaard, NOR   1:12:26.40
1998

50 KILOMETERS
1924 Thorleif Haug, NOR   3:44:32.00
1928 Per Erik Hedlund, SWE   4:52:03.00
1932 Veli Saarinen, FIN   4:28:00.00
1936 Elis Wiklund, SWE   3:30:11.00
1948 Nils Karlsson, SWE   3:47:48.00
1952 Veikko Hakulinen, FIN   3:33:33.00
1956 Sixten Jernberg, SWE   2:50:27.00
1960 Kalevi Hämäläinen, FIN   2:59:06.30
1964 Sixten Jernberg, SWE   2:43:52.60
1968 Ole Ellefsaeter, NOR   2:28:45.80

1972 Pål Tyldum, NOR   2:43:14.75
1976 Ivar Formo, NOR   2:37:30.05
1980 Nikolai Zimyatov, SOV   2:27:24.60
1984 Thomas Wassberg, SWE   2:15:55.80
1988 Gunde Svan, SWE   2:04:30.90
1992 Bjorn Daehlie, NOR   2:03:41.50
1994 Vladimir Smirnov, KAZ   2:07:20.30
1998

40 KILOMETERS RELAY
1924–1932 not held
1936 FIN   2:41:33.00
1948 SWE   2:32:08.00
1952 FIN   2:20:16.00
1956 SOV   2:15:30.00
1960 FIN   2:18:45.60
1964 SWE   2:18:34.60
1968 NOR   2:08:33.50
1972 SOV   2:04:47.94
1976 FIN   2:07:59.72
1980 SOV   1:57:03.46
1984 SWE   1:55:06.30
1988 SWE   1:43:58.60
1992 NOR   1:39:26.00
1994 ITA   1:41:15.00
1998

COMBINED CROSS-COUNTRY & JUMPING
1924 Thorleif Haug, NOR
1928 Johan Gröttumsbråten, NOR
1932 Johan Gröttumsbråten, NOR
1936 Oddbjörn Hagen, NOR
1948 Heikki Hasu, FIN
1952 Simon Slåttvik, NOR
1956 Sverre Stenersen, NOR
1960 Georg Thoma, GER
1964 Tormod Knutsen, NOR
1968 Franz Keller, GER
1972 Ulrich Wehling, GDR
1976 Ulrich Wehling, GDR
1980 Ulrich Wehling, GDR
1984 Tom Sandberg, NOR
1988 Hippolyt Kempf, SWI
1992 Fabrice Guy, FRA
1994 Fred Barre Lundberg, NOR
1998

CROSS-COUNTRY SKIING · WOMENS

5 KILOMETERS
1924–1960 not held
1964 Claudia Boyarskikh, SOV   17:50.500
1968 Toini Gustafsson, SWE   16:45.200
1972 Galina Koulacova, SOV   17:00.500
1976 Helena Takalo, FIN   15:48.690
1980 Raisa Smetanina, SOV   15:06.920
1984 Marja-Liisa Hämäläinen, FIN 17:04.000
1988 Marjo Matikainen, FIN   15:04.000
1992 Marjut Lukkarinen, FIN   14:13.800
1994 Ljubov Egorova, RUS   14:08.815
1998

10 KILOMETERS
1924–1948 not held
1952 Lydia Wideman, FIN   41:40.00
1956 Lyubov Kosyreva, SOV   38:11.00
1960 Maria Gusakova, SOV   39:46.60
1964 Claudia Boyarskikh, SOV   40:24.30
1968 Toini Gustafsson, SWE   36:46.50
1972 Galina Koulacova, SOV   34:17.82
1976 Raisa Smetanina, SOV   30:13.41
1980 Barbara Petzold, GDR   30:31.54
1984 Marja-Liisa Hämäläinen, FIN 31:44.20
1988 Vida Venciene, SOV   30:08.30
1992 Lyubov Egorova, EUN   25:53.70
1994 Lyubov Egorova, RUS   27:30.10
1998

16 KILOMETERS
1924–1988 not held
1992 Lyubov Egorova, EUN   42:20.80

1994 Manuela Di Centa, ITA   0:39:44.50
1998

20 KILOMETERS
1924–1980 not held
1984 Marja-Liisa Hämäläinen, FIN 1:01:45.00
1988 Tamara Tikhonova, SOV   0:55:53.60

30 KILOMETERS
1924–1988 not held
1992 Stefania Belmondo, ITA   1:22:30.10
1994 Manuela Di Centa, ITA   1:25:41.60
1996

20 KILOMETERS RELAY
1924–1952 not held
1956 FIN (15 km.)   1:09:01.00
1960 SWE (15 km.)   1:04:21.40
1964 SOV (15 km.)   0:59:20.20
1968 NOR (15 km.)   0:57:30.00
1972 SOV (15 km.)   0:48:46.15
1976 SOV   1:07:49.75
1980 GDR   1:02:11.10
1984 NOR   1:06:49.70
1988 SOV   0:59:51.10
1992 EUN   0:59:34.80
1994 RUS   0:57:12.50
1998

SKI JUMPING

TEAM SKI JUMPING
1924–1984 not held
1988 FIN
1992 FIN
1994 GER
1998

SKI JUMPING, LARGE HILL*
1924 Jacob Thams, NOR
1928 Alfred Andersen, NOR
1932 Birger Ruud, NOR
1936 Birger Ruud, NOR
1948 Petter Hugsted, NOR
1952 Arnfinn Bergmann, NOR
1956 Antti Hyvärinen, FIN
1960 Helmut Recknagel, GDR
1964 Toralf Engan, NOR
1968 Vladimir Beloussov, SOV
1972 Wojciech Fortuna, POL
1976 Karl Schnabl, AUT
1980 Jouko Törmänen, FIN
1984 Matti Nykänen, FIN
1988 Matti Nykänen, FIN
1992 Toni Nicminen, FIN
1994 Jens Weissflog, GER
1998

TEAM NORDIC COMBINED
1924–1984 not held
1988 GDR
1992 JPN
1994 JPN
1998

SKI JUMPING, NORMAL HILL
1924–1960 not held
1964 Veikko Kankkonen, FIN
1968 Jiri Raska, CZE
1972 Yukio Kasaya, JPN
1976 Hans-Georg Aschenbach, GDR
1980 Anton Innauer, AUT
1984 Jens Weissflog, GDR
1988 Matti Nykänen, FIN
1992 Ernst Vettori, AUT
1994 Espen Bredesen, NOR
1998

NORDIC COMBINED, INDV.
1924 Thorleif Haug, NOR
1928 Johan Grottumsbråten, NOR
1932 Johan Grottumsbråten, NOR
1936 Oddbjorn Hagen, NOR
1948 Heikki Hasu, FIN
1952 Simon Slåttvik, NOR
1956 Sverre Stenersen, NOR
1960 Georg Thoma, GER
1964 Tormod Knutsen, NOR
1968 Franz Keller, GER
1972 Ulrich Wehling, GDR
1976 Ulrich Wehling, GDR
1980 Ulrich Wehling, GDR
1984 Tom Sandberg, NOR
1988 Hippolyt Kempf, SWI
1992 Fabrice Guy, FRA
1994 Fred Barre Lundberg, NOR
1998

SHORT TRACK SPEEDSKATING

MEN'S 1000 METERS
1924–1960 not held
1992 Kim Ki-Hoon, KOR   1:30.76
1994 Kim Ki-Hoon, KOR   1:34.57
1998

MEN'S 5000-METER RELAY
1924–1988 not held
1992 KOR   7:14.02
1994 ITA   7:11.74
1998

WOMEN'S 500 METERS
1924–1988 not held
1992 Cathy Turner, USA   0:47:04
1994 Cathy Turner, USA   0:45.98
1998

WOMEN'S 3000-METER RELAY
1924–1988 not held
1992 CAN   4:36.62
1994 KOR   4:26.64
1998

INDEX

ACKNOWLEDGMENTS

Tehabi Books gratefully acknowledges the generous support and contributions provided by the following individuals to *The Olympic Spirit*. Without their commitment this project would not have been possible. Tom Angelillo, Southern Progress Corporation; Bruce Akin, Dianne Mooney, Carolyn Smith and Rebecca Fitzgerald, *Southern Living* Books; Fernando Riba, Jean-Francois Pahud, Dr. Doris Vanhove, Claude Jaccard, Catherine Fasel, and Sylvia de Techtermann, Olympic Museum, Lausanne, Switzerland; Jenny Barry, Maura Carey Damacion and Jenny Collins, Collins Publishers San Francisco; Carlos Duran, Galeria Senda, Barcelona, Spain; Dr. Vladimir Mateveyeu, Hermitage Museum, Saint Petersburg, Russia; Bernard Knox, Center for Hellenic Studies, Washington, D.C.; Walt Wilson and the staff of the USOC's Center for Sports Technology, and Barry King, Maxine Fleming and the staff at the USOC's Public Information Office, Colorado Springs, Colorado; George Ortiz and Laurentia Leon of The George Ortiz Collection, Switzerland; Dr. Alfred Bernhard-Walcher and Dr. Tscrwantner, Kunsthistorisches Museum, Austria; Professor Ruurd B. Halbertsma, Rijks Museum, Holland; Amy Freehour and the Sculpture Society, New York; Todd Toth and GT Bicycles, Santa Ana, California; Steve Sutton and Andy Kiss, Duomo Photography, New York; Allsport Photography, Los Angeles; Maggie Lavin, ISL Marketing, Atlanta; Andrew Clarke, Leo Chu and Raymond Shing, Mandarin Offset, Washington, D.C. and Hong Kong; Sanjay Sakhuja, Scott Runcorn, Maria Sota, Luke VanMeter and the staff at Digital Pre-Press International, San Francisco; Greg della Stua, PrintNet, San Francisco; Andy Gutierrez, Kara Thoman and Kathleen Wilkinson.

SELECTED BIBLIOGRAPHY

Carlson, Lewis H., and Fogarty, John J. *Tales of Gold*. Chicago: Contemporary Books, 1987.

Coe, Sebastian. *The Olympians*. London: Pavilion Michael Joseph, 1984.

Connors, Martin; Dupuis, Diane L.; and Morgan, Brad. *The Olympics Factbook*. Detroit: Visible Ink Press, 1992.

Finley, M.I., and Pleket, H.W. *The Olympic Games: The First Thousand Years*. New York: The Viking Press, 1976.

Guttmann, Allen. *The Olympics: A History of the Modern Games*. Urbana and Chicago: University of Illinois Press, 1992.

Pausanias. *Guide to Greece*. Translated by Peter Levi, S.J. Harmondsworth. Middlesex, England: Penguin Books, Ltd., 1971.

Suite Olympic Centennial: A History of Modern Olympism. Barcelona: Editorial Centennial, 1992.

Schaap, Richard. *An Illustrated History of the Olympics*. New York: Alfred A. Kopf, 1963.

Schöbel, Heinz. *The Ancient Olympic Games*. London: Studio Vista Limited, 1966.

Sweet, Waldo E. *Sport and Recreation in Ancient Greece*. New York: Oxford University Press, 1987.

Wallechinsky, David. *The Complete Book of the Olympics*. Boston: Little, Brown and Company, 1992.